*Introduction*
*to*
*Music  Research*

PRENTICE-HALL INTERNATIONAL, INC., London
PRENTICE-HALL OF AUSTRALIA, PTY. LTD., Sydney
PRENTICE-HALL OF CANADA, LTD., Toronto
PRENTICE-HALL OF INDIA PRIVATE LTD., New Delhi
PRENTICE-HALL OF JAPAN, INC., Tokyo

# Introduction
# to
# Music Research

RUTH T. WATANABE

*Sibley Music Library*
*Eastman School of Music*
*University of Rochester*

PRENTICE-HALL, INC., *Englewood Cliffs, New Jersey*

To Pauline Alderman and Anne Theodora Cummins

© 1967 by PRENTICE-HALL, INC.
Englewood Cliffs, New Jersey

*Library of Congress Catalog Card No.: 67–20360*

*Current printing (last digit):*

*10   9   8   7   6*

# *Preface*

*Introduction to Music Research* is intended as a practical handbook treating the basic procedures and tools of investigative studies. As a college teacher, the author has been prompted to write the work by the many questions put to her by her own students and by students over the country who have requested assistance. As librarian of a music collection serving both undergraduates and graduates, she has observed their methods and has considered the need for a guidebook pointing the way through the bibliographical maze. She has drawn upon her experiences as a student, a professor, and a librarian.

Research has become so much a part of graduate curricula in the arts that musicians are expected to be scholars as well as creators and performers. Essentially the same methods of investigation may be employed whether the presentation of the study is to be oral (as in a seminar report), performed (as in a lecture-recital), or written (as in a thesis). This book contains an account of these methods, and if it leans in the direction of the written product, it is because the thesis or dissertation causes the greatest anguish among music students.

This book is neither a thesis manual nor a style sheet, for each college has its own, and prescribed practices in the mechanics of writing vary from institution to institution. Its principal purpose is to present some down-to-earth suggestions on how to do research in a way that will make the most of the investigative phase of graduate study, for every worthy endeavor should add to the knowledge and appreciation of the subject. Because the book is directed to the young graduate student rather than the seasoned researcher, little attempt has been made to include materials requiring extensive knowledge of foreign languages or technical proficiency in theoretical or historical research. Some of the procedures outlined are intended as a review of those already encountered in previous experiences but now presented in the context of research studies.

The first part of the book deals with library orientation. It is based upon questions constantly being asked of librarians and members of the reference staff. The second part is concerned with bibliographical and formal problems, as well as some matters of professional etiquette. The third part is a survey of research materials generally found in American libraries. It is not an annotated bibliography of materials, for that need is excellently served by Vincent Duckles's *Music Reference and Research Materials* (Free Press of Glencoe, 1963). The items included in *Introduction to Music Research* serve as examples or representatives of the most important types of reference works. The section on current periodicals is included in response to many inquiries into the nature of journal literature.

The bibliographies which conclude most of the chapters document the text. They list sources of more detailed information than is possible to present in a handbook. The Index to Works Mentioned in the Text carries only brief entries because full bibliographical details are presented in both footnote references and the bibliographies.

The handbook may be used as an aid to thesis writing in conjunction with style manuals and guides to the mechanics of research; it may serve as a basic text for courses in research methods; it may also be consulted as a bibliographical aid.

The author acknowledges with sincere thanks the advice and encouragement given her by Dr. Pauline Alderman, the late Dr. Catherine K. Miller, Mr. John R. Russell, and the members of the staff of the Sibley Music Library. Special appreciation is expressed to Lilian Levinson, Catherine McDermott, Elizabeth O. Matthews, Ann R. Schramm, and Elizabeth S. Addams.

R. W.

# Contents

## PART TWO    THE RESEARCH PAPER

## PART THREE    SURVEY OF RESEARCH MATERIALS

*Introduction
to
Music Research*

*Part One*

# LIBRARY ORIENTATION

# 1

## Approaches to
## Music Research

### The Place of Research in Music

Although science seemingly receives major emphasis today, increasing importance is being given also to the fine arts. Discoveries in technology and mechanization have released leisure hours to a large part of our population, enabling many people to turn as competent amateurs to some sort of artistic expression. With growing public interest, the arts have acquired a place of prominence in the curricula of schools on all levels. The responsibility of the professional artist has likewise grown: he must be an educated, articulate citizen in addition to being a proficient practitioner of his craft.

Simultaneously, graduate education has become a necessity for a professional career. A bachelor's degree is no longer an open sesame to a good position. For a teacher in the schools a master's degree is a meal-ticket, and for a professor a doctorate is both job insurance and a stepping-stone toward a higher academic rank and tenure in colleges and universities. Even for the creative artist—the composer, conductor, or performer who in former years was considered "free"—a permanent affiliation with some institution is desirable for economic and professional security. Both educators and public may object to this as being wrong. But there is no denying the fact that earning degrees is an essential part of one's training, be he creator, performer, teacher, or critic.

Graduate departments are expanding to accommodate the increasing number of students seeking advanced degrees. Surely the demand for M.A.'s and Ph.D.'s can never be satisfied by mass production of highbrow mediocrity. It is still a privilege to be a graduate student, and in earning a

3

degree one must put forth a measure of honest work which will make him able to cope with the conditions of his profession.

Musicians have found that they cannot afford to be merely good performers or good composers, all financial and status considerations aside. The best artists know the most about music and are the most articulate about it. Although students aspiring to a concert career may rebel at research, knowledge does not interfere with artistry. On the contrary, the results of research aid in authentic performance; witness Rosalyn Tureck and her studies of Bach. The late pianist Alfred Cortot contributed analyses of Chopin's music. Harpsichordist Ralph Kirkpatrick is the author of a Scarlatti biography. Composers Howard Hanson and Walter Piston are outstanding writers on music theory. Picked at random, these leaders offer proof that, far from detracting from a musician's ability, organized knowledge adds to his effectiveness as an artist. To make research an integral part of music education is therefore valid.

## The Nature of Music Research

The importance of the arts in every culture notwithstanding, research in this field sometimes lacks tangible results. Unlike the findings of research in some areas of science, which may be truly dramatic or even earth-shaking, the results of scholarly endeavor in the fine arts cannot be expected to be spectacular. It is characteristic of the artistic field that fresh facts are additive rather than replacive, tending more to increase the body of knowledge than to displace or nullify data previously accumulated. Each study, no matter how small, should contribute something to the sum of human learning and appreciation. Because the investigator is a force in the dissemination of his art, his work should be engaging to the reader. If his paper is prepared with enthusiasm and is well done, so that he transmits his interest to his reader—the professor, the graduate committee, or another investigator—his efforts are both musically and intellectually worthwhile.

American colleges and universities offer advanced degrees in music education, theory, history and literature, musicology, composition, performance, and therapy, with each field overlapping several others. Because no one area can exist alone, a researcher must expect his studies to cut across the limits of his specific subject into other fields.

When research is undertaken as a class assignment, the results may be presented as a course paper or an oral report. The time spent on it may be less than one semester. But when investigation is carried on for a thesis or a dissertation, the time spent is rarely less than two semesters and may extend over a period of years. Regardless of the magnitude of the project, research is a logical process: it is the pursuit of facts and ideas, the organization of the data to point to some possible conclusions, the evaluation of the results, and the presentation of the whole in an intelligible fashion.

## Some Basic Methods

Studies may be conducted and their conclusions presented in a variety of ways. One may analyze a composition with the aid of research materials to present the findings orally. One may consider a work in relation to its background, style, and aesthetic value to perform it in a recital. One may compare pedagogical procedures to evaluate them philosophically or critically. One may delve into the history of a subject to write an account of what he has learned. All such methods are valid and all constitute research.

Whether the presentation of the study is to be oral, performed, or written, essentially the same procedures may be followed in gathering and handling data. In spite of such variable elements as overlapping subject areas and differences of opinion and temperament among scholars, there are some basic methods of research in music:

1. The historical, in which a chronological account of the subject is given.
2. The developmental, in which the evolutionary processes of the subject are studied.
3. The theoretical, in which the subject is related to such concepts as form, harmony, counterpoint, and devices of composition.
4. The analytical, in which the subject is taken apart and reconstructed to learn why and how it functions.
5. The comparative, in which several elements may be examined for points of similarity; and conversely, the contrastive, in which points of difference are noted.
6. The experimental, in which tests are made in the hopes of discovering a physical or psychological phenomenon.
7. The critical, in which some criteria of judgment are established and applied to an evaluation of the subject.
8. The statistical, in which results of analyses or surveys or answers to questionnaires are tabulated to reach some conclusion or to prove or disprove a theory.
9. The speculative, in which a philosophy or theory may be formulated.[1]

[1]The speculative method is in danger of becoming too subjective only when the researcher allows himself to be carried away by an unsubstantiated idea.

10. The descriptive, in which a subject or a condition is systematically and fully described.

Other methods exist. Moreover, for most research projects several approaches must be used, either simultaneously or consecutively. Methods may differ, also, depending upon the relative complexity of the subject or the depth of the study.

No matter which method is employed, the writer needs to exercise imagination, judgment, and good taste to arrive at a logical conclusion and to account for his findings. Academic honesty is to be taken for granted. Self-reliance and originality, as opposed to slavish repetition of material already put forth by someone else, is required. Exactly where to draw the line between dependence upon another's authority and striking out on one's own is perhaps the nicest question of all and the most difficult to answer. In most cases the line of demarcation is not revealed until most of the fact-finding has been accomplished.

Libraries play an important role in the preparation of a report or thesis, for good results are well-nigh impossible without consulting many books, periodicals, and scores. Upon the wise use of library facilities rests not only the excellence of the final product but the speed and efficiency of research as well. In the chapters immediately following some useful information on library orientation is presented.

# 2

## The Music Library

### The Development
### of Music Libraries

Libraries everywhere are becoming increasingly important, and great effort is being expended to improve their services to scholars. The objective of the librarian is to make knowledge or the tools of knowledge available as quickly and efficiently as possible.

The library is a stockpile of knowledge in the form of books, manuscripts, maps, microprints, periodicals, pictures, recordings, and tapes; pamphlets and clippings may also be included, as well as such special materials as slides and filmstrips. It is an agency developed especially for convenience and economy. Where else but in a library can one expect to find a corpus of materials for his studies chosen with discrimination, classified and cataloged with care, and organized and shelved? Students may avail themselves of all its resources if they know how to get to them and, in some cases, if they have paid a nominal fee which is but an infinitesimal portion of what it would cost in time, energy, and money to search for and collect the necessary items themselves.

It takes years upon years to amass a research library, even a small one. In the large, illustrious libraries of Europe the process of accumulation has continued for many centuries. In America, many libraries have been collecting material for several decades, often sending agents to other parts of the world to search for and procure desired books. On the other hand, libraries in some areas of the United States and Canada have only recently begun their development, and it may be some time before they can become large research centers.

No matter what kind of library one encounters, he may be sure that

7

someone there has gone to much trouble to investigate the readers' needs, search out publishers and dealers, and arrange for the purchase of scores, journals, books, or whatever materials are wanted. Someone has worked to classify and catalog the acquisitions before arranging them on the shelves for the prospective user. If one is disappointed in a library because it lacks a desired piece of music or a particular periodical, he may feel inclined to complain about the collection or malign the librarian. It is more realistic instead to be thankful for the material the library contains that he can use without first having had to search for it and purchase it himself. Regardless of size, location, and arrangement, a library represents a capital investment which often runs into millions of dollars. Moreover, thousands of professional hours have been expended upon it.

The United States being a comparatively young nation, the development of its music libraries (or music sections within libraries) is of recent occurrence. The majority of the collections have been instituted since the beginning of the present century. Indeed, fifty years ago, except in the most favored cities, it was almost impossible to find a well-stocked music library in America, and scholars were obliged to travel to Europe to do their research.

Fortunately the situation has improved. Before 1940 several music libraries had developed: collections in the New York Public Library, Boston Public Library, Grosvenor Library in Buffalo, New York (now part of the Buffalo and Erie County Library), the Sibley Music Library in Rochester, New York; the music divisions of the Carnegie Library in Pittsburgh, the Free Library of Philadelphia, the Cincinnati Public Library, the Newberry Library in Chicago, the Detroit Public Library, the Los Angeles and San Francisco Public Libraries, and the Henry E. Huntington Library in San Marino, California, to name some at random. The Music Division of the Library of Congress has long been the most outstanding collection of music in the Western Hemisphere and one of the greatest in the world.[1]

Hand in hand with the phenomenal growth of universities and colleges following World War II has come a proportionate expansion of research facilities. The establishment of important collections in the great university and public libraries of the Far West, Southwest, and Middle West is a

---

[1]For accounts of outstanding music libraries in all countries, see Charles L. Cudworth, "Libraries and Collections," in *Grove's Dictionary of Music and Musicians*, 5th ed. (London: Macmillan, 1954), V, 160–223; Supplement (1961), 266–267; and Alfons Ott and Richard Schaal, "Musikbibliotheken und Sammlungen," in *Die Musik in Geschichte und Gegenwart* (Kassel: Bärenreiter-Verlag, 1949–    ), IX, cols. 1034–1078. For information about libraries in the United States and Canada which include music in their collections, see also Anthony T. Kruzas, ed., *Directory of Special Libraries and Information Centers* (Detroit: Gale Research Co., 1963).

comparatively recent phenomenon—a dramatic development in a large section of the country where research sources in music had heretofore been few and widely scattered. Still, because of the geography of our national progress, with population building up first in the East, the music libraries with the richest and largest holdings of historical significance are (with a few notable exceptions) found in the cities of the Atlantic seaboard.

Some important, basic differences exist between the contents of European and American libraries. Of long standing and showing a national, institutional, or personal bias, the collections of Europe are well stocked with historical materials (manuscripts, incunabula, part-books, theoretical treatises, early editions of both music and books, and possibly some periodicals) originating in or having to do with the place in which they are located. National, royal, or state libraries reflect the output of specific countries. Libraries in conservatories contain works of their masters and students. Libraries in theaters may represent the repertory of the operatic companies that have played there. Cathedral libaries, amassed through the centuries, are working collections of music performed in religious services, while monastery libraries are repositories for the writings of the scholar-monks. Private collections may be the result of a nobleman's hobby or favorite cultural interest. Modern books about music may not be included, because of the absence of practical necessity for them or possibly a lack of funds for their acquisition. Recordings are customarily not a part of the collection.

On the other hand, American libraries, supported by annual appropriations and maintained for current study purposes, are stocked with secondary sources: reference works, books, and periodicals. Scores and sheet music are likely to be of recent issue, and recordings are nearly always a part of the collection. Two major factors are responsible for this: (1) In spite of the trend among the large, well-established libraries to acquire manuscripts and early editions of European music, the average American music library has been unsuccessful in competing with European libraries for the possession of primary sources. For reasons of availability and economy, the procurement of scores, historical sets, journals, and treatises published before World War II has been difficult. (2) Because the American college library must reflect institutional curricula and subject interests of the faculty, materials in greatest demand for implementing classes are acquired before others are considered for purchase. The public library is similarly obliged to obtain books and music most useful to its patrons. By necessity rather than by preference, therefore, some libraries in the United States consist mainly of secondary sources, books in English, music of domestic production, and reprints of standard works.

The doctoral candidate in musicology or theory may profit by selecting an institution which maintains both a strong department of instruction and a well-stocked library for research. Although he may acquire materials through such cooperative schemes as interlibrary loan, there is no substitute for locally available resources. Wherever the student may be, however, to know how to reach the contents of libraries is important, and the first step is to learn the operations of music collections in general and of the local institution in particular.

## The Location of Music Materials in the Library

The collection and housing of music materials in a college is influenced by its size and academic policies. Some libraries contain only a few hundred volumes; others contain hundreds of thousands. In schools where music is part of a humanities or liberal arts course, the music materials (scores, books, periodicals, and recordings) may all be placed in the general library and the items recorded by entries in the general catalog. The student may locate his sources in one building by consulting one catalog. Depending upon the classification system in use, he may find scores and sheet music arranged in one section of the library, while reference works and books about music may be intershelved with books on other subjects; or he may find scores, recordings, and books about music occupying a separate section of their own in the library stacks. In rare instances, all music materials may be interfiled in a single numerical or alphabetical sequence. In a one-library college the collection is usually so compact that materials are easily accessible no matter what their arrangement may be. The librarian in charge is not necessarily a music specialist. He is likely to be an all-around scholar capable of advising students of varying interests.

If the music division is part of a school of fine arts, the music sources are often integrated into an arts library supervised by a specialist in music or a specialist in art. Some universities with a separate school of music maintain a departmental collection of scores and recordings supervised by a music specialist and housed within the music building; books about music may be found in the general university library. In other universities music currently in print may constitute the music library, while the rare books and out-of-print works may be part of the university's research collection. On some large campuses, separate undergraduate and graduate libraries may be maintained in buildings of their own, both containing music materials on appropriate levels. The investigator may have to consult several catalogs and visit several buildings in quest of his sources, but he will be rewarded by a larger selection of references than he probably would encounter in a one-library institution.

The ideal situation, admittedly existing in only a few large schools of music, is the relatively autonomous music library in which all materials form a single collection housed in one building. Such a library is large, and adequate for most of the research needs of graduate students. It may include rare books, incunabula, and manuscripts. Its selection of scores and books in print tends to be all-inclusive. The researcher may enlist the services of well-trained librarians who are both competent musicians and scholars.

Various arrangements similar to those outlined above are found in public libraries, with the size and organization determined by the nature of the community, flexibility of civil-service regulations for employees, and availability of funds. In many large cities the music division of the public library is expected to offer research opportunities to students from several neighboring colleges and high schools in addition to making music available to the public. Such services require a superior collection of materials as well as an efficient staff.

Because of burgeoning public and college libraries and the necessity for maintaining order, departmentalization is becoming more common. A student must become acquainted with the operations of special departments, each with its own regulations. Some libraries maintain a reference department in which dictionaries, encyclopedias, and bibliographical tools for many subjects are kept, and a staff member trained in the use of such materials is in charge. Reference books customarily are consulted within departmental quarters and are not withdrawn for home use. Many libraries have a periodical room housing journals and newspapers. Some institutions serving a clientele of scholars may also maintain a microtext department, with equipment for reading microfilms and microcards. Others may make provision for the mechanical retrieval of data. In public libraries, an important department is the audiovisual or record room for films and recordings. Where such departmentalization takes place, the student may find music sources in several different sections of the library.

# Libraries Containing
# Special Music Sources

Although some "ordinary" music and books may be included in such collections as the Henry E. Huntington Library in San Marino, the Newberry Library in Chicago, the Pierpont Morgan Library in New York, and the Folger Shakespeare Library in Washington, the greater portion of these libraries' holdings is "special," consisting of unusual or even unique works of historical or cultural significance: manuscripts, incunabula, first or early editions, and special printings. Nearly all such items are valuable, and many are priceless. Similar treasures are housed in rare-book divisions of the Library of Congress and some of the large public and university libraries, and they often include music sources.

Almost without exception, rare and antiquarian books are reserved for study by the advanced scholar, who must use them within premises subject to security measures. Neither such regulations nor the distance he might have to travel to a special library should deter the serious researcher from seeking original sources. Even when facsimiles and reprints are available, it is rewarding, particularly in historical investigation, to see the genuine article.

Possibilities for locating materials exist beyond the music library. Items of local interest, found in township libraries and collections of historical societies, may prove useful for research in early American music. Libraries devoted to cultural history—the Frank V. de Bellis Collection, for example[2]—often possess important books on music in addition to works in peripheral areas which may have bearing upon one's research project. A subject collection, such as one devoted to the life and works of da Vinci, may be rich in musical resources. Libraries in museums possessing instrument collections or showing interest in musical iconography usually contain useful reference works. One may consult the *American Library Directory*,[3] *The World of Learning*,[4] the *Directory of Special Libraries and Information Centers*,[5] and the *International Library Directory*,[6] as well as lists of museums and libraries issued by Chambers of Commerce to determine the location of such resources.

Although librarians and their assistants may be present to assist their patrons, the student can learn to help himself. Each library may differ slightly from all others, but in spite of seeming diversity there is an appreciable degree of conformity in principles of operation. On the whole, libraries in the United States and Canada are more likely than their

[2] A description of this library, a collection of Italian cultural contributions to Western civilization now a part of the San Francisco State College, is given in *The Frank V. de Bellis Collection in the Library of San Francisco State College* (San Francisco: San Francisco State College, 1964).

[3] *American Library Directory* (24th ed.), (New York: R. R. Bowker Company, 1964).

[4] *The World of Learning, 1965–66* (16th ed.), (London: Europa Publications, Ltd., 1965). A volume is issued annually.

[5] Kruzas, Anthony T., ed., *Directory of Special Libraries and Information Centers* (Detroit: Gale Research Co., 1963).

[6] *International Library Directory* (London: A. P. Wales Organization, 1963). Though international in coverage, the entries include many special and local libraries.

European counterparts[7] to present a uniform appearance and to function under nearly similar conditions. Comparatively new, serving a large public, and striving for efficiency, they tend to adopt practices common to other institutions of their kind. With a knowledge of basic procedures, therefore, a student can work profitably in almost any American collection.

# BIBLIOGRAPHY

*American Library Directory* (24th ed.), ed. Eleanor F. Steiner-Prag. New York: R. R. Bowker Company, 1964.

Cudworth, Charles L., "Libraries and Collections," in *Grove's Dictionary of Music and Musicians* (5th ed.), V, 160–223; Supplement (1961), 266–267, ed. Eric Blom. London: Macmillan & Co., Ltd., 1954.

*The Frank V. de Bellis Collection in the Library of San Francisco State College.* San Francisco: San Francisco State College, 1964.

*International Library Directory.* London: A. P. Wales Organization, 1963.

Kruzas, Anthony T., ed., *Directory of Special Libraries and Information Centers.* Detroit: Gale Research Co., 1963.

Ott, Alfons and Richard Schaal, "Musikbibliotheken und Sammlungen," in *Die Musik in Geschichte und Gegenwart*, IX, cols. 1034–1078, ed. Friedrich Blume. Kassel: Bärenreiter-Verlag, 1949–    .

*The World of Learning, 1965–66* (16th ed.). London: Europa Publications Ltd., 1965.

---

[7]Many European libraries were originally special depositories and reflect varying and sometimes unusual tastes of private owners. Other collections, not operated as public libraries, have adopted different procedures most suited to their patrons.

# 3

# Library Catalog Cards

## Types of Library Catalogs

After locating various departments within a library, one approaches their contents through the catalog, the purpose of which is to indicate what items are available and where they are shelved. Library catalogs vary in appearance, content, and format, according to the nature of the collection and the systems under which they operate.

A detailed catalog is not necessary in some European libraries whose curators, through long tenure of office, know where things are, and whose patrons have both patience and the time to wait for books to be brought to them. Handwritten lists of books or myriad slips pasted into volumes may constitute a catalog. Although they are not catalogs in the sense that the American library patron envisions catalogs, they are reminders to the curator of the holdings of his institution.

Many European catalogs are printed. They range from slender books of brief entries to large tomes of full, scholarly, descriptive entries.[1] Although printed volumes in multiple copies have the advantage of being accessible, portable, and compact, they suffer from being inflexible. Revisions and additions cannot be made without issuing a supplementary volume or preparing a new edition of the catalog. The volumes with abbreviated entries, moreover, are not fully descriptive of the items they represent and may do little justice to the importance of the collection.

In the typical American library, with rapid employee turnover and

[1]An example of a catalog serving both as a catalog per se and as a reference tool is *The Catalogue of Printed Music in the British Museum. Part 53: Music in the Hirsch Library* (London: The Trustees of the British Museum, 1951).

14

patrons who are numerous in their demands and always in a hurry, the catalog must be accessible and specific, giving complete identification of each item in the collection. The catalog should be intelligible to patrons and staff alike, especially where stacks are open and the clients must locate their own books.

The chief type of public catalog in America is the *card catalog* in which printed or typed cards are filed according to some arbitrary system. Even in the large libraries which issue departmental catalogs in book form by mechanical print-out, the master catalog remains on cards. As cumbersome as a card catalog can become, with heavy cabinets needed to accommodate the entries, the use of cards has been justified by practical considerations: (1) The uniformity achieved by cards of a standard size is pleasing to the client who is already accustomed to working with similar files in other contexts. (2) American college libraries, faced with expanding curricula and changing student needs, are inclined toward a fluctuating collection. Public libraries, geared to shifting popular tastes, are likewise subject to rearrangement. Americans are more likely than Europeans to add and discard books.[2] In a card file a librarian may add, shift, revise, and discard entries without disturbing the rest of the catalog, a convenience that has not gone unnoticed by the many foreign librarians who now subscribe to the card catalog system.

## Types of Cards

In the card catalog system, each item available in the library is represented by several cards, of which the following types are the most important:[3]

1. The *author card*. When the author is known, a card is made with his name as the heading. The *composer card* for a piece of music is equivalent to the author card.
2. The *title card*. A card is made with the title as heading if the title is distinctive (uniquely descriptive, unusual, startling, or humorous, as in *Golliwog's Cakewalk* by Claude Debussy or *The Well-Tempered Listener* by Deems Taylor). A title card is made also for an anonymous work.

[2]In Europe, where most readers buy their own books, the institutional libraries can remain comparatively stable. Americans tend to borrow books for collateral and leisure-time reading as well as for research, thereby compelling libraries to stock items which may be of ephemeral value, subject to being discarded once their popularity has waned.

[3]If the catalog is in book form, each item is represented by several entries in the book. The information given is similar to that on cards.

3. The *subject card*. A card is made with the subject as heading to indicate what is available on that subject to a reader who is not looking for a specific title or writer. A card for a piece of music may show its medium, the type, and/or form (BALLET MUSIC; PIANO MUSIC —SONATAS; CLARINET MUSIC—STUDIES).[4] If a work deals with several subjects, or a composition represents several forms (prelude and fugue, for example), a card is prepared for each subject or form of music.

A book may be represented by several other cards, such as those for a joint author, editor, translator, or compiler. Moreover, the catalog may contain a variety of special cards, which will be discussed below.

## The Author Card

An author card for a book may look like Figure 3–1.

**Figure 3-1  An Author Card for a Book.**

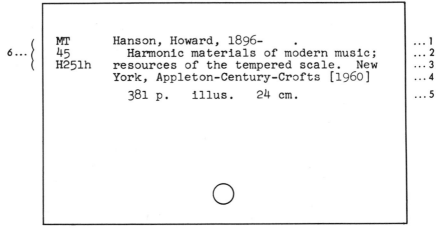

1. Hanson, Howard, 1896–     . (the *author*)

The name of the author is indicated, with his last name first, followed by his given name(s). The date of birth (and, if applicable, of death) may be given, although vital statistics need not be included unless the cataloger wishes the card to be complete in detail or to give information helpful to

[4]Capital letters are used here to indicate subject headings, a practice found in many catalogs.

the patron. Dates are given as a rule, however, when several writers of the same name appear in the catalog and the individuals must be identified:

Bradley, George, 1688–1751.
Bradley, George, 1856–1910.
Bradley, George, 1922–    .

2–3. Harmonic materials of modern music; resources of the tempered scale.    (the *title*)

Following the author's name, the title of his book is given. Usually it is quoted from the title page.[5] If the title is in a foreign language, the text is likely to be in that language.[6] Sometimes a title is so long that the cataloger may wish to shorten it; ordinarily, however, the complete title is given, as in Figure 3–1.

3–4. New York, Appleton-Century-Crofts [1960]    (the *imprint*)

The imprint is a statement of where, by whom, and when the work was published or copyrighted. On lines 3 and 4 of the example, the imprint shows that the book was published in New York by Appleton-Century-Crofts in 1960. On some cards the publication date is enclosed in brackets, indicating that the information came from a source other than the title page (e.g., the copyright notice, the preface, or the reverse side of the title page). If the date given is the copyright date (which may be different from the date of printing), the notation is generally preceded by "c" (e.g., c. 1960).

5.    381 p.    illus.    24 cm.    (the *collation*)

The collation indicates the number of pages contained in the book, the presence of such important items as illustrations and facsimiles, and any other characteristics which might prove useful in describing a book. The information here is clear: the book contains 381 pages, includes illustrations, and stands 24 centimeters high. Items listed in the collation include charts, diagrams, frontispiece, facsimiles, illustrations, maps, musical examples, plans, plates, portraits, and tables. The physical dimensions of the book give a quick mental image of the volume; it is convenient to know how tall an item stands in libraries where folios or miniature scores may occupy special shelves. The number of pages in a book shows its relative thickness.

[5]The title page is the page in front of the book, on which information is given concerning the author, title, and (usually) the publisher and the place and date of publication. It is the page by which the book can easily be identified.
[6]For example, in a book entitled *Die Geschichte der Musik*, the account of the history of music probably will be in German.

6.   MT   (the *call number*)
     45
     H251h

The various letters, numbers, and other devices usually placed in the upper left-hand corner of the catalog card constitute the call number, a set of symbols used to identify and locate a specific book in a specific place. To the average library patron the call number indicates where to find the item among other books of its kind.[7] Because the holdings of any library are different from those of every other, each collection arbitrarily assigns its own call numbers to its own books. Call numbers therefore vary with the institution. A book may bear one set of symbols in Library X, while another copy of the same work will have a different series of symbols in Library Y. Sometimes such notations as "Rare Book Room," or "Reference" are added to a call number to show the department within the library where the book is found. One must copy each detail when filling out a call slip to request a book, for every symbol of the call number carries a definite and specific meaning.

Some catalog cards look more complicated than others. The degree of complexity is usually determined by the amount of descriptive material necessary to identify the book.

**Figure 3-2   A More Complex Card for a Book.**

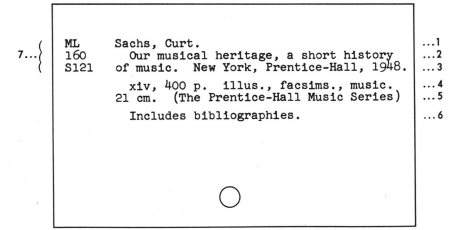

1.   Sachs, Curt.   (the author)

[7]To the professional librarian or advanced research specialist the call number may also have further connotations of classification by subject, size, or order of accession, the author's name, and a suggestion of the title and edition, but these technical considerations are beyond the scope of this handbook.

2–3.  Our musical heritage, a short history of music.    (the title)

3.    New York, Prentice-Hall, 1948.    (the imprint)

4–5.  xiv, 400 p.  illus., facsims., music.  21 cm.  (The Prentice-Hall Music Series)  (the collation)

In Figure 3–2 the collation is more complicated than that in Figure 3–1: the main portion of the text, consisting of 400 pages and including illustrations, facsimiles, and music, is preceded by 14 preliminary pages. The book is 21 centimeters in height. It forms part of a publisher's series called The Prentice-Hall Music Series.

6.    Includes bibliographies.    (the *note*)

The note is an added feature to indicate that the book contains such research aids as bibliographies, discographies, thematic indexes, and the like. A *contents note* may be used on cards representing books made up of a number of individual works (an anthology) or of several well-defined sections, each by a separate author (see Figure 3–7). In other words, the notes record distinguishing features of the book which are not already given in the body of the catalog card.

7.    ML   (the call number)
      160
      S121

A catalog card representing a musical composition contains essentially the same elements as one for a book (see Figure 3–3).

Figure 3-3   A Catalog Card for a Piece of Music.

```
 ┌──────────────────────────────────────────────────────────┐
 │                                                          │
 │   M        Hovhaness, Alan Scott.                  ...1  │
8...│   1045       Concerto no. 8, for orchestra, op.    ...2  │
 │   H845c.8m  117.  New York, C. F. Peters Corp.,     ...3  │
 │   c. 1958.                                          ...4  │
 │                                                          │
 │            73 p.  19 cm.  (Edition Peters no.      ...5  │
 │         6049)                                            │
 │                                                          │
 │            Miniature score.                         ...7  │
 │                                                          │
 │                                                          │
 │                         ◯                                │
 │                                                          │
 └──────────────────────────────────────────────────────────┘
```

1.    Hovhaness, Alan Scott.   (the composer)

2–3.  Concerto No. 8, for orchestra, op. 117.   (the title)

3–4.  New York, C. F. Peters Corp., c. 1958.   (the imprint)

5–6.  73 p.   19 cm.   (Edition Peters no. 6049)   (the collation)

7.    Miniature score.   (the note)

8.    M   (the call number)
      1045
      H845c.8m

The same methods of interpretation may be used for reading a card representing a piece of music. In Figure 3–3, the note (Miniature score.) means that the music is in small format with reduced-size print, as contrasted to the full score in large format and normal type.

## The Conventional Title

Most music catalogs contain *conventional titles*. In order that the cards for any and all forms of a given composition may be filed in the same place regardless of how the title pages may read, the cataloger may arbitrarily choose one title under which the various editions of the work, the arrangements of it, and the excerpts from it are to be brought together. This title, known as the conventional title, appears in brackets following the composer's name. It may be a distinctive title, as in Figure 3–4. It may also be a form title; if Beethoven's well-known symphony bears title page designations like *Eroica Symphony*, *Third Symphony*, or *Symphony in E-Flat*, the cataloger may use *Symphony No. 3* as the conventional title, under which all the cards will be filed to save the reader the trouble of looking under "Eroica" and "Third" as well as "Symphony."

In Figure 3–4, the conventional title chosen by the cataloger is *Le nozze di Figaro*, which appears at line 2 on all three cards. This opera by Mozart is also known as *Figaro*, *Figaros Hochzeit*, *The Marriage of Figaro*, and *Les noces de Figaro*. In the absence of a conventional title, the reader would have to look under all versions of the title, as well as the title of the excerpt (*Porgi amor* at line 2, Figure 3–4C). Because it may be difficult to hit upon the right conventional title when one is searching in a catalog, the cataloger provides *see cards* (see Figure 4–1) to lead the patron from each of the title variants to the conventional title.

Card A in Figure 3–4 represents an English score with an English title; card B, a French score with a French title; and card C, an excerpt from the opera. All are brought together in the catalog under Mozart, Wolfgang Amadeus and the single title: *Le nozze di Figaro*. The cards also illustrate some rather detailed entries used in cataloging music. In card A, lines 2 to 6, the score represented by the card is fully described with regard to the number of acts, name of the librettist, translator, arranger, and the format (vocal score). Card B gives the names of the translators and the format (partition piano et chant). Such details are sometimes helpful in identifying an edition of a work if the composition has been published in several

**Figure 3-4    Three Cards with Conventional Title.**

A

```
M          Mozart, Wolfgang Amadeus.                    ...1
1503          [Le nozze di Figaro].  The marriage      ...2
M93nBoR    of Figaro.  Opera in four acts by Wolf-     ...3
           gang Amadeus Mozart. Words by Lorenzo       ...4
           da Ponte. English version by Edward J.      ...5
           Dent. Vocal score by Ernest Roth.  New      ...6
           York, Boosey and Hawkes, Inc., [1947]       ...7

              354 p.  Pub. pl. no. B. and H. 15960.    ...8
           27 cm.                                      ...9
```

B

```
M          Mozart, Wolfgang Amadeus.                    ...1
1503          [Le nozze di Figaro].  Les noces de      ...2
M93bH      Figaro. De W. A. Mozart. Traduction         ...3
           française rhythmée par A. van Hasselt et    ...4
           J.-B. Rongé. Partition piano et chant.      ...5
           Braunschweig, Litolff, [185-?]              ...6
              224 p.  Pub. pl. no. 88.  28 cm.         ...7
```

C

```
M          Mozart, Wolfgang Amadeus.                    ...1
1508           [Le nozze di Figaro].  Porgi amor        ...2
M939LP     (Mighty love).  For voice and piano, in      ...3
           D.  Edited by Edgardo Lèvi.  London,         ...4
           Ascherberg, Hopwood and Crew, Ltd.,          ...5
           [1912]                                        ...6
               6 p.   36 cm.
```

different forms by different publishers, or if it has been issued in several versions. In card C, lines 2 to 4 carry the title of the excerpt, its English translation, the arrangement (for voice and piano), the key, and the name of the editor, clearly distinguishing it from any other edition of the same excerpt.

At line 6, card B, the date of the imprint reads: [185–?]. Because the publication date did not appear on the title page, brackets are used. The cataloger, unable to locate a printing or copyright date anywhere on the score, has resorted to a dash and question mark to suggest an approximate (and even questionable) date. In the opinion of the cataloger the piece was probably published in the 1850's.

At line 8, card A, and line 7, card B, the *publisher's plate number* is given in the collation to aid in identification and dating of the scores. An explanation of this device appears in Chapter 11.

## The Joint Author

If two or more authors collaborate on a book, the author whose name appears first on the title page is considered the "first" writer and the heading appears under his name. In *Music in History* by Howard D. McKinney and W. R. Anderson, "McKinney" appears first on the title page and is the name used for the author entry, in spite of the fact that "Anderson" comes first in the alphabet. Anderson's name appears as an added entry and he is designated as joint author (see Figure 3–8).

Figure 3-5    Author Entry for a Collaboration.

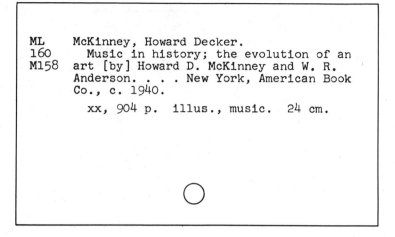

Figure 3-6    An Organization as Author.

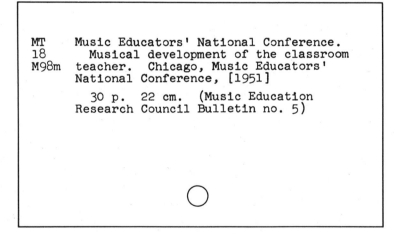

If the book was not written by an individual but is the work of an organization, a committee, or an agency (e.g., Music Educators' National Conference, Figure 3–6), the name of the group is used as the author.

The cards described above, with the author's name as the heading, are *author cards*. When they are placed in a catalog, they represent the *author entry* or *main entry*. The author card using an organization heading is also

called a *corporate entry*. The cards are filed in alphabetical order by whatever appears first on the card (excluding the call number):

> Hanson
> Hovhaness
> McKinney
> Mozart
> Music Educators' National Conference
> Sachs

## Other Types of Cards:
## Added Entries

Cards of other types may be found in the catalog. An example of an
*editor card* is shown in Figure 3–7.

**Figure 3-7   An Editor Card.**

```
ML      Reeser, Eduard, 1908-    , ed.              ...1
295.5      Music in Holland; a review of contempo-   ...2
H329m   rary music in the Netherlands.  Authors:     ...3
        Wouter Paap [and others]. Trans. by Ian F.   ...4
        Finlay. Amsterdam, J.M. Meulenhoff, [1959]   ...5
           x, 247 p.  illus., ports., music.         ...6
        25 cm.                                        ...7
           Contents.-Composers, by W. Paap.-Musical  ...8
        performers, by J. Wouters.-Musical educa-    ...9
        tion, by J. Daniskas.-Organizations, by E.  ...10
        Brautigam.-Popular and light music, by A.   ...11
        Swart.                                       ...12
```

1.    Reeser, Eduard, 1908–    , ed.   (the *editor*)

The name appearing as the heading is that of an editor rather than of
an author. The book, consisting of sections by various writers, is edited
by Eduard Reeser, whose name is given with the proper designation.

2–3.  Music in Holland; a review of contemporary music in the Nether-
      lands.   (the title)

3–4.  Authors: Wouter Paap [and others].

Several authors, including Wouter Paap, who wrote the first section, are involved in the preparation of the book. A listing of all the writers would be excessive. The cataloger has indicated in brackets that others besides Paap are included.

4–5.  Trans. by Ian F. Finlay.   (the *translator*)

Originally in Dutch, the work was translated into English by Ian F. Finlay, who is designated as the translator. The information about the several authors and the translator is included on the catalog as further description.

5.     Amsterdam, J. M. Meulenhoff, [1959].   (the imprint)

6–7.  x, 247 p.   illus., ports., music.   25 cm.   (the collation)

8–12. Contents.-Composers, by W. Paap.-Musical performers, by J. Wouters. . . . (the *contents note*)

Because the book contains sections or separate essays by several writers, the cataloger has made a *contents note* in which the title and author of each are given. A glance at the note provides the reader with an idea of the scope of the volume.

Such a card is an *editor card*, treated as the main entry in lieu of the author card. The example above should be filed in the catalog under "R" for Reeser. Entries may be made for a compiler in case the book is a compilation, and then the *compiler card* becomes the main entry.

When, as in the text by McKinney and Anderson (see Figure 3–5), the book is a collaboration, a card may be made for the joint author, as shown in Figure 3–8.

Figure 3-8   A Card for a Joint Author.

```
        Anderson, W   R    , jt. author.
ML      McKinney, Howard Decker.
160        Music in history, the evolution of an
M158    art [by] Howard D. McKinney and W. R.
        Anderson. . . . New York, American Book
        Co., c. 1940.
           xx, 904 p.   illus., music.   24 cm.
```

A card for the *translator* (abbreviated "tr." or "trans.") may be made, especially if the translation is in itself an important work of literary or scholarly value. A card may be made for the *librettist* of an opera, operetta, or oratorio, as well as for the *lyricist* or writer of the text of a song.

The editor, joint author, and translator cards are *added entries*. While they may not be the most important cards in the file, they function to provide information and increase avenues of approach to a given book or composition. No matter how many added entries there may be, the basic elements on the cards remain the same.[8] The cataloger prepares a *unit card*, the master card in the form of a main entry, from which any number of copies may be made, and the appropriate heading is then typed or printed above the main entry. This *unit card system* provides for unified and organized growth of the library catalog.

## The Title Card

*Title cards* are prepared for works with a distinctive title (e.g., Debussy's *Golliwog's Cakewalk*). If a work is anonymous, there must naturally be a title card in order to identify the book. A typical title card may look like the example in Figure 3–9. In accordance with the unit card system, everything about the card follows the arrangement of the author entry, except that the title is added at the head of the card. When a con-

Figure 3-9   A Typical Title Card.

```
                    Through an opera glass.
        ML          Gass, Irene.
        1700            Through an opera glass, by Irene Gass
        G251TW       and Herbert Weinstock.  London, New
                     York, Abelard-Schuman, [1958]
                        166 p.  illus.  21 cm.




                                    O
```

[8]Similar information also appears in entries in "book" catalogs which are arranged in volumes instead of on cards.

ventional title (see above, Figure 3–4) is used, all the title cards bear the conventional title as their heading, no matter what the respective title pages contain (see Figure 3–10).

**Figure 3-10   Conventional Title Card.**

```
          Le nozze di Figaro.
M         Mozart, Wolfgang Amadeus.
1503         [Le nozze di Figaro]. The marriage
M93nBoR   of Figaro. Opera in four acts by Wolf-
          gang Amadeus Mozart. Words by Lorenzo
          da Ponte. English version by Edward J.
          Dent. Vocal score by Ernest Roth.  New
          York, Boosey and Hawkes, Inc., [1947]

             354 p.  Pub. pl. no. B. and H. 15960.
          27 cm.
```

## The Subject Card

Among the various types of added entries are *subject cards*, indicating subject matter of a book. Two subject cards for the same book are shown in Figure 3–11. A book may deal with several subjects. A separate card

**Figure 3-11   Typical Subject Cards.**

```
          MUSIC - HISTORY AND CRITICISM - 20TH CENT.
ML        Machlis, Joseph, 1906-     .
197          Introduction to contemporary music.
M149I     New York, W. W. Norton, [1961]

             714 p.  illus.  24 cm.

          Includes bibliography and discography.
```

```
              MUSIC - APPRECIATION.
  ML       Machlis, Joseph, 1906-
  197          Introduction to contemporary music.
  M149I    New York, W. W. Norton, [1961]

              714 p.   illus.   24 cm.

              Includes bibliography and discography.



                            ◯
```

is made for each. The number and nature of the subject headings depend upon the scope of the work and upon the system of headings adopted by the library. From several existing schemes or lists of subject headings each library chooses one which best fits its needs.[9] The adoption of a list means that the specific subject headings are arbitrarily used to avoid variation and elaboration, and it is necessary for the reader to know the scheme used in his library.[10]

The subject headings are typed in red in some libraries and in capital letters or boldface in others, depending upon the custom of the institution. The cards are filed in alphabetical order by the heading, so that when they are in their proper arrangement, they indicate all the books available in the library on a given subject. (For their use in a subject catalog, see Chapter 5.)

People as well as things may be subjects of study. In Figure 3–12 Franz Liszt is the subject.

Cards equivalent in function to subject cards are prepared for musical compositions. Properly speaking, they cannot be called subject cards, for they indicate the type of music, the medium of expression, or the form of the work, as shown in Figures 3–13 to 3–15.

[9]Many American libraries use *Music Subject Headings Used in Printed Catalog Cards of the Library of Congress* (Washington: Library of Congress, 1952). Some smaller libraries use Minnie Earl Sears, comp., *List of Subject Headings for Small Libraries* (8th ed.), ed. Bertha M. Frick (New York: The H. W. Wilson Company, 1959). In some libraries the list of subject headings is devised by the subject catalogers. Usually a printed or typed list is posted for the convenience of the readers.

[10]If the list of subject headings used in the library is not posted, the student should ask the catalogers for information. Every catalog department has a master list from which subject cataloging is done.

Figure 3-12    A Card Showing a Person as Subject.

LISZT, FRANZ, 1811-1886.

ML      Westerby, Herbert.
410       Liszt, composer, and his piano works.
L77W52  Descriptive guide and critical analysis
        . . . By Herbert Westerby . . . London,
        W. Reeves, Ltd., [1936]

          xxii, 336 p.   front., illus., music,
        ports.   19 cm.

Figure 3-13    A Card for a Type of Music.

BALLETS.

M       Bondon, Jacques.
1520      La coupole; tableaux fantastiques
B711cm  d'un monde étrange.   Paris, Heugel,
        [c. 1929]

          76 p.   19 cm.

          Miniature score.

          Contents.-I. La coupole.-II. Jenkins.-
        III. Las horlas.

The card in Figure 3–13 will be filed under "B," along with entries for other ballets. By looking through the catalog a person may find all the ballet music available in the collection. A student wishing to know what compositions are available for horn may look under HORN MUSIC to find a complete file of such works available in the library. One looking for piano sonatas may look under PIANO MUSIC—SONATAS.

The heading HORN MUSIC in Figure 3–14 represents an undivided heading, while PIANO MUSIC—SONATAS in Figure 3–15 represents a

Figure 3-14   A Card for a Musical Medium.

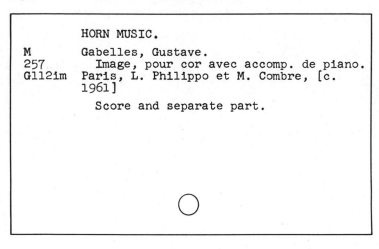

```
          HORN MUSIC.
M         Gabelles, Gustave.
257          Image, pour cor avec accomp. de piano.
G112im    Paris, L. Philippo et M. Combre, [c.
          1961]
            Score and separate part.
```

Figure 3-15   A Card for a Musical Medium and a Form.

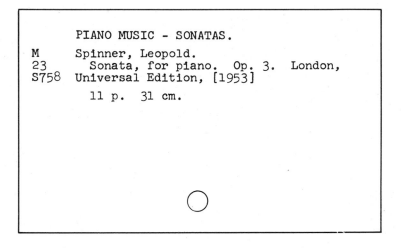

```
          PIANO MUSIC - SONATAS.
M         Spinner, Leopold.
23           Sonata, for piano.  Op. 3.   London,
S758      Universal Edition, [1953]
            11 p.   31 cm.
```

subdivided heading. Headings for "small" subjects (i.e., those with comparatively few items in the library) are usually undivided. Headings for "large" subjects (with many items in the library) are likely to be subdivided: PIANO MUSIC—BALLADES; PIANO MUSIC—CONCERTOS; PIANO MUSIC—DANCES.

# Summary: Relationship
# of Cards to Each Other

In the card catalog the author card is ordinarily the *main entry*. If there is no author card, but an editor card takes its place (Figure 3–7), the editor card is the main entry. If the work is anonymous, the title card becomes the main entry. The main entry is simply the first card in importance to the cataloger and identifies the book. The other cards are added to provide several avenues of approach to a work and to increase efficiency in locating various kinds of materials in a library catalog; hence their designation, "added entries." If the reader wishes to know the number and nature of the added entries for any given book or composition, he may look on the bottom of the printed main entry card[11] or on the reverse side of the typed one. He will find *tracings* or notations indicating the added entries used in the specific library.

The cards so far discussed describe a book or a piece of music by recording its physical features and identifying characteristics as well as its author, title, and subject(s). Although they constitute the majority of cards found in the catalog, there are still other types of cards serving additional purposes. Special cards are explained in the next chapter.

## BIBLIOGRAPHY

*The Catalogue of Printed Music in the British Museum. Part 53: Music in the Hirsch Library*. London: The Trustees of the British Museum, 1951.

*Music Subject Headings Used in Printed Catalog Cards of the Library of Congress*. Washington: Library of Congress, 1952.

Sears, Minnie Earl, comp., *List of Subject Headings for Small Libraries* (8th ed.), ed. Bertha M. Frick. New York: The H. W. Wilson Company, 1959.

[11]Many libraries use printed cards issued by the Library of Congress, while other libraries use cards typed by the staff or reproduced by some copying device.

# 4

## Cross-Reference
## and Special Cards

### The See Card

Some special cards, differing in appearance and purpose from those discussed in Chapter 3, are found in nearly all catalogs. They aid efficiency and speed in locating desired items. While most libraries adhere to basic general practices of cataloging, they differ in matters of form, spelling, and subject headings. To guide the reader to the proper entries when such variants are involved, each institution prepares its own set of special cards. Perhaps the most numerous of them are the *see cards*, used for cross-reference. If one has looked under a name or subject heading but has failed to find entries, a see card may indicate where he should have looked. The see card carries the message, "Don't look here; look there."

Such cards are filed in the catalog by the name given first on the card (under "T" for Tschaikovsky; under "Sc" for Scriabin). They have evolved as a result of some arbitrary practices existing by necessity in all libraries. A problem arises when a cataloger must determine which of several acceptable spelling variants he will adopt for his catalog. In the first example (Fig. 4–1), the cataloger selected "Chaikovskii," the variant used on the printed cards issued by the Library of Congress, as the spelling to be used throughout the catalog. All the cards for the composer bear this spelling, no matter what variants may appear on the title-pages of the many works by and about him, and they are filed under "Chaikovskii." But many people habitually spell the name "Tschaikovsky" and will look under "Tschaikovsky." A cross-reference or see card inserted into the catalog carries the message, "Don't look under 'Tschaikovsky'; look under 'Chaikovskii.' " In the second example the reader is advised to look under "Skryábin" rather than under "Scriabin."

**Figure 4-1   Some Typical See Cards.**

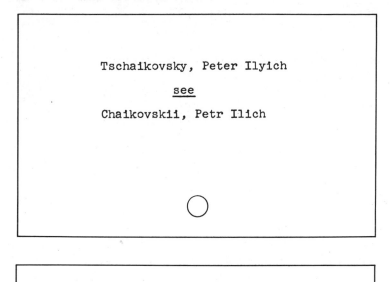

Difficulties arising from hyphenated names have prompted catalogers to use cross-references like that shown in Figure 4–2. This card indicates

**Figure 4-2   Cross-Reference Card for a Hyphenated Name.[1]**

Warden, Bruno Hardt-
*see*
Hardt-Warden, Bruno

[1]In this and some following examples representing card entries, only the pertinent information will be given.

that one should look under "Hardt-Warden" to find entries in the catalog.

To avoid confusion resulting from compound names, the cataloger may provide see cards as shown in Figure 4–3.

Figure 4-3    Cross-Reference Cards for Compound Names.

Williams, Ralph Vaughan
*see*
Vaughan Williams, Ralph

Robbins Landon, Howard Chandler
*see*
Landon, Howard Chandler Robbins

Names including "de," "von," or "van" (or variants thereof) may cause confusion, for the disposition and spelling of such names differ with their nationality and period of origin. Cross-reference cards are usually placed in the catalog to clarify the practice within a given library catalog (see Figure 4–4).

Figure 4-4    Cross-Reference Cards for Names with "de."

Machault, Guillaume de
*see*
Guillaume de Machault

d'Indy, Vincent
*see*
Indy, Vincent d'

Although works are sometimes issued under a pseudonym[2] or pen name which may become so well known as to have an "identity," books are customarily cataloged under the real name of the author. The cataloger adds a see card with a notation referring the reader from the pseudonym to the real name (see Figure 4–5). Peter Warlock is the pseudonym of Philip Heseltine. Because works are cataloged under the author's real name, the reader should look under "Heseltine" although "Warlock" may appear on the book.

[2]A pseudonym is a name, not his own, adopted by a person to conceal his real name.

**Figure 4-5    Cross-Reference Card for Pseudonym.**

Warlock, Peter
*see*
Heseltine, Philip

Names are not the sole reason for see cards. A card with the notation:

LIEDER
*see*
SONGS

shows that because *Lieder* means essentially the same as *songs*, the entries for Lieder are filed with entries for songs. This practice is sensible in libraries containing many compositions of similar type but bearing different designations in their titles. By bringing entries together under one heading, the cataloger unifies the catalog and saves the researcher's time.

Subject headings peculiar to a given library may be explained by a see card. In libraries where music for the Mass is filed under the heading of SACRED MUSIC, a card may be furnished with the notation:

MASSES
*see*
SACRED MUSIC

If SACRED MUSIC has been divided into smaller categories, the card may read:

MASSES
*see*
SACRED MUSIC—MASSES

showing the subdivision under which to look for entries. In still other collections, the heading SACRED MUSIC may not be used in the catalog but entries may be filed under CHURCH MUSIC. The see card may then read:

SACRED MUSIC
*see*
CHURCH MUSIC

In essence this card says, "For entries representing sacred music, see CHURCH MUSIC."

Translations, especially of titles, call for see cards, for example:

Threepenny Opera

*see*

Dreigroschenoper

Kurt Weill's *Threepenny Opera* was originally called *Dreigroschenoper*. In libraries where the score is cataloged under the German title, a see card may refer the reader from the English title to the German.

When a work is known under several names, as in the case of an opera translated into many languages, and the cataloger chooses one as the conventional title (see Figure 3–4), cross-reference cards are made, referring from the composer and title-page title to the composer and conventional title (see Figure 4–6). Mozart's opera has been translated into several

**Figure 4-6   See Cards for Conventional Title.**

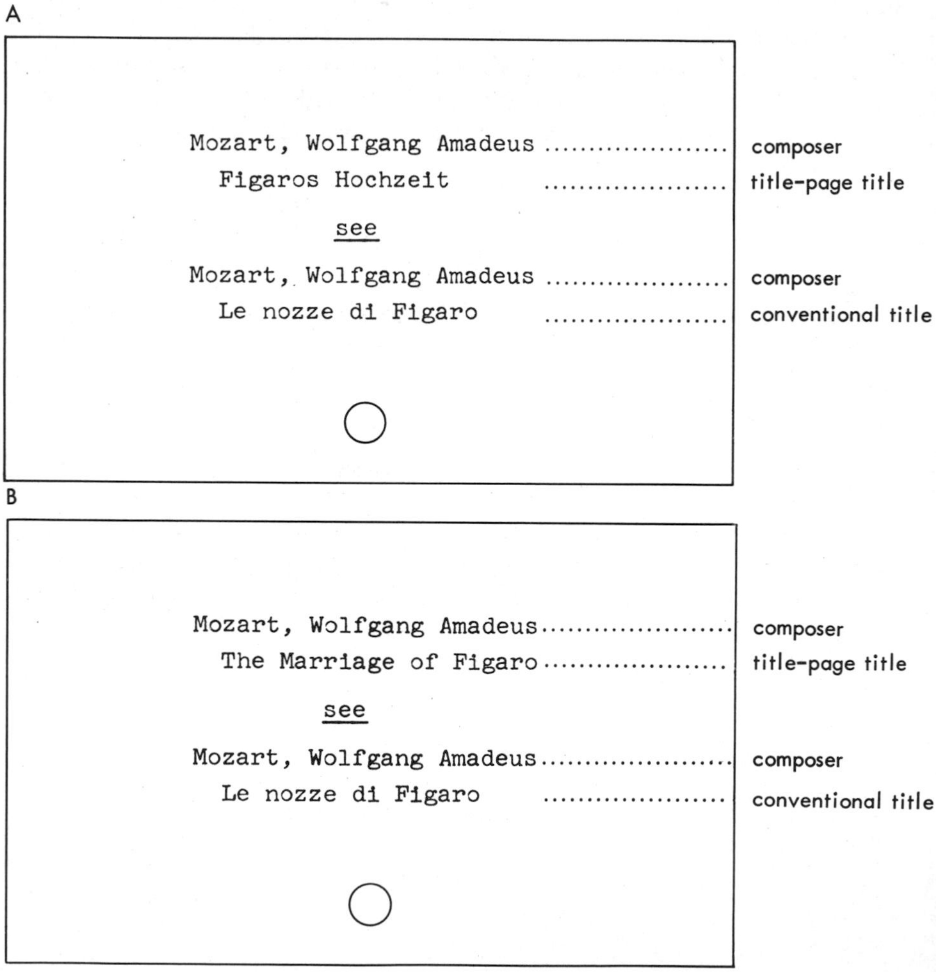

A

```
Mozart, Wolfgang Amadeus ...................... composer
   Figaros Hochzeit          ...................... title-page title

              see

Mozart, Wolfgang Amadeus ...................... composer
   Le nozze di Figaro        ...................... conventional title
```

B

```
Mozart, Wolfgang Amadeus...................... composer
   The Marriage of Figaro ...................... title-page title

              see

Mozart, Wolfgang Amadeus...................... composer
   Le nozze di Figaro        ...................... conventional title
```

languages (*Figaros Hochzeit, The Marriage of Figaro, Les noces de Figaro*). If entries were filed under the titles of these translations, they would be scattered. In the example, *Le nozze di Figaro* has been adopted as the conventional title. No matter what appears on the title page, every version is entered under this title. Card A in Figure 4–6 points from the German title to the Italian; card B points from the English title to the Italian.

## The See Also Card

The *see also card* is a device indicating additional places to find entries. A reader searching for books on dances and looking under the subject heading DANCES may be disappointed at the dearth of material. A see also card, filed in front of the section on dances, may indicate that other items are to be found under FOLK-DANCES, in which case the card reads:

DANCES

*see also*

FOLK-DANCES

A see also card may bear several suggestions. A person looking for a variety of part-songs may find a card reading:

PART-SONGS

*see also*

GLEES

MADRIGALS

ROUNDS

According to this card he may find desired items by looking under PART-SONGS, GLEES, MADRIGALS, and ROUNDS.

## The Series Card

Many catalogers offer further assistance by indicating (1) the contents of books or scores published as a large series and (2) the individual compositions or volumes which constitute a series. Cards known as *series cards* are made as a quick reference to such large bodies of materials as *Nagels Musik Archiv, Hortus musicus,* or *Das Chorwerk* (three examples of musical score series) or the Master Musicians, Lives of Great Composers, or the Norton History of Music Series (three examples of literature series). A glance at these convenient cards, filed alphabetically in the catalog by the title of the series, enables the researcher to know which individual volumes of a large series the library owns. Ordinarily the cataloger lists only the items contained in his library. In a few cases in which all parts of a series are listed (as if the catalog were a bibliography), he indicates by some clear symbol the volumes found in the library. As an example, an excerpt from information contained in series cards for the *Hortus musicus* is given in Figure 4–7.

Figure 4-7    Excerpt from Series Cards.

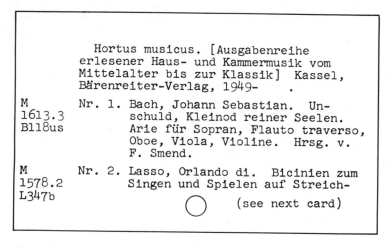

Hortus musicus. [Ausgabenreihe erlesener Haus- und Kammermusik vom Mittelalter bis zur Klassik] Kassel, Bärenreiter-Verlag, 1949-    .

M 1613.3 B118us    Nr. 1. Bach, Johann Sebastian. Un- schuld, Kleinod reiner Seelen. Arie für Sopran, Flauto traverso, Oboe, Viola, Violine. Hrsg. v. F. Smend.

M 1578.2 L347b    Nr. 2. Lasso, Orlando di. Bicinien zum Singen und Spielen auf Streich-    (see next card)

Card 2.

Hortus musicus. und Blasinstrumenten. Hrsg. v. G. Pinthus.

M 322 H236sd    Nr. 3. Handel, Georg Friedrich. Sonate D-dur für Flöte (Oboe, Violine) und Basso continuo. Hrsg. v. W. Hinnenthal.

The series is composed of separate compositions. In the library from which the above cards are taken each work is individually classified and cataloged. The cataloger has made series cards on which he has indicated the number of each issue, its composer, title, and editor. He has given the call number for each, so that the patron may easily locate the desired work. To look up individual issues would be a huge undertaking indeed, for almost 200 pieces have already been published, with many more to appear.

The thousands of cards filed in the catalog constitute a tool by which the student may learn what is available in a given library and where the items are located in that institution. It is necessary to know the filing system to make efficient use of the cards, and that we shall study in the next chapter.

# 5

## The Library Catalog

As a rule in American institutions the catalog is accessible to the public and consists of cards filed in a cabinet according to some system. The system must be explored by the researcher new to a library, and its special features understood. Generally, one of the procedures described below makes a good starting point.

To locate all the works by a given author, the reader should first look for his name in the catalog, where cards for all the books by him contained in the library are arranged in alphabetical order by title:

Einstein, Alfred.
Beispielsammlung zur Musikgeschichte[1]

Einstein, Alfred.
Geschichte der Musik

Einstein, Alfred.
Gluck

Einstein, Alfred.
Greatness in music

Einstein, Alfred.
The Italian madrigal

If the book is anonymous or the reader does not know the author's

[1] Each of these items represents the first lines on a card. Similar lists are used also on subsequent pages.

name, he must look for the title in the catalog.[2] A person searching for various books or compositions bearing the same name may find them by looking for the title. The cards for a given title will be arranged by the name of the author or composer:

> Faust.
> Gounod, Charles.
> > Faust. Opera in 5 acts
>
> Faust.
> Lassen, Eduard.
> > [Faust]. Musik zu Goethes Faust
>
> Faust.
> Schumann, Robert.
> > Faust. Scenes from Goethe's Faust, for solo voices
>
> Faust.
> Spohr, Ludwig.
> > Faust. Grosse Oper in 3 Aufzuegen

To find several books on a given subject, one may look under the subject heading, where he will see entries for all the appropriate items arranged in alphabetical order by the name of their authors. As we have said, subject headings differ with each institution, depending upon the source used by the cataloger for compiling his subject list.[3]

## The Dictionary Catalog

Not all catalogs are arranged in the same manner. The cataloger may be influenced in his choice of system by such practical considerations as the size of the collection, type of library, system of classification, and the nature of the clientele. Many libraries have a *dictionary catalog*, in which all cards for all items are filed, dictionary fashion, into one all-inclusive alphabet by whatever appears on the heading (excluding, of course, the call number), whether it is the name of the author, the title of the work, or the subject(s) treated. To avoid confusion, libraries with large catalogs adopt certain conventional methods of filing, although these practices are by no means mandatory.

[2]When the title is commonplace or nondescriptive (e.g., *History of Music, Sonata for Violin*), no title card is made. The reader must look under the subject: MUSIC —HISTORY AND CRITICISM, VIOLIN MUSIC—SONATAS.

[3]In some libraries subject headings are listed for public reference. Otherwise it is advisable to consult the librarian for assistance. In the absence of a list and the librarian, one may find possible subject headings by consulting *Music Subject Headings Used in Printed Catalog Cards of the Library of Congress.*

Usually the cards for works written *by* a person appear first under his name and are arranged in alphabetical order by their titles.[4] They are followed by cards representing the works *about* a person (i.e., a person as subject, see Figure 3–12), which are arranged in alphabetical order by their authors' names. In catalogs in which both literary and musical works are filed in one alphabet, the cards for such works by Franz Liszt as *Années de pèlerinage, Concerto in E-flat, Correspondence, Life of Chopin,* and *Mephisto Waltz* are filed before the cards for books about him. A *guide card* may precede the entries to facilitate the search:[5]

Works by Liszt, Franz (*guide card*)

Liszt, Franz.
  Années de pèlerinage

Liszt, Franz.
  Concerto in E-flat

Liszt, Franz.
  Correspondence

Liszt, Franz.
  Life of Chopin

Liszt, Franz.
  Mephisto waltz

Works about Liszt, Franz (*guide card*)

Bory, Robert.
  La vie de Franz Liszt

Calvocoressi, M. D.
  Biography of Franz Liszt

Gottschalg, A. W.
  Franz Liszt in Weimar

Westerby, Herbert.
  Liszt, composer, and his piano works

In catalogs in which literary works are separated from musical compositions, there may be two alphabetical arrangements of works by a person, each following an appropriate guide card:[6]

[4]If a person is a compiler, editor, or joint author as well as an author, the cards for works compiled, edited, or jointly written by him come next in the order given here: Smith, John, comp.; Smith, John, ed.; Smith, John, jt. auth.; with entries in alphabetical order by title under each designation.

[5]A guide card bears the name, subject, or form of items represented by cards which immediately follow.

[6]This separation constitutes a modification of strict dictionary filing but is considered practical for some libraries.

Liszt, Franz (*guide card*)
    Literary Works

Liszt, Franz.
    Correspondence

Liszt, Franz.
    Life of Chopin

Liszt, Franz (*guide card*)
    Musical Compositions

Liszt, Franz.
    Années de pèlerinage

Liszt, Franz.
    Concerto in E–flat

Some catalogers file cards for the collected editions of a person's works first under his name. These cards are followed by cards representing individual works by him, arranged in alphabetical order by their titles:

Bach, Johann Sebastian (*guide card*)
    Collected Editions

Bach, Johann Sebastian.
    Neue Ausgabe sämtlicher Werke

Bach, Johann Sebastian.
    Werke

Bach, Johann Sebastian (*guide card*)
    Individual Compositions

Bach, Johann Sebastian.
    Kunst der Fuge

Bach, Johann Sebastian.
    Orgelbüchlein

Bach, Johann Sebastian.
    Suite in B minor

Cards for authors whose names begin with Mc and Mac are grouped together as though they were all spelled Mac and the rest of the "Mac" cards are interfiled with them:

> MacArthur
> McBean
> Macbeth
> McCarthy
> Macchi

Subject cards are filed alphabetically by author under the appropriate subject heading. If a library contains a few books on a general subject (OPERA in the example below), the entries might be filed under the subject heading thus:

OPERA
Briggs, Thomas H.
    Opera and its enjoyment

OPERA
Ella, John.
    Lectures on dramatic music

OPERA
Taubman, Hyman Howard.
    Opera—front and back

But if a library possesses many books on the subject, the entries may be subdivided into such subheadings as those shown below. Under the subject heading of OPERA, the subheadings are filed in alphabetical order, with cards arranged by author under them:

OPERA—ANALYTICAL GUIDES
                    (*subject heading and subheading*)

Hughes, Frank C.
    Famous Mozart operas

OPERA—ANALYTICAL GUIDES
Marini, R. B.
    La Turandot di G. Puccini

OPERA—ANALYTICAL GUIDES
Rinaldi, Mario.
    Lo Straniero di Ildebrando Pizzetti

OPERA—BIBLIOGRAPHY
                    (*subject heading and subheading*)
Central Opera Service.
    Opera manual

OPERA—BIBLIOGRAPHY
Morton, C. A.
    Modern drama and opera. A reading list

OPERA—DICTIONARIES
                    (*subject heading and subheading*)
Clément, Félix.
    Dictionnaire des opéras

OPERA—DICTIONARIES
Lessing, Gotthold E.
  Handbuch des Opern-repertoires

OPERA—DICTIONARIES
Loewenberg, Alfred.
  Annals of opera

OPERA—DICTIONARIES
Towers, John.
  Dictionary-catalogue of operas

OPERA—HISTORY AND CRITICISM
                    (*subject heading and subheading*)
Apthorp, William F.
  The opera, past and present

OPERA—HISTORY AND CRITICISM
Gass, Irene.
  Through an opera glass

OPERA—HISTORY AND CRITICISM
Grout, Donald Jay.
  A short history of opera

Finally, the catalog contains the geographical arrangement of the subject, with cards under the subject heading in alphabetical order by place and the individual works for each place filed alphabetically by author:

OPERA—BERLIN
Fetting, Hugo.
  Die Geschichte der deutschen Staatsoper

OPERA—BERLIN
Kapp, Julius.
  Geschichte der Staatsoper Berlin

OPERA—FRANCE
Dauriac, L. A.
  La psychologie dans l'opéra français

OPERA—FRANCE
Martine, Jacques D.
  De la musique dramatique en France

OPERA—LONDON
Mander, Raymond.
  The theatres of London

OPERA—LONDON
Northcott, Richard.
  Gounod's operas in London

## The Divided Catalog

Some catalogs are not arranged in one great alphabet but are divided into several clearly defined sections, each complete in itself. One section may contain the author cards in alphabetical order (the *author catalog*); another may contain the title cards in alphabetical order (the *title catalog*); and still another may contain the subject cards in alphabetical order (the *subject catalog*). In such an arrangement the patron looks into the author catalog for works by a composer or author; into the title catalog for a particular title; and into the subject catalog for the available books on a given subject. While this means investigating several separate catalogs, the procedure is essentially the same as the consultation of the dictionary catalog.

In some libraries the author cards and title cards are interfiled in one catalog, forming the *author-and-title catalog*, while the subject cards are filed in another (the *subject catalog*). Where such a system is employed the cataloger may provide an index of subject headings in some convenient form as an aid to locating material in the subject catalog; the reader may thereby determine which subjects related to his research are present in the library.

Other arrangements are possible. Practices vary and the division of the catalog is not governed by hard and fast rules. The method of division, if there is one, is left to the discretion of the librarian, who is guided by matters of policy, convenience, preference, economy, or even by tradition. If the student encounters difficulty in using the catalog, he may consult members of the library staff for assistance. Once he becomes familiar with the local library, he will find that the catalog, if it is a good one, can be an important bibliographical tool if he uses it well.

# BIBLIOGRAPHY

*Music Subject Headings Used in Printed Catalog Cards of the Library of Congress.* Washington: Library of Congress, 1952.

*Subject Headings Used in the Dictionary Catalogs of the Library of Congress.* Washington: Library of Congress, 1957.

# 6

## Interlibrary Loan and
## Regional Library Cooperation

### Interlibrary Loan

Interlibrary loan has been developed as a means of pooling the resources of libraries throughout the country. If the local library does not own a book or journal which the student considers indispensable to his research, his librarian may request it on loan from another library that has it.

The philosophy of interlibrary cooperation is sound. No matter how extensive the collection, it is rarely possible and certainly not practical for any one library to have everything pertaining to a subject. Even if the material were all obtainable at once, it would be financially impossible to acquire all of it and impossible to find space for it. But with many libraries cooperating in acquisition so that purchases are divided among them, a large stock of available sources is built up, even though the individual items may be housed in buildings miles away from each other. By sending the material from one library to another, the needs of many scholars may be met without overtaxing any one institution. Interlibrary loan has developed into such an important function that in some libraries a professional staff member is in charge of a department of interlibrary relations. In small libraries the reference department or the circulation department handles interlibrary loans.

If one needs something on interlibrary loan, he consults the person in charge, giving complete bibliographical identification of the desired book: author, title, imprint, and, in the case of an article from a journal, the volume number, date, and specific pages on which the material is found. For verification he should also supply the source of his data (e.g., a bibliographical list in a reference work). Such information is recorded by the librarian on an interlibrary loan request form which is sent to the appropriate lending library.[1] When the request has been processed, the book arrives at the student's library, where he may use it for a prescribed time under conditions set forth by the owner. Usually the sole expense to the user is the postage required to have material sent to him and returned at the end of the loan period.[2]

Naturally, the largest, best-stocked collections must bear the heaviest burden of interlibrary lending. Most major institutions consider it part of their service program, in some cases even paying the postage to the borrowing library (the return postage being borne by the borrower). Some libraries, however, are not permitted by conditions of their charters, stipulations of their donors, or some administrative policy, to engage in the interlibrary loan program. Inability to participate does not mean unwillingness to cooperate. In compensation for the lack of lending services, an efficient photoduplication department may be maintained to aid research by supplying copies of requested material, provided such material is in the public domain (see Chapter 7). The charges are nominal, rarely more than the cost of supplies and labor.

The practices of interlibrary loan, determined by the policy-making group within the library, necessarily vary with each institution. The degree to which a library participates is a matter of individual discretion rather than compulsion. Librarians are usually quick to send material on loan if it is in print, in good condition, and rugged enough to travel. In case of loss in transit, a book in print can be replaced; in case of rough handling, a sturdy book can survive. Librarians hesitate to send early editions, volumes from sets, and fragile items. They are loathe to lend bound periodicals, and they rightfully will refuse requests for unique items and manuscripts. Exceptions may be made only if circumstances are extraordinary. Recordings and tapes are not customarily sent on interlibrary loan.

For obvious reasons, a librarian cannot send materials which are in use by his own patrons. Sometimes he is forced to refuse also if he has received so many requests for the same books that the chances of a student's having access to them in time to profit by them are negligible. The borrower may be advised to ask for the items again if he still wishes to use them after a

---

[1]By consulting union lists and catalogs, the librarian finds which collections own the desired items. In some instances the requests go directly to a state library or regional bibliographical center. In other cases, several libraries may be contacted. If the student knows the location of the books he wants, he should by all means assist the librarian by furnishing this information at the time he requests the loan.

[2]Some libraries do not charge postage. On the other hand, some libraries charge a small service fee. Practices differ with individual libraries, depending upon financial condition, policies, and administrative reasons.

specified period has elapsed. A librarian, especially in a busy institution, must consider the nature of the request before complying. Because he feels his first loyalty to the professional researcher and the graduate student working on a thesis or dissertation, he may be obliged to refuse loans for purposes of an undergraduate paper or a term report. Indeed, some borrowing librarians will not request items on loan except for graduate research.

As a rule, librarians in institutions which subscribe to the University Microfilms service of microfilming dissertations in their collections (see Chapter 7), ask that the student or his library purchase a copy directly from Ann Arbor[3] rather than borrow the original works from the library. This policy is justified because (1) the original typescript of a dissertation serves archival purposes and should neither leave the campus nor be subjected to the wear and tear of repeated mailings; (2) carbon copies soon become smudged and illegible; and (3) the comparatively small cost of the microfilm or Xerox copy is sometimes little more than the postage and supplies necessary to send the dissertation on loan.

In addition to accepting refusals in good spirit, one is expected to abide by conditions imposed by the lending library. If he is asked to sign a slip indicating his use of a book, he must sign. If he is requested to read the material only within the library, he must honor this stipulation. The borrowing library assumes full responsibility for the book while it is on loan. One must never embarrass his own librarian by asking for the special privilege of home use, which cannot be granted without breaking faith with the lending library.

Many institutions make provision for international loans. As communication becomes easier, researchers become increasingly dependent upon international library cooperation to obtain bibliographical sources. At present, difficulties of transportation still exist in some quarters, as do complications attending customs clearance across international borders. Librarians may prefer not to request loans from other countries if it is possible to purchase microfilm or photocopies of desired items owned by foreign libraries.

If the interlibrary loan restrictions seem excessive, they are not intended to be discouraging. They have been enumerated here so that the prospective borrower may understand the reasons for any disappointments he may experience. Actually, one stands a good chance of obtaining most of the desired material if he is reasonable and sometimes a few items received on interlibrary loan make the difference between successful research and an undistinguished paper.

[3]University Microfilms, Inc., Ann Arbor, Michigan.

## Regional Cooperation

Closely allied with interlibrary loan is cooperation on a regional basis, established in some parts of the country to aid scholarly research by rapid distribution of source materials. The working principles underlying this function are: (1) the cooperative use of the holdings of participating libraries within a given geographic area, and/or (2) cooperative ownership of materials by a number of institutions. Cooperation may take many forms, depending upon the number and nature of the collections involved, the types of library clientele, topography, and communications systems.

Perhaps the most highly organized system of regional cooperation is found in the nonprofit bibliographical centers found in various parts of the country. Such centers usually consist of an office or offices in which a union catalog is maintained together with a collection of bibliographical tools. A union catalog, as the term clearly implies, is a catalog recording materials of all sorts—books, periodicals, scores, and manuscripts— owned by the participating libraries within the region. It indicates what is available and where it is located. Bibliographical tools are such helpful items as bibliographies, checklists, catalogs, indexes, and reference books which are used to identify and to locate materials. A trained staff keeps the catalog up to date, consults the bibliographical tools as needed, and helps to implement the services offered by the center.

A scholar may expect bibliographical centers to render the following services:

1. Locate materials either within their own region or elsewhere.
2. Direct him to institutions which are most likely to have important material related to his subject.
3. Assist in identifying authors, titles, and editions when he has gone as far as he is able with the resources at his command.
4. Help interpret bibliographical entries.
5. Facilitate and expedite interlibrary loans by routing requests to the proper sources.
6. Facilitate acquisition of photocopy and microfilm.

An example of the type of bibliographical center described above is the Pacific Northwest Bibliographic Center, located in the University of Washington Library in Seattle.[4] Established in 1940 with a Carnegie Foundation

[4]For full details, see Raynard Swank, "The Pacific Northwest Bibliographic Center," in *Libraries and Librarians of the Pacific Northwest*, Pacific Northwest Library Association (Seattle: University of Washington Press, 1960), pp. 220–239.

grant, it is operated by the Pacific Northwest Library Association and supported by libraries on a subscription basis. Serving the states of Oregon, Washington, Idaho, Montana, and Alaska in the United States and the province of British Columbia in Canada, the center maintains a large union catalog of author entries for the holdings of 40 libraries in the area, plus entries for the John Crerar Library in Chicago, and the Library of Congress. The center gives extensive interlibrary loan service, not only by supplying the location of the wanted items but also by referring the requests to the proper holding libraries.

Another large center is the Bibliographical Center for Research—Rocky Mountain Region, located at the Denver Public Library and serving Colorado, Wyoming, Utah, Nebraska, and New Mexico. Its union catalog lists the holdings of 250 libraries. Other centers maintaining union catalogs for similar purposes (although perhaps not operating exactly in the same way) include the Philadelphia Bibliographical Center and Union Library Catalogue, located in Logan Hall of the University of Pennsylvania and listing the holdings of 171 libraries in its catalog; the Cleveland Regional Union Catalog at Western Reserve University (60 libraries); and certain state centers like those of California (California State Library, Sacramento), Nebraska (Nebraska Public Library Commission, Lincoln), New Hampshire (Concord), Ohio (Columbus), and Vermont (Montpelier). Other regional union catalogs and bibliographical centers exist.[5]

Operations of some regional bibliographical centers may be further implemented by a basic book stock housed on the premises or by a collection of material on microfilm or microcards which may be lent for the use of individuals doing research at any one of the member libraries. A regional center may be a center for information retrieval, with data stored in a computer "brain." In other cases regional cooperation may function through a federation of several libraries, each owning outstanding collections in certain subjects and working through an office to exchange research services. Although bibliographical centers vary in organization and method of operation, their common aim is to provide information quickly, hopefully to save the scholar's time and effort and to give him access to the largest possible number of known sources. In many instances cooperation is not limited to one geographic area but extends to states beyond regional borders. The local librarian or the thesis adviser should be able

[5]See *American Library Directory* (22nd ed.), (New York: R. R. Bowker Company, 1960), pp. 1051ff.; *American Library Directory* (24th ed.), (New York: R. R. Bowker Company, 1964), pp. 1237ff. Though not up to date, the following articles contain descriptions of regional centers: Ralph T. Esterquest, "Regional Library Centers, 1946–47," *College and Research Libraries*, IX (July, 1948), 215–220; "Regional Library Centers Today: A Symposium," *College and Research Libraries*, VIII (January, 1947), 54–69.

to indicate centers located close enough for profitable use and give instructions on how to request assistance.

State libraries constitute another form of cooperative agency, although they may not be cooperative in the sense that participating libraries pool their resources in a regional center. Many states maintain a tax-supported library with a book and microfilm stock to fill requests from the libraries of that state. In some cases, as with New York State Library at Albany, an interlibrary loan request may be placed by telephone or wire rather than by mail, and if the desired item is in stock, it is immediately dispatched to the borrowing library. Some states are fortunate in having both a state library and a regional bibliographical center at their service. In the Pacific Northwest area a state library is found in Oregon and in Washington, bibliographically the two most active states participating in the Pacific Northwest Bibliographic Center. This does not mean a duplication of effort or of financial investment, for the resources of the various agencies differ. If the state library cannot fill a request, one of the member libraries of the regional bibliographic center may be of assistance. Conversely, if an item cannot be supplied by the members of the regional center, the state library may be able to provide it.

In still another form of regional cooperation a published union catalog gives data on the location of library holdings even where no central bibliographical office exists. An example is *Reference Works in Music and Music Literature in Five Libraries of Los Angeles County,* edited by Helen W. Azhderian.[6] Issued in 1953, it is a union catalog of research holdings in music of the Los Angeles Public Library, the University of Southern California Library, the library of the University of California at Los Angeles, the William Andrews Clark Library, and the Henry E. Huntington Library. Each library has its own specialties, and each represents a distinctive type of collection,[7] yet the union is possible because of the common interest in materials of music and the willingness to pool

[6]Helen W. Azhderian, ed., *Reference Works in Music and Music Literature in Five Libraries of Los Angeles County* (Los Angeles: University of Southern California, 1953). The union catalog is being kept up to date by Joan Meggett, Music Librarian, University of Southern California, although no plans for the issue of a new edition have been formulated.

[7]The Los Angeles Public Library has a large Art and Music Department; the University of Southern California is a private university with a music library serving a college of music; the University of California at Los Angeles is a state university with a music library; the William Andrews Clark Library, now affiliated with the University of California at Los Angeles, was founded as a private special collection of seventeenth- and eighteenth-century humanities sources; the Henry E. Huntington Library, in San Marino, is an independent private research library. The Huntington Library's early music has been cataloged: Edythe N. Backus, *Catalogue of Music in the Huntington Library Printed before 1801* (San Marino, Calif.: Huntington Library, 1949). This work has not been duplicated in the Azhderian union catalog.

resources. By means of the catalog a researcher may know where he may find references without having to travel from one library to another to consult their individual catalogs. The ease with which books may be traced is in itself a boon to the busy scholar.

Union catalogs are maintained in countries where resources for research exist in several or many libraries. An example is the *British Union-Catalogue of Early Music Printed before the Year 1801*, in which holdings of more than a hundred libraries in the British Isles are listed and indexed.[8]

The *National Union Catalog*, maintained in Washington, is so enormous as to be in a class by itself. It has two forms: (1) It is a catalog of millions of cards filed in the Library of Congress, recording holdings of more than 500 research libraries and including also entries for distinctive materials in the Philadelphia, Cleveland, and North Carolina regional catalogs. (2) It is, in addition, a printed catalog in book form, issued under various titles.[9] Librarians have frequent use for this catalog, the largest in the country, in locating sources for their patrons.

The *Union List of Serials*[10] and the *Union List of Microfilms*[11] show the location of periodicals and microfilms, respectively, to be found in the libraries throughout the country. Ricci and Wilson's *Census of Medieval and Renaissance Manuscripts in the United States and Canada*[12] indicates which collections own manuscript material. Although they are of a general nature, these lists include items in music. Specifically in the field of music, the *International Inventory of Musical Sources*[13] will eventually list materials in the many research libraries over the world. These great national and international bibliographical tools tend to make interlibrary cooperation progressively easier and more effective. They are likewise valuable in implementing photocopy and facsimile reproduction.

A major problem faced by agencies preparing such catalogs is main-

---

[8]Edith B. Schnapper, ed., *British Union-Catalogue of Early Music Printed before the Year 1801* (London: Butterworth Scientific Publications, 1957).

[9]For the contents and titles of volumes, see Bohdan S. Wynar, *Introduction to Bibliography and Reference Work*, 3rd ed. (Denver: Libraries Unlimited, Inc., 1966), pp. 77ff.

[10]Winifred Gregory, ed., *Union List of Serials in Libraries in the United States and Canada* (2nd ed.), (New York: The H. W. Wilson Company, 1943). Includes "Bibliography of Union Lists of Serials." Supplements for 1941–1943 and 1944–1949 were issued in 1945 and 1952, respectively. *New Serial Titles: A Union List of Serials Commencing Publication after December 31, 1949* (Washington: Library of Congress, 1953–      ) is to be used in conjunction with the *Union List of Serials*.

[11]Philadelphia Bibliographical Center and Union Library Catalog, *Union List of Microfilms: Cumulation, 1949–1959* (Ann Arbor: Edwards Brothers, Inc., 1961).

[12]Seymour de Ricci and W. J. Wilson, *Census of Medieval and Renaissance Manuscripts in the United States and Canada* (New York: The H. W. Wilson Company, 1935–1940).

[13]*Répertoire international des sources musicales (International Inventory of Musical Sources)*, (München: G. Henle Verlag, 1960–      ).

taining the tools once they have been started and keeping the entries up to date. New cards must be made for additions and old cards withdrawn for discarded or lost books. Printed lists must be reprinted with revisions. The work never ceases.

As new devices are perfected, data may be transmitted by electronic means from a source to a patron many miles away. Differences of opinion may exist regarding the possible value of mechanical methods to the musical scholar, but experimentation offers interesting speculations and promises for the future. At present, as limited as communication may seem, students may be sure that interlibrary cooperation is at least a step in the right direction.

# BIBLIOGRAPHY

*American Library Directory* (22nd ed.). New York: R. R. Bowker Company, 1960. 24th ed., 1964.

Azhderian, Helen W., ed., *Reference Works in Music and Music Literature in Five Libraries of Los Angeles County*. Los Angeles: University of Southern California, 1953.

Backus, Edythe N., *Catalogue of Music in the Huntington Library Printed before 1801*. San Marino, Calif: Huntington Library, 1949.

Esterquest, Ralph T., "Regional Library Centers, 1946–47," *College and Research Libraries*, IX (July, 1948), 215–220.

Gregory, Winifred, ed., *Union List of Serials in Libraries in the United States and Canada* (2nd ed.). New York: The H. W. Wilson Company, 1943. Supplements, 1945, 1952.

*New Serial Titles: A Union List of Serials Commencing Publication after December 31, 1949*. Washington: Library of Congress, 1953–    .

Philadelphia Bibliographical Center and Union Library Catalog, *Union List of Microfilms: Cumulation, 1949–1959*. Ann Arbor: Edwards Brothers, Inc., 1961.

"Regional Library Centers Today: A Symposium," *College and Research Libraries*, VIII (January, 1947), 54–69.

Ricci, Seymour de, and W. J. Wilson, *Census of Medieval and Renaissance Manuscripts in the United States and Canada*. New York: The H. W. Wilson Company, 1935–1940.

*Répertoire international des sources musicales (International Inventory of Musical Sources)*. München: G. Henle Verlag, 1960–    .

Schnapper, Edith B., ed., *British Union-Catalogue of Early Music Printed before the Year 1801*. London: Butterworth Scientific Publications, 1957.

Swank, Raynard, "The Pacific Northwest Bibliographic Center," in *Libraries and Librarians in the Pacific Northwest*, Pacific Northwest Library Association. Seattle: University of Washington Press, 1960, pp. 220–239.

Wynar, Bohdan S., *Introduction to Bibliography and Reference Work* (3rd ed.). Denver: Libraries Unlimited, Inc., 1966.

# *7*

# *Copying and Photoreproduction*

## Introduction

Recent technical developments have enabled the researcher to obtain copies of materials otherwise out of his reach. If one learns of a distant source valuable to his study, if items requested on interlibrary loan are restricted, or if one must work with the contents of a manuscript or rare book, he may ask that a reproduction be made for him. Often he has a choice of the type of copy. The image may be full size, reduced size, or microscopic size; it may be negative (light characters on a dark background) or positive (dark characters on a light background); it may be on paper, on cards, or on film. The number of copying devices in use is amazing, using photographic, contact, and electrostatic processes. To describe even the most representative of them is unfortunately beyond the scope of this book. Suffice it to state that most librarians have access to some sort of equipment for making copies of books, music, and journals.

## Copyright[1]

Before the student orders copies, however, he must consider certain limitations, the principal one being that of copyright. According to the

[1]For a detailed discussion, see W. J. Leaper, *Copyright and Performing Rights* (London: Steven & Sons Ltd., 1957); Harriet F. Pilpel and Morton D. Goldberg, *A Copyright Guide* (2nd ed.), (New York: R. R. Bowker Company, 1963); Howard L. Walls, *The Copyright Handbook for Fine and Applied Arts* (New York: Watson-Guptil Publications, 1963).

present law in the United States, a person complying with the regulations and following the procedures prescribed by the Copyright Office may register his books or his compositions for 28 years, with the possibility of a renewal for a second 28 years: a total of 56 years' protection against copying or pirating.[2] A copyright notice—a designation of when and by whom the item is copyrighted—must appear on each work thus protected.[3] Anything bearing a copyright date within the last 56 years may be still in copyright and not yet in the public domain; this means that it may not legally be reproduced.

Much discussion has recently taken place concerning "fair use"—the concept that reproduction of a copyrighted work is permissible if it does not prove harmful to the copyright owner. The term, however, does not appear in the wording of the present law, and although it is mentioned in the proposed revision of the law, it is still subject to dispute. The concept of fair use has developed around a few cases brought to court and is largely based upon the wishful thinking of many who believe the law should allow copying for research or other private use as long as no sale is involved and the copyright owner appears to lose nothing by it. As a result of the heavy pressure of research, especially in the vital scientific and industrial fields in which information is needed almost before it is in print, scholars have been put to inconvenience and expense by the strict application of the law. Librarians as well as investigators themselves have sought a solution. A study was made of the photocopy situation by a committee of experts. As an outcome of the publication of the report of this Joint Committee on Fair Use in Photocopying in the *Bulletin* of the American Library Association[4] and its subsequent approval by the American Library Association Council on July 13, 1961,[5] many librarians follow the recommendation contained in the report that a library should provide a single photocopy of any published work or portion thereof. If a librarian subscribes wholeheartedly to this concept, the student may be able to procure a copy of almost any article in a journal or parts of any book that he might request for research purposes.

[2]The revision of the copyright law, introduced in Congress on February 4, 1965, provides for the duration of copyright for the life of the author and 50 years after his death. This is in line with the law of European countries generally.

[3]At present it must be on the title page or the reverse side (*verso*) of the title page in a book. In a periodical it must appear on the title page or masthead page (the one containing data about the publishers, owners, and editors, together with the address of editorial and advertising offices) or the first page of text. In a piece of music it belongs on the title page, its verso, or the first page of music. The revised law proposed in 1965 is not so specific.

[4]"[Joint Committee on Fair Use in Photocopying] Report, American Library Association," *Bulletin* LV (June, 1961), 571–573.

[5]*Ibid.* (September, 1961), 680.

On the other hand, the approval of the report of the Joint Committee is not synonymous with the enactment of a new copyright law—far from it. While the report points up the fact that copying of material for research is desperately needed in some critical fields, while it shows that copying for research is not necessarily detrimental to the copyright owner, and while it recommends a change in the existing law, it still leaves the individual librarian both morally and legally responsible for what goes on in his library.[6] Strictly speaking, any infringement of copyright, no matter for what reason, is still unlawful and actually not honest. If a librarian does not wish to give permission to copy a work, one must abide by his decision. Moreover, because of the involvement of performance rights and the difference in situation between authors and composers, the recommendation of the report of the Joint Committee cannot very well apply to music as freely as it might to nonmusic materials. It is doubtful whether any librarian will indiscriminately grant permission to reproduce music which is protected by copyright.[7]

But to get back to what one may obtain with impunity, any material which is in the public domain (either because it was not copyrighted or because its copyright has expired) may be made available in some form of reproduction provided the owner has access to a copying device and the original book is in condition to be copied. Such factors as fragility and brittleness of pages, the absence or presence of color, the clarity of print, and the condition of the bindings on books and journals may determine the ability to obtain a good copy. In general, the results are not only clearly legible, but sometimes easier to read than the original.

When one has a choice of the type of copy he may order, he should consider cost, bulk, and legibility. If the desired item is brief, it is practical to request a full-sized positive reproduction, requiring no reading equipment and presenting few storage problems. The rate per print, depending upon the size of the image and the type of process used, may range from a few cents to about 35 cents. (The more expensive photostatic process is not discussed here, for other systems cost less and are readily available.) But if the material desired is a lengthy treatise or a long composition, a microfilm copy with images much reduced in size may be preferable, since it is less expensive and more compact. The average rate per frame of microfilm is about 5 to 8 cents, and if the size of the original permits, two pages may be filmed on a single frame.

[6]The fair-use clause included in the revision of the copyright law does not spell out the definition of the term, thus leaving the librarian almost as he has been: morally and legally responsible for interpreting fair use.

[7]Recordings are also protected. Dubbing on a tape recorder from a recorded disc owned by a library is illegal, and most librarians will refuse permission to copy.

## Microfilm and Microfilm Archives

Microfilm is a photographic reproduction in which the image is reduced to fit a frame of 35mm or 16mm film. The film may be either positive or negative; of the two the positive is easier to read. The frames, each containing a single page or a double page of a book, depending upon the size of the original, are arranged in strips which are wound onto a metal or plastic spool for storage. In order to be read, the spool is put on a microfilm reader—a sort of projector—and the strip is fed through a slot or channel. The image is thrown onto a reading surface and simultaneously magnified.

Microfilm copies sometimes come in microfiche form—a few frames mounted on a standard-sized card, forming a unitized type of medium. Microfiche readers, while differing somewhat from microfilm readers, operate on the same basic principles of projection and magnification.

Because of rapidly expanding libraries with their attendant space problems, microfilm has become important. Many institutions maintain large collections of materials in this compact form: long runs of periodicals, multivolume sets, and older treatises and musical part-books. Some recently founded music libraries depend heavily upon microfilm for a considerable part of their historical sources, thus saving shelf space and the expense involved in procuring out-of-print or rare books.

Libraries possessing valuable early editions often make microfilm copies for circulation in order to preserve the original books for archival purposes. Because microfilm copies of sources from distant localities may be gathered in one place, some institutions have conscientiously accumulated collections on special subjects or historical periods. The sixteenth- and seventeenth-century music on microfilm in the Isham Memorial Library at Harvard, the sixteenth-century prints and manuscripts on film in the Music Library of the University of Illinois, and the Renaissance and Baroque theoretical treatises on film at the Sibley Music Library of the Eastman School of Music are examples. Other libraries have material on microfilm which they may be willing to copy for research. The *Union List of Microfilms*[8] may be consulted to locate the holdings of institutions, and from time to time *Notes* of the Music Library Association (available in most music libraries) carries information about significant film collections.

Two microfilm archives, whose existence attests to the importance of film, must be mentioned. The Knights of Columbus Vatican Library at St. Louis University is a research center containing film copies of the manuscripts from the several Italian collections constituting the complex

[8]Of the Philadelphia Bibliographical Center.

Vatican Library.[9] A general collection covering many fields, it also includes items valuable for music research.

The Archive of German Music History is a large collection of microfilm copies of manuscripts and printed sources pertaining to the history of German music from *ca.* 1450 to *ca.* 1700.[10] Original books and scores belonging to a number of libraries, museums, and private collections in both Europe and America have been copied, and the film deposited at Kassel. In 1959 there were already some 2,500 works on some 550,000 exposures of 35mm film, of which 80 per cent were musical compositions and 20 per cent theoretical works; 75 per cent were printed sources and 25 per cent manuscripts. More items are being filmed constantly.[11] Copies of the film are supplied upon request from any bona fide researcher engaged in a study of German music or allied fields, and no further release is necessary from the institutions owning the original books. The service represents a forward step in the movement toward free access to study materials.[12]

A joint commercial and scholarly enterprise for the collection and dissemination of materials is the University Microfilms archive of theses and doctoral dissertations, drawing from all fields in which advanced degrees are granted in the United States. Research studies accepted by the participating universities are sent to University Microfilms (Ann Arbor, Michigan) to be transferred to a master film from which microfilm and/or Xerox copies may be made as needed. To indicate available titles and their contents, together with the price of the copy, the firm issues three publications: *Masters Abstracts, Dissertation Abstracts*,[13] and the yearly summary, *American Doctoral Dissertations*. (See Chapter 8 for further description of the project and discussion of the bibliographical uses to which the microfilm services may be put.)

Microfilm, although useful and comparatively inexpensive, admittedly suffers from some limitations, of which the necessity for using a mechan-

[9]The collection of music materials in the archive is described by the musicologist who worked on the project: Ernst C. Krohn, "Music in the Vatican Film Library at St. Louis University," *Notes* XIV (1957), 317–324; "Vatican Music Collections on Microfilm at Saint Louis University," *Caecilia* LXXXIV (1957), 95–98.

[10]For description, see Harald Heckmann, "Archive of German Music History," *Notes* XVI (1958), 35–39.

[11]Catalogs are being issued for this archive: Harald Heckmann, comp., *Deutsches musikgeschichtliches Archiv: Katalog der Filmsammlung*. (Kassel: Bärenreiter-Verlag, 1955–    ).

[12]When the research is completed and the writer wishes to publish his work, it is in order for him to ask permission to include materials taken from the film. Publication and private research are two different things. Proper acknowledgment of sources is a moral obligation.

[13]*Doctoral Dissertations, Music, 1949–1964* (Ann Arbor: University Microfilms, Inc., 1965), is a list of works extracted from *Dissertation Abstracts* and *Microfilm Abstracts*. Some music libraries which do not subscribe to the all-inclusive *Dissertation Abstracts* may have this selective book.

ical reader may be one. A person sometimes experiences difficulty in finding available reading equipment at the time he wishes to study, if the research schedule has become congested. Another limitation, pertaining to negative microfilm, is the eye fatigue caused by reading white characters on a dark background. The light factor may also be a slight problem. For some types of reading equipment, the room must be partially darkened, making note-taking and transcription trying. Such hardships may be avoided by having portions of the film strip put through a Xerox Copyflo which makes paper copies the same size as the original. Though perhaps too expensive for processing the complete film, the Copyflo process is a great help in research requiring the careful perusal of a limited number of important or closely printed pages.

## Microcards

The microcard is a form of reproduction first developed for the preservation of bulky documents and tomes of proceedings which would otherwise occupy many cubic feet of shelf space. Its working principle is microphotography, by which the image of a page is so greatly reduced that 40 to 60 pages of textbook size may be printed on one side of a 3" x 5" card. The card is read through equipment which magnifies the image, projecting it on a slightly tinted surface.

An advantage of microcard over microfilm is that the equipment may be used in a lighted room; notes can be taken and music transcribed with no darkening of the reading area. To this advantage is added another: because one deals with a small card rather than a long strip of film, it is a simple matter to locate specific pages. A heading clearly visible to the naked eye is placed on each card, giving complete bibliographical data on the original book and the specific pages which appear on that card.

Several hundred titles in music are available on microcards.[14] Four continuing projects were listed as early as 1961–1962 in the *Catalog of Microcard Publications.*[15] The University of Rochester Press[16] has been issuing three series of cards containing reproductions of (1) music periodicals, including the *Allgemeine musikalische Zeitung;* (2) early books on music, principally historical and theoretical treatises from the Renaissance

[14]See, for example, *Guide to Microforms in Print, 1966* (Washington: Microcard Editions, Inc., 1966).

[15]*Catalog of Microcard Publications No. 3, 1961–1962* (Washington: Microcard Editions, Inc., 1962).

[16]University of Rochester Press, Mrs. Margaret Toth, editor, c/o Rush Rhees Library, River Campus Station, Rochester, New York 14620. A catalog is available: *Microcard Publications in Music* (Rochester: University of Rochester Press, 1965). See also Eva Maude Tilton, *A Union List of Publications in Opaque Microforms* (2nd ed.), (New York: Scarecrow Press, 1964).

and Baroque periods; and (3) representative American theses and dissertations in music education, music history, theory, and performance.

The J. S. Canner Company[17] has published microcard reproductions of the *Musical Quarterly*. There are several such microprint publication projects in various research areas: education, law, library science, medicine, and the humanities.

The microcard is inexpensive, costing about 25 to 35 cents per card, or less than 1 cent per page. A rare but important work like the *Syntagma musicum* of Michael Praetorius, listed at nearly $1,000 on the antiquarian book market, may be had in microcard copy for less than $10.

Because a card reader is necessary in using microcards, and scholars may not always have access to one, the Microcard Corporation (West Salem, Wisconsin) has developed equipment to produce a normal-sized photographic copy of any page on a microcard. While it may not be practical to have all the pages thus enlarged, a student may profit by having the most important portions of the microcard copies for use without the reading equipment.

## Xerox

Within recent years the Xerox process has been developed.[18] An electrostatic principle is employed to produce life-sized copies of books, manuscripts, music, journals, and charts on paper stock. The association of University Microfilms with the Xerox Corporation has created a new agency for research assistance. University Microfilms, with Xerox equipment, can produce full-sized copies on paper from a microfilm. A student may profit from having Xerox reproductions made of those films or parts of films containing material important to his study, even when availability of a microfilm reader is no problem. For transcription of music, perusal of manuscripts, or extensive note-taking, the Xerox copy is considerably easier to manage than film.

Theses and dissertations submitted to University Microfilms for inclusion in the research archives may be obtained in either microfilm or Xerox copy. In *Masters Abstracts* and *Dissertation Abstracts* (see below, pp. 70–71 prices are quoted for both forms of reproduction. The convenience of handling may offset the difference in price between microfilm and Xerox copies; most students prefer Xerox reproductions.

By supplementing the holdings of local libraries with interlibrary loans, and the use of regional cooperative programs and various copying methods, one may obtain much material. A person studying where adequate library

[17]J. S. Canner and Co., Inc., 618 Parker Street, Roxbury, Mass.
[18]Xerox Corporation, Rochester, New York, has developed the process and manufactures the copying equipment.

facilities are lacking must rely heavily upon such aids. Even the favored researcher, working in an area rich in resources, is sometimes obliged to use one or all of these services. With rapid developments in copying, transmission of information, and publication, the time and effort necessary for research may be minimized in years to come.

# BIBLIOGRAPHY

*Catalog of Microcard Publications No. 3, 1961–1962.* Washington: Microcard Editions, Inc., 1962; *No. 4, 1962–1963,* 1963.

*Dissertation Abstracts; Abstracts of Dissertations and Monographs in Microform.* Ann Arbor: University Microfilms, Inc., 1938–    . Until 1951 the title was *Microfilm Abstracts.*

*Doctoral Dissertations, Music, 1949–1964.* Ann Arbor: University Microfilms, Inc., 1965.

*Guide to Microforms in Print, 1966.* Washington: Microcard Editions, Inc., 1966.

Heckmann, Harald, "Archive of German Music History," *Notes* XVI (1958), 35–39.

———, comp., *Deutsches musikgeschichtliches Archiv: Katalog der Filmsammlung.* Kassel: Bärenreiter, 1955–    .

*Index to American Doctoral Dissertations.* Ann Arbor: University Microfilms, Inc., 1956–    .

"[Joint Committee on Fair Use in Photocopying] Report. American Library Association," *Bulletin* (June, 1961), 571–573.

Krohn, Ernst C., "Music in the Vatican Film Library at St. Louis University," *Notes* XIV (1957), 317–324.

———, "Vatican Music Collections on Microfilm at Saint Louis University," *Caecilia* LXXXIV (1957), 95–98.

Leaper, W. J., *Copyright and Performing Rights.* London: Stevens & Sons, Ltd., 1957.

*Masters Abstracts.* Ann Arbor: University Microfilms, Inc., 1962–    .

*Microcard/Microfiche Catalog No. 6.* Washington: Microcard Editions, Inc., 1965.

*Microcard Publications in Music.* Rochester: University of Rochester Microprint Press, 1965.

Philadelphia Bibliographical Center and Union Library Catalog, *Union List of Microfilms: Cumulation, 1949–1959.* Ann Arbor: Edwards Brothers, Inc., 1961.

Pilpel, H. F., and M. D. Goldberg, *A Copyright Guide* (2nd ed.). New York: R. R. Bowker Company, 1963.

Tilton, Eva Maude, *A Union List of Publications in Opaque Microforms* (2nd ed.). New York: Scarecrow Press, 1964.

Walls, Howard L., *The Copyright Handbook for Fine and Applied Arts.* New York: Watson-Guptil Publications, 1963.

*Part Two*

# *THE RESEARCH*
# *PAPER*

# 8

## Selection of
## a Research Topic

### Introduction

The selection of a subject is the first step in the research process unless, as in term papers and reports, the topic is assigned by the instructor. Selection involves considerable preliminary study. Far from being merely a formality, this may be interesting and enlightening, and may open up vistas hitherto unperceived by the student.

The investigator needs motivation. In addition to some previous background in the research area as a prerequisite to understanding his work, he should have a lively interest in the subject. He may pursue a topic because it pricks his curiosity and offers possibilities for exploration. If the subject is a comparatively new one, the student may strive for a discovery or the formulation of an original concept in the hope of contributing creatively to his field. He may, on the other hand, continue research already begun by someone else, hoping to advance, criticize, re-evaluate, or correct the existing work.

The student needs to budget his time. As interesting as a topic may appear, he has only a certain number of months for work on his thesis or dissertation. Institutions set limits on the number of years one may take to achieve a graduate degree, and it is foolhardy to attempt a project which is too extensive for the allotted time. But because a thesis must be of a certain magnitude to be accepted, some attention must be paid to the breadth of a proposed study. The faculty adviser should be able to give counsel on this matter.

The researcher must have easy access to enough material for his study to make the project practical. While all the necessary books and scores need not be available locally, one should know where to find them and how to obtain them through interlibrary loan or photocopy.

After some thought and preliminary investigation, the student may consider several topics as possibilities and make a list of them, bearing in mind the necessity for narrowing down the field to satisfy departmental requirements and to avoid duplication of effort in case someone else has done similar work.

## The Principle of Nonduplication

Although some departments and colleges may be inclined toward lenience in the matter of essays and some theses for the master's degree, a universal principle of limitation governs the doctoral dissertation: universities strictly prohibit the duplication of effort on any topic known to be written or in progress. If, for example, it is established that a person at University X is writing a dissertation on the orchestral innovations of Berlioz, a doctoral candidate at University Y must not embark upon the same project. Obviously, this may preclude the adoption of an interesting subject just because someone else got to it first. While on the surface it may seem unfair, the student must accept the condition, for by the same token, once he has selected his topic and has had it approved, he is protected in his turn from what may appear to be the predatory instincts of other dissertation writers.

The student is free to base his research upon the work of others or to use pre-existing dissertations as a springboard for his own investigation if a study already written can be enlarged upon, followed up, refuted, or corrected.

## The Local Survey

To find out what has already been treated and what is currently in progress is a primary step in topic selection. Most graduate departments keep accurate, up-to-date records of their research. Thesis bibliographies—which may be maintained as card catalogs, mimeographed booklets, or checklists—generally list (1) authors and titles of research completed in the department, (2) authors and titles of research in progress, and (3) authors and titles of topics accepted by the department for treatment in the immediate future.

Some universities publish retrospective lists, with or without abstracts, of works written within their departments and schools. A few random examples will suffice here. The University of Rochester's *Check List of Masters' and Doctors' Theses*[1] gives authors, titles, and degrees for all theses and dissertations accepted by the university within a stipulated period. The works are listed by subject field under the individual schools within the university. An author index appears at the end of the checklist. Ohio University's *Abstracts of Theses and Dissertations*[2] is an annual compilation, giving authors and titles of the studies, with an abstract or condensation of the basic findings and conclusions of each work accepted for a degree during the particular academic year.

Some large music departments and schools of music issue their own lists independently of the university. The School of Music at Northwestern University has a *Bibliography of Research* compiled by Hazel B. Morgan,[3] listing authors, titles, degrees, and dates of research papers—essays, theses, and dissertations—presented for the master's and doctor's degrees with music concentration since the first granting of such degrees at Northwestern. The main compilation is augmented by a list of works in progress, and a subject index is included.

Such card files, lists, and bibliographies of research done locally are kept in departmental offices or in reference sections of libraries. Large libraries sometimes have records of research completed in institutions other than their own. By referring to such sources, the writer becomes aware of the extent to which study has been carried on. He finds that his own list of topic possibilities may need to be trimmed because of work already completed or being carried on by others; conversely, he may be struck by new possibilities with which he may augment his list.

In most colleges the research papers submitted and accepted for degrees are housed within the library, where they may be consulted. A title which is obscure or misleading on a checklist may become meaningful when the work itself is read. Because of discrepancies sometimes occurring between the title of a thesis and its contents, the papers should be scanned or their abstracts studied to determine what has been accomplished and what has

---

[1]University of Rochester Library Staff, *Check List of Masters' and Doctors' Theses* (Rochester, N. Y.: University of Rochester, 1933–    ). The checklists are issued at approximately five-year intervals to record works during a specific period. In addition to the checklist, two up-to-date card files list the research in music, one maintained in the office of the Graduate Department of the Eastman School of Music and the other in the Sibley Music Library, where they may be consulted.

[2]Ohio University, *Abstracts of Theses and Dissertations* (Athens, Ohio: The Graduate College, 1939–    ). Until 1959 the publication was entitled *Abstracts of Masters' Theses*.

[3]Hazel B. Morgan, comp., *Bibliography of Research* (Evanston, Ill.: School of Music, Northwestern University, 1958).

yet to be done. If opportunities for the expansion of a subject become apparent, additional possible topics may be listed.

## The National Survey

National thesis bibliographies enable the researcher to expand his survey of subject possibilities. The following titles, important in music education, are available in most libraries: *Bibliography of Research Studies in Music Education, 1932–1948*, and *Bibliography of Research Studies in Music Education, 1949–1956*. Both are prepared by William S. Larson,[4] and list masters' and doctors' studies pertaining primarily to the teaching of music. The entries are arranged by states and indexed by topics.

The Larson lists were followed, with some modification, by Roderick Gordon's "Doctoral Dissertations in Music and Music Education, 1957–1963," and supplements in the *Journal of Research in Music Education*.[5] Devoted exclusively to doctoral papers, the list contains, in addition to studies in music, works related to the teaching of music: acoustics, therapy, psychology, speech, and tests and measurements, as well as dissertations submitted in the form of compositions and transcriptions. Although some musicological studies are included, the historical works given in the Hewitt list (see below, note 10) are not duplicated. Works in progress have purposely been omitted because of major changes often taking place during the writing of a dissertation which tend to alter the results. Availability of individual theses in microfilm, microcard, or Xerox copy is indicated, and agents are listed through whom desired items may be procured. A topical index concludes the list.

Another tool with national coverage is Alan P. Merriam's annotated bibliography of masters' theses and doctoral dissertations in ethnomusicology and folk music,[6] including 180 works submitted and accepted by American institutions. Short statements of the nature of the research are

---

[4]William S. Larson, *Bibliography of Research Studies in Music Education, 1932–1948* (Chicago: Music Educators' National Conference, 1949), incorporating the *Bibliography of Research Studies in Music Education, 1932–1944*, ed. by Arnold M. Small (Iowa City: State University of Iowa Press, for the Music Educators' National Conference, 1944). William S. Larson, *Bibliography of Research Studies in Music Education, 1949–1956* (Washington: Music Educators' National Conference, 1957), appearing in *Journal of Research in Music Education*, V (Fall, 1957), 64–225.

[5]Roderick D. Gordon, "Doctoral Dissertations in Music and Music Education, 1957–1963," *Journal of Research in Music Education*, XII (Spring, 1964), 4–112; supplement, 1963–1964, in XIII (Spring, 1965), 45–55; supplement 1964–1965, in XIV (Spring, 1966), 45–57.

[6]Alan P. Merriam, "Special Bibliography: An Annotated Bibliography of Theses and Dissertations in Ethnomusicology and Folk Music Accepted at American Universities," *Ethnomusicology*, IV (January, 1960), 21–25.

given. The first supplement, by Frank J. Gillis,[7] is a continuation of the Merriam bibliography, with the addition of dissertations written in other countries.

Johannes Riedel's "Dissertationen zur Hymnologie und Kirchenmusik in Nordamerika" in the *Jahrbuch für Liturgik und Hymnologie*[8] is a classified cumulative bibliography of dissertations in the field of sacred music accepted by universities in the United States.

The issue of the *Journal of Music Therapy* for June, 1964, is devoted to research abstracts in the subject field.[9] Of the 170 items abstracted, more than 40 are theses and dissertations. The abstracts are short and to the point.

On a more general subject basis is a compilation by Helen Hewitt, called *Doctoral Dissertations in Musicology*.[10] "Musicology" in this title means not merely history of music but also theory, music literature, philosophy, pedagogy, and science pertaining to the development of some movement, form, style, or phenomenon—physical or psychological—in music. The entries represent dissertations written and accepted in the United States for the Doctor of Philosophy and Doctor of Sacred Music degrees since the first granting of musical doctorates.[11] Accounts of works in progress are also given.

The dissertation topics are classified by historical periods (e.g., Antiquity, Middle Ages, Renaissance), as well as by broad subject areas (e.g., ethnomusicological and national subjects, instruments, philosophy, theory). There are an author index and a subject index with small subdivisions (e.g., Abaco, Abel, *a cappella* composition, accentuation). The

---

[7]Frank J. Gillis, "Special Bibliography: An Annotated Bibliography of Theses and Dissertations in Ethnomusicology, Supplement I," *Ethnomusicology*, VI (September, 1962), 191–214.

[8]Johannes Riedel, "Dissertationen zur Hymnologie und Kirchenmusik in Nordamerika," *Jahrbuch für Liturgik und Hymnologie*, VII (1962), 326–335.

[9]Margaret L. Sears and William W. Sears, comps., "Abstracts of Research in Music Therapy," *Journal of Music Therapy*, I (June, 1964), 33–60.

[10]Helen Hewitt, *Doctoral Dissertations in Musicology* (Denton, Tex.: Music Teachers' National Association, 1953); supplements in *American Music Teacher*, II (May-June, 1953), 10, 16–17; III (May-June, 1954), 8–9, 16; *Journal of the American Musicological Society*, VII (1954), 131–140; VIII (1955), 116–122; IX (1956), 202–209. 2nd ed., (Baldwin, N. Y.: Music Teachers' National Association, 1958); 1958–1959 supplement in *Journal of the American Musicological Society*, XI (1958), 217–226; 1960 supplement in same journal, XII (1959), 215–224 (the discrepancy in dates results from the delayed publication of the *Journal*, while the numbering and date of the issues remained unbroken; the 1959 volume actually appeared in 1961). 3rd ed., (Philadelphia: American Musicological Society, 1961), including statement of availability of works in microfilm or microcard copy; supplements in *Journal of the American Musicological Society*, XV (1962), 330–346; XVI (1963), 382–393. 4th ed., (Philadelphia: American Musicological Society, 1965).

[11]Dissertations submitted for the Doctor of Musical Arts degree are not included. The Gordon list (see above, note 5) does have entries for D.M.A. dissertations.

compiler constantly revises and brings *Doctoral Dissertations in Musicology* up to date, making it a practical reference for American music research on the doctoral level.

Another tool—one that is paradoxically more general in scope than the Hewitt list (because all subject areas are included) but more exclusive in content (because not all universities submit works)—is *Dissertation Abstracts*, published monthly by University Microfilms.[12] Cooperating institutions (some 160 in May, 1966)[13] send their doctoral dissertations to University Microfilms to be photographed on a master film from which microfilm and Xerox copies may be made as desired. *Dissertation Abstracts* is two things at once: (1) a catalog of works available in microfilm or Xerox copy, together with their prices, and (2) a compilation of abstracts of studies by students in many universities throughout the country.[14] The abstracts are arranged by broad subject areas such as mathematics, music, pharmacology, and philosophy, and their titles are entered in a subject index under detailed subdivisions such as concertos, sonatas, and symphonies.

Upon completion of each twelve-month fiscal period, an index giving a cumulative account of the year's work is published as Part II of the June issue of *Dissertation Abstracts*. A listing of works by subject, using subject headings assigned by the Library of Congress upon perusal of the abstracts, appears first, followed by an alphabetical list of authors.

Also at the end of the academic year a volume entitled *American Doctoral Dissertations* is published.[15] Compiled from commencement programs of various schools, the index attempts a complete listing of doctoral dissertations accepted by universities in the United States and Canada, regardless of participation in the microfilming project and including many works other than those abstracted in *Dissertation Abstracts*. The volume for 1964–1965 lists 15,693 studies by broad subject fields, arranged under the name of the degree-granting institution; among them are 155 studies in music. An author index follows the subject list.

Begun in 1956 with the list of works accepted during the academic year 1955–1956, *American Doctoral Dissertations* is in a sense a continuation and successor to *Doctoral Dissertations Accepted by American*

---

[12]*Dissertation Abstracts: Abstracts of Dissertations and Monographs in Microform* (Ann Arbor: University Microfilms, Inc., 1938–    ). Until 1951 the title was *Microfilm Abstracts*.

[13]This number includes eight foreign universities (Canadian, French, Chilean, and Australian).

[14]Although participation in the microfilm project is voluntary and not all institutions take part, the enrollment of additional schools each year makes *Dissertation Abstracts* increasingly effective as a research tool.

[15]*American Doctoral Dissertations* (Ann Arbor: University Microfilms, Inc., 1956–    ). The introduction contains useful information, including a list of current university serial publications abstracting dissertations (e.g., Ohio University's *Abstracts of Theses and Dissertations*).

*Universities*, published annually from 1934 to 1955 by The H. W. Wilson Company. This publication in turn had overlapped and then superseded the *List of American Doctoral Dissertations*, a record of works accepted between 1912 and 1938, which had been issued by the Library of Congress and published by the United States Government Printing Office from 1913 to 1940.[16] There has thus been a continuous listing of American dissertations since 1912: for works to 1938, the *List of American Doctoral Dissertations*; for works between 1934 and 1955, *Doctoral Dissertations Accepted by American Universities*; and for those since 1956, *American Doctoral Dissertations*.[17]

In summer, 1962, University Microfilms began the publication of *Masters Abstracts*, designed to serve the same purpose for masters' theses as *Dissertation Abstracts* serves for doctoral research. In the first issue eight theses on music were listed. The importance of *Masters Abstracts*, while not equal to that of *Dissertation Abstracts* as a bibliographical tool, is bound to increase as more theses are submitted.

## The International Survey

Students working toward the doctorate should investigate research done in countries other than their own. Such an expanded survey is likewise advisable for some masters' theses. National bibliographical tools (e.g., *Catalogue des thèses et écrits académiques*, for France;[18] *Jahresverzeichnis der deutschen Hochschulschriften*, for Germany[19]), similar to the *Index to American Doctoral Dissertations*, are published in most of the countries of Europe and are described in Keith Mixter's *General Bibliography for Music Research*.[20] Many general bibliographies also exist, from which dissertations on music subjects may be extracted. The best guide to their

[16]*List of American Doctoral Dissertations*, Vols. I–XXVII (1912–1938), (Washington: Library of Congress, 1913–1940), and *Doctoral Dissertations Accepted by American Universities*, Vols. I–XXII (1933/34–1954/55), (New York: The H. W. Wilson Company, 1934–1955) are available in reprint copy through Kraus Reprint Corp., 16 East 46th Street, New York.

[17]If the local library does not subscribe to *American Doctoral Dissertations*, the student may find *Doctoral Dissertations, Music, 1949–1964* (Ann Arbor: University Microfilms, Inc., 1965) useful. Found in many music libraries, it is a list extracted from *Dissertation Abstracts* and *Microfilm Abstracts* of studies in the field of music.

[18]*Catalogue des thèses et écrits académiques, 1884/85–* (Paris: Ministère de l'Education nationale, 1885– ). Years 1–60 (1884/85–1943) are available in reprint through Kraus Reprint Corp.

[19]*Jahresverzeichnis der deutschen Hochschulschriften, 1885/86–* . Years 1885/86–1906/07 are available in reprint through Kraus Reprint Corp.

[20]Keith E. Mixter, *General Bibliography for Music Research*, Detroit Studies in Music Bibliography No. 4 (Detroit: Information Service, Inc., 1962), pp. 26–28.

contents is Constance Winchell's *Guide to Reference Books.*[21] To avoid duplication of material already well presented and available in many libraries, only bibliographies pertaining to  dissertations in music are cited in the present chapter.

Lists from Germany are more numerous than those from other European countries. German universities, long active in music research, have many dissertations in music history, theory, aesthetics, philosophy, psychology, and pedagogy. The fact that German institutions insist upon publication of doctoral papers in book or monograph form adds to their availability. *Die Musikforschung,* a periodical found in many libraries, contains annual lists entitled "Im Jahre—angenommene musikwissenschaftliche Dissertationen," giving data on musicological works starting with the academic year 1948/49.[22] A list compiled by Richard Schaal and printed in the *Jahrbuch der Musikwelt,* is a reference source for retrospective listing from 1885 to 1948.[23] A third German bibliography is the series of lists originally contained in the *Jahrbuch der Musikbibliothek Peters,* published first in 1922[24] and continued in the *Deutsches Jahrbuch der Musikwissenschaft* under the title, "Verzeichnis der im Berichtjahr—bei der deutschen Bücherei zu Leipzig registrirten musikwissenschaftlichen Dissertationen und Habilitationsschriften."[25] The list for 1960 (appearing in 1961) was compiled by Ortrun Landmann and contains 46 items.[26]

For Austrian dissertations one may consult "Verzeichnis der seit 1955 am Musikwissenschaftlichen Institut der Universität Wien approbierten Dissertationen," in *Studien zur Musikwissenschaft.*[27] Although it includes only studies accepted at Vienna since 1955, it represents the institution most productive of research in Austria. Music dissertations from other Austrian universities (mainly Innsbruck) are given in part in the *Oesterreichische Bibliographie.*[28]

[21]Constance M. Winchell, *Guide to Reference Books* (7th ed.), (Chicago: American Library Association, 1951); supplements 1950–1952 (1954); 1953–1955 (1956); 1956–1958 (1960); 1959–1962 (1963).

[22]*Die Musikforschung* (Kassel: Bärenreiter-Verlag, 1948–    ). The list of material accepted in that year is the first of the annual bibliographies and appears in Vol. III (1950).

[23]Richard Schaal, "Verzeichnis der musikwissenschaftlichen Dissertationen in Deutschland, 1885–1948," *Jahrbuch der Musikwelt* (Bayreuth: J. Steeger, 1949), pp. 58–103.

[24]*Jahrbuch der Musikbibliothek Peters* (Leipzig: C. F. Peters, 1894–    ). The list begins in Vol. 29 (1922). Commonly called *Peters Jahrbuch,* Vols. 1–47 (1894–1940) are available in reprint. The yearbook was discontinued after 1940.

[25]*Deutsches Jahrbuch der Musikwissenschaft* (Leipzig: C. F. Peters, 1957–    ). *Habilitationsschriften* mentioned in the title are inaugural dissertations.

[26]*Ibid.,* (1961), pp. 97–99.

[27]"Verzeichnis der seit 1955 am Musikwissenschaftlichen Institut der Universität Wien approbierten Dissertationen," *Studien zur Musikwissenschaft,* XXIII (1956), 188.

[28]*Oesterreichische Bibliographie* (Vienna: various publishers, 1946–    ). This is a general bibliography from which music items must be extracted.

Richard Schaal's *Verzeichnis deutschsprachiger musikwissenschaftlicher Dissertationen, 1861–1960*, is a large retrospective listing of works in the German language.[29] The writings are not limited to those submitted to universities in Germany but include also those approved at institutions in Switzerland, Austria, and Sweden. Following the list of 2,819 studies is a subject index. No author index is provided, presumably because the subjects rather than the authors are the more important consideration. In the introduction the compiler gives bibliographical data on the indexes from which his information was extracted.

The 1958 volume of *Acta musicologica* contains an excellent review of musicological research in France since 1945.[30] Following an account of research conditions and accomplishments, the author has furnished a three-page list of doctoral dissertations, including works on acoustics, theory, history, pedagogy, and folk material.

The terms *Musikwissenschaft* and *musicologie* in the titles above may probably best be translated as "musicology." Contrary to the popular American conception, musicology is a broad field embracing the systematic study of music in its many aspects. Historical studies are but one phase of the subject area, which also includes pedagogy, theory, philosophy, psychology, acoustics, and aesthetics. In some countries musicology is synonymous with music criticism and propaganda, and musicologists are concerned with current concert repertoire and contemporary music.

For ethnomusicology, in which interchange of ideas between scholars over the world is brisk, the supplement to "An Annotated Bibliography of Theses and Dissertations in Ethnomusicology," contained in *Ethnomusicology*, has been expanded to include research papers written in the Americas, Europe, and Asia, as well as those accepted in the United States.[31]

The classified "Literaturbericht zur Hymnologie," a regular feature of the *Jahrbuch für Liturgik und Hymnologie*,[32] is an international bibliography listing dissertations on church music as well as books and articles in journals.

The careful perusal of references mentioned above (or tools like them) provides the prospective writer with a fund of knowledge. He finds his appreciation of music research deepened and realizes the extent to which his preferred topics have been studied, both in his own country and abroad. He may draw interesting comparisons and contrasts between personal preferences, methods, and avenues of approach. To gain this over-all perspective is an important step in research.

[29]Richard Schaal, *Verzeichnis deutschsprachiger musikwissenschaftlicher Dissertationen, 1861–1960* (Kassel: Bärenreiter-Verlag, 1963).
[30]François Lesure, "La musicologie française depuis 1945," *Acta musicologica*, XXX (1958), 3–17.
[31]Gillis, "Special Bibliography."
[32]*Jahrbuch für Liturgik und Hymnologie* (Kassel: J. Stauda-Verlag, 1955–    ).

## Some Final Considerations

When the student has eliminated from his list of tentative topics any items which are not free, he should investigate the comparative availability of materials on subjects remaining as possibilities. No one can hope to locate all the sources he desires; accessibility of books, journals, scores, and recordings varies. In cities maintaining well-stocked libraries one may require little assistance from interlibrary loans or photocopy. A student in a less favorable situation may have to rely heavily upon these services (see above, Chapters 6 and 7). It stands to reason that topics for which materials are within reach are more practical than those for which only a few sources can easily be found.

Language is another consideration. No matter how interesting a topic may be, it is folly to attempt it if most of the literature exists only in a language which the student does not know. To learn a new language for the sake of a thesis may prove too time-consuming to warrant the effort. Enlisting the services of a translator is not satisfacory unless the translator knows enough about all aspects of the subject to grasp the full import of what he reads. Even under the best conditions the translator and the writer must work together to reach complete understanding of the material. A possible exception to the no-translator principle is the inclusion of a few items in a foreign language to supplement numerous basic sources available in a language the writer reads easily.

Two other factors should be recognized. First, depending upon where the student is enrolled, the choice of a thesis topic may be partly determined by the academic policies of the college, by the relative strength of the department in specific subject areas, and even by the interests of members of the faculty. If strong biases exist, they must be considered fairly. Although no instructor or graduate committee should force a student to pursue a subject against his will, it is legitimate and often helpful for a professor to suggest a certain topic. Some advisers, however, quite rightly prefer to have the student take the initiative. Such a preference is not a lack of interest in the candidate's welfare, although he might appreciate helpful steering in the right direction; making suggestions is a professor's prerogative rather than his duty.

Second, depending upon the college and the topic, the need may arise for interdepartmental cooperation. Some problems of acoustical research, for example, may require the assistance of the physics department, or studies in musical therapy may require the aid of the psychology department. The student must ascertain the availability of such assistance. He must be prepared to straddle two departments and to reconcile their differences of opinion and method. Inability to reach a complete understanding jeopardizes the research.

Having finally narrowed his list of topic possibilities to a few which seem interesting and practical, the student is ready for guidance in arriving at his final choice. The adviser should be willing to give assistance in his selection and definition of the topic. When the choice has been made, the writer may compile his bibliography and prepare the outline for his research. In most graduate schools he will be asked to submit for approval by the graduate committee an explanation of his topic, a proposed or tentative bibliography, and an outline of procedure and contents of his research paper.

## BIBLIOGRAPHY

*American Doctoral Dissertations.* Ann Arbor: University Microfilms, Inc., 1956– .

*Catalogue des thèses et écrits académiques, 1884/85–* . Paris: Ministere de l'Education nationale, 1885– .

*Deutsches Jahrbuch der Musikwissenschaft.* Leipzig: C. F. Peters, 1957– .

*Dissertation Abstracts.* Ann Arbor: University Microfilms, Inc., 1938– .

*Doctoral Dissertations, Music, 1949–1964.* Ann Arbor: University Microfilms, Inc., 1965.

*Doctoral Dissertations Accepted by American Universities,* Vols. I–XXII (1933/34–1954/55). New York: The H. W. Wilson Company, 1934–1955.

Gillis, Frank J., "Special Bibliography: An Annotated Bibliography of Theses and Dissertations in Ethnomusicology, Supplement I," *Ethnomusicology,* VI (September, 1962), 191–214.

Gordon, Roderick D., "Doctoral Dissertations in Music and Music Education, 1957–1963," *Journal of Research in Music Education,* XII (Spring, 1964), 4–112; supplement, 1963–1964, in XIII (Spring, 1965), 45–55; supplement, 1964–1965, in XIV (Spring, 1966), 45–57.

Hewitt, Helen, *Doctoral Dissertations in Musicology* (4th ed.). Philadelphia: American Musicological Society, 1965.

*Jahrbuch der Musikbibliothek Peters,* Vols. 29–47 (1922–1940). Leipzig: C. F. Peters, 1923–1941).

*Jahrbuch für Liturgik und Hymnologie.* Kassel: J. Stauda-Verlag, 1955– .

*Jahresverzeichnis der deutschen Hochschulschriften, 1885/86–* . Reprinted by Kraus Reprint Corp., New York.

Larson, William S., *Bibliography of Research Studies in Music Education, 1932–1948.* Chicago: Music Educators' National Conference, 1949.

———, *Bibliography of Research Studies in Music Education, 1949–1956.* Washington: Music Educators' National Conference, 1957, appearing in *Journal of Research in Music Education,* V (Fall, 1957), 64–225.

Lesure, François, "La musicologie française depuis 1945," *Acta musicologica*, XXX (1958), 3–17.

*List of American Doctoral Dissertations*, Vols. I–XXVII (1912–1938). Washington: Library of Congress, 1913–1940.

*Masters Abstracts*. Ann Arbor: University Microfilms, Inc., 1962–    .

Merriam, Alan P., "Special Bibliography: An Annotated Bibliography of Theses and Dissertations in Ethnomusicology and Folk Music Accepted at American Universities," *Ethnomusicology*, IV (January, 1960), 21–25.

Mixter, Keith E., *General Bibliography for Music Research*, Detroit Studies in Music Bibliography No. 4. Detroit: Information Service, Inc., 1962.

Morgan, Hazel B., comp., *Bibliography of Research*. Evanston, Ill.: School of Music, Northwestern University, 1958.

*Die Musikforschung*. Kassel: Bärenreiter-Verlag, 1948–    .

*Oesterreichische Bibliographie*. Vienna: various publishers, 1946–    .

Ohio University, *Abstracts of Theses and Dissertations*. Athens, Ohio: The Graduate College, 1939–    .

Riedel, Johannes, "Dissertationen zur Hymnologie und Kirchenmusik in Nordamerika," *Jahrbuch für Liturgik und Hymnologie*, VII (1962), 326–335.

Schaal, Richard, *Verzeichnis deutschsprachiger musikwissenschaftlicher Dissertationen, 1861–1960*. Kassel: Bärenreiter-Verlag, 1963.

———, "Verzeichnis der musikwissenschaftlichen Dissertationen in Deutschland, 1885–1948," *Jahrbuch der Musikwelt*. Bayreuth: J. Steeger, 1949, 58–103.

Sears, Margaret L., and William W. Sears, comps., "Abstracts of Research in Music Therapy," *Journal of Music Therapy*, I (June, 1964), 33–60.

Small, Arnold M., *Bibliography of Research Studies in Music Education, 1932–1944*. Iowa City: State University of Iowa Press, 1944.

University of Rochester Library Staff, *Check List of Masters' and Doctors' Theses*. Rochester, N. Y.: University of Rochester, 1933–    .

"Verzeichnis der seit 1955 am Musikwissenschaftlichen Institut der Universität Wien approbierten Dissertationen," *Studien zur Musikwissenschaft*, XXIII (1956), 188.

Winchell, Constance M., *Guide to Reference Books* (7th ed.). Chicago: American Library Association, 1951; supplements, 1954, 1956, 1960, 1963.

# *9*

# *Bibliography: Books*

## General Nature
## of a Bibliography

Although research may be a lengthy process involving books, periodicals, pamphlets, and scores, much can be accomplished through organization to give direction to the study and to shorten the time required. As groundwork for his reading, the student should compile a basic bibliography, a list or file of all the items he hopes to consult. Because a music project may require perusal of scores, sheet music, and instrumental or vocal parts, the bibliography tends to become more complex than that for a liberal-arts study, for which books and periodicals represent most of the source material. Moreover, if recordings and sound tapes are used in the investigation, one may also need a discography.

Music bibliographies may be divided into several sections: (1) books, (2) periodicals, and (3) scores and/or sheet music. If there is a discography, it may either be compiled separately or constitute a fourth section of the bibliography. Because these materials must be located by various methods and in various places, and their entries rearranged, most thesis advisers recommend the use of cards (3″ x 5″ or slightly larger) to note bibliographical data, a separate card for each item. Cards are desirable for the speed they make possible in adding new entries, deleting unwanted ones, and alphabetizing the remainder.

The following are basic steps usually taken in the preparation of a bibliography: A list is made of materials on the subject; the items are evaluated and rearranged in some logical order; the number of sources available in the immediate vicinity is determined, and plans are made for the acquisition of the rest through photocopy or interlibrary loan. Such steps may occupy many hours, depending upon the research subject. No matter how tedious the work may seem at the outset, however, time given to it is well spent. An immature student, unable to resist the temptation to read immediately upon finding a reference appropriate to his topic, may become confused by the variety of books encountered or frustrated by lack of information which he feels should be readily available. His research may suffer from indirection. It is much safer instead to compile a good bibliography by which to check progress and budget valuable time, while simultaneously being guided to well-ordered reading.

## General Sources

One starting point for a discussion of bibliography is book material, although any of the source media might be taken first and several types (e.g., books and periodicals) may be found together in the same bibliographical tools.

From the catalogs of the local library the researcher may gather information about several "book" types (books, monographs, and cataloged pamphlets), which may constitute the largest portion of the bibliography for some projects. When an appropriate work is found, the following data may be noted on a bibliography card: the name of the author, last name first (for easy alphabetizing later); the complete title of the work (for positive identification in case the author has written several books on the same or similar subjects); its imprint (place of publication, publisher, and date of publication or copyright); collation (number of pages or number of volumes); and call number in the library in which the student is working. He should make such notes as "includes bibliography," "discography, pp. 152–160," or "index of compositions, Appendix A," which are useful for future reference. If facilities of several libraries are being used, the cards should show the specific places in which each source is found.

Because the bibliography is to be a list of what one hopes to consult and not necessarily what he has available on the spot, the student should continue with possibilities other than those appearing in local library catalogs. As a beginning he may study the bibliographical notes contained in books which are already on his list and in his own library. The note, "Bibliography: pp. 305–312," in Figure 9–1 indicates that Redlich has an eight-page bibliography in his study of Berg. By checking the works listed there, the student may find some sources which, although perhaps not available in his immediate vicinity, can be obtained quickly through interlibrary loan.

One may consult the bibliographical notes appended to leading articles

Figure 9-1    A Bibliographical Notation.

```
Redlich, Hans Ferdinand
Alban Berg, The Man and His Music
New York: Abelard-Schuman, 1957
316 pp.
Catalog of works: pp. 287-298
Discography: pp. 299-304
Bibliography: pp. 305-312
In Library X: ML 410 B493R31 (Music Dept.)
In Library Y: 927.8 B49 (General Library)
```

on the topic in dictionaries and encyclopedias.[1] Such lists are usually selected from among works worthy of a researcher's attention, including books and articles in periodicals in all languages. Taking Berg as an example, one finds nine sources given in Grove, four in Riemann, and eight in Baker—all in bibliographical notes following the article on the composer. Several items appear in all three, indicating that the compilers agreed as to the value of these books and articles. For a composer like Beethoven, for whom the bibliographical notes in standard reference tools run into several columns, a larger difference of opinion as well as more points of agreement may be found.

## Additional Sources

When or before the resources of local libraries have been exhausted, the bibliography of books may be sufficient for some studies. The breadth of a bibliography naturally depends upon the magnitude of the topic, the purpose for which the paper is written, and the degree of ability of the

[1]Some recommended sources: *Grove's Dictionary of Music and Musicians* (5th ed.), (London: Macmillan & Co., Ltd., 1954); supplement (1961). Every edition of Grove is different and bibliographical notes vary. Hugo Riemann, *Musik Lexikon* (Mainz: B. Schott's Söhne, 1959). *Baker's Biographical Dictionary of Musicians* (5th ed.), (New York: G. Schirmer, Inc., 1958). Willi Apel, *Harvard Dictionary of Music* (Cambridge, Mass.: Harvard University Press, 1956). *Die Musik in Geschichte und Gegenwart: Allgemeine Enzyklopädie der Musik* (Kassel: Bärenreiter-Verlag, 1949–    ). Commonly known as *MGG*, this encyclopedia is in German and has excellent coverage and well-organized bibliographical notes.

individual to handle the research problem. The nature of the subject also influences the size of the bibliography: a person studying Beethoven must consult more references than one working on Berg, for obviously more has been written about Beethoven than about Berg.

The advanced scholar will very likely need to pursue further materials to do justice to all phases of his subject. Large catalogs of holdings in national libraries are a fruitful source of information. The multivolume *Library of Congress Catalog . . . Books: Subjects, 1950–1954* and supplements,[2] a subject index compiled from the printed catalog cards issued by the Library of Congress, is an example. The individual volumes are arranged by broad subject fields, with entries containing bibliographical data under each heading. Akin to the *Library of Congress Catalog* are the several catalogs of European national libraries (e.g., the British Museum's *Catalogue of Printed Books*[3] and *General Catalogue of Printed Books*[4] or the Bibliothèque Nationale's *Catalogue général des livres imprimés: Auteurs*[5]). They are mammoth compilations, in which music is but one of the subjects included among many other research areas. Large university and public libraries usually possess such catalogs, which may be housed in the catalog department or the reference room.

Catalogs of music collections in large libraries, both local and national, provide information about a wide variety of books on music. The dictionary catalog of music holdings in the New York Public Library has been issued by G. K. Hall and Company of Boston and may be available in some libraries as a reference tool. Vincent Duckles lists a number of catalogs issued by various libraries (see his *Music Reference and Research Materials*[6]), making further discussion unnecessary here.

The following bibliographical sources, usually available in general libraries and in large bookstores, may be useful in locating books in print: *Cumulative Book Index: A World List of Books in the English Language*;[7] *Books in Print: An Index to the Publishers' Trade List Annual*, together with the *Subject Guide to Books in Print*;[8] and *Paperbound Books in*

[2]*The Library of Congress Catalog . . . Books: Subjects, 1950–1954* (Ann Arbor: J. W. Edwards, Inc., 1955); *1955–1959* (Paterson, N. J.: Pageant, 1960); *1960* (Washington: Library of Congress, 1961); *1960–1964* (Ann Arbor: Edwards, 1965).

[3]British Museum, Department of Printed Books, *Catalogue of Printed Books* (London: Clowes, 1881–1900); supplements (1900–1905).

[4]British Museum, Department of Printed Books, *General Catalogue of Printed Books* (London: various publishers, 1931–    ).

[5]Bibliothèque Nationale, *Catalogue général des livres imprimés: Auteurs* (Paris: Imprimerie Nationale, 1897–    ).

[6]Vincent Duckles, *Music Reference and Research Materials* (New York: The Free Press of Glencoe, 1964), pp. 196–259.

[7]*Cumulative Book Index: A World List of Books in the English Language* (New York: The H. W. Wilson Company, 1938–    ).

[8]*Books in Print: An Index to the Publishers' Trade List Annual* (New York: R. R. Bowker Company, 1948–    ); *Subject Guide to Books in Print* (1957–    ).

*Print.*[9] These lists can be approached by author, title, and subject. Directions on their use are found in the front pages of each volume.

Printed national bibliographies (lists of books on all subjects received by the national library and/or issued by the nation's publishing houses) exist for many countries. Their coverage of music has been explained by Donald W. Krummel and James B. Coover in an article in *Notes*,[10] which may serve as a guide.

Brief comments on a few representative lists devoted primarily to books on music are presented on the following pages. *The British Catalogue of Music*[11] contains a section on books, including those published in Britain during a specified year. The items are indexed by author and title.

Jean Leguy's *Catalogue bibliographique des livres de langue française sur la musique*[12] is useful as a source for books in French. Properly speaking, it is not a national catalog but a trade list of books available at E. Ploix-Musique. Nevertheless, it effectively serves a bibliographical purpose. Books on music are classified by major areas: history of music; life and works of musicians; instruments, orchestra and orchestration; the song; musical forms; sacred music; music pedagogy; miscellaneous studies; treatises and large didactic works; writings by musicians; dance and ballet; fine editions and musical novels; and reviews and periodicals. Each area is subdivided, with appropriate headings under which books are listed; the catalog is indexed by author. Although the majority of works are French in origin, many stem from French-speaking Belgium and Switzerland.

The *Bibliographie des Musikschrifttums*[13] gives a broad international view of books and journals in many languages. The work was begun in the mid-thirties by Kurt Taut. After his death two years later, it was continued by Georg Karstädt until 1941. Four volumes were published, listing literature about music (books and journals) issued from 1936 to 1939. During World War II and the reconstruction years (1941–1949) the bibliography was suspended; there is no listing of materials published during the forties. In 1954, under the direction of Wolfgang Schmieder, the second phase of publication began with the volume covering literature

[9]*Paperbound Books in Print* (New York: R. R. Bowker Company, 1956–    ).

[10]Donald W. Krummel and James B. Coover, "Current National Bibliographies; Their Music Coverage," *Notes* XVII (1960), 375–388. See also Mixter, *General Bibliography for Music Research*, Chap. 2, for a list of national bibliographies.

[11]*The British Catalogue of Music* (London: Council of the British National Bibliography, 1957–    ).

[12]Jean Leguy, *Catalogue bibliographique des livres de langue française sur la musique* (Paris: Ploix, 1954). *Fascicule complémentaire . . . et supplément 1954–1959* (1959).

[13]*Bibliographie des Musikschrifttums* (Leipzig: F. Hofmeister, 1936–1941; 1954–    ). Sometimes referred to as the *Schmieder Bibliography*, after its present editor.

published in 1950–1951, and subsequent issues have continued to appear.

The *Bibliographie des Musikschrifttums* is an annual cumulation. Each volume encompasses the entire field of music research, including bibliography, theory, and musicology; music history; contemporary music (including "new music," its theory, composers, and pedagogy); instruments; and individual musicians. The 1956–1957 issue, published in 1961, contains 7,187 entries indexed by subjects, places, and proper names. From the standpoint of convenience, the most serious drawback to the *Bibliographie* is the long interval (averaging four years) between the issue of the works listed and the appearance of the bibliographical volume. This time lag is offset by the thoroughness of the work and the extent of its coverage. Being of German origin, its emphasis is upon literature from German sources, although its scope is international.

A helpful list of books of non-German origin is the *Neuerwerbungen ausländischer Musikliteratur*,[14] one of the printed catalogs of the Deutsche Staatsbibliothek in Berlin. While it indicates only the holdings of that particular library, these include works of Russian, Polish, Czech, and Hungarian origin as well as some from the West. With increasing interest in the music of the Middle and East European nations, this type of bibliography may grow in importance.

For a project involving subjects related to music (e.g., aesthetics, psychology, philosophy, literature) one may investigate the *Bibliographie einiger Grenzgebiete der Musikwissenschaft*.[15] Unlike the *Bibliographie des Musikschrifttums*, which is an annual cumulation, this work is retrospective, striving for as complete a listing as possible of source materials in peripheral areas published from 1800 to *ca.* 1961. There are 3,519 entries, indexed by subjects and proper names.

If the library does not possess the above-mentioned bibliographical tools[16] the student has recourse to the lists of new books found in some music journals. A few examples are cited here. The "Quarterly Book List," a feature of the *Musical Quarterly* for many years, contains entries for current books arranged by language. A representative selection of works on music, it serves the purpose of the average music researcher. The sections on new books in the *Notes* of the Music Library Association are more extensive, including a greater variety of publications in many different languages. They are useful to the musicologist and theorist as well as to the student. The *Musical Quarterly* and *Notes*, both considered a necessary part of the music periodical collection, have wide circulation among

---

[14]*Neuerwerbungen ausländischer Musikliteratur (1954–1955)*, Deutsche Staatsbibliothek bibliographische Mitteilungen 12; (Berlin: Deutsche Staatsbibliothek, 1956).

[15]Mecklenburg, Carl Gregor, Herzog von, *Bibliographie einiger Grenzgebiete der Musikwissenschaft* (Baden-Baden: Verlag Heitz, 1962).

[16]These works may be deemed too specialized for inclusion in some libraries.

libraries and are among the best guides for both the practical musician and the research student.

For books on music issued in the 1930's and 1940's one may look into the "Index novorum librorum" of *Acta musicologica*, the organ of the International Musicological Society. Containing information about books on music, with entries by subject classification, this list was unfortunately discontinued in 1952. As far as it goes, it is useful. *Fontes artis musicae*, the journal of the International Association of Music Libraries, contains a selective international checklist of music materials by country of origin. In a sense, the lists in *Fontes* begun in 1954 may function as continuations of those in the *Acta* in spite of some differences in format and selection. The *Acta* and *Fontes* are found in most research and music libraries.

## Special Subject Lists

Students in some specialized subjects are fortunate in having a published bibliography. Some examples, representing several different fields, are given here. The Basart bibliography of serial music[17] fills a need for a definitive listing of references to twelve-tone and electronic music. However, in contemporary composition, with its rapid developments, so many new studies are being published that no bibliography can remain up to date. Basart provides data on the majority of necessary materials, and after selecting the items needed from this list, the student may add literature issued since the publication of the list. Similar treatment may be necessary for all bibliographies, although the speed at which new items appear varies with the subject.

In twentieth-century American composition, the book entries in *Some Twentieth-Century American Composers* by John Edmunds and Gordon Boelzner[18] give some idea of works written by and about a selected group of outstanding creators.[19] The first appendix to Volume II suggests where to look in standard reference works for biographies of a number of composers in America.

Some representative special lists on music performance are the Garretson bibliography on string chamber-music performance,[20] the Rutan bibliog-

[17]Ann Phillips Basart, *Serial Music: A Classified Bibliography of Writings on Twelve-Tone and Electronic Music* (Berkeley: University of California Press, 1961).

[18]John Edmunds and Gordon Boelzner, *Some Twentieth-Century American Composers* (New York: The New York Public Library, 1959–1960).

[19]See also Storm Bull, *Index to Biographies of Contemporary Composers* (New York: Scarecrow Press, 1964).

[20]Homer E. Garretson, *An Annotated Bibliography of Written Material Pertinent to the Performance of Chamber Music for Stringed Instruments* (Ann Arbor: University Microfilms, Inc., 1961). Doctoral dissertation submitted to the University of Illinois for the Ed.D. degree, 1961.

raphy on brass and percussion chamber music,[21] and the Squire bibliography on woodwind chamber music.[22] Other similar bibliographies, listing books and articles from periodicals, with helpful annotations and some indication of content, are in preparation.

The bibliographical section of the *Mozart-Handbuch*[23] is an example of a comprehensive list (3,871 entries) of known sources on one person. The student needs only to consider the effort expended by its compilers in gathering and confirming data and sorting them into a workable bibliography to realize what a time-saver the compilation is. Among the thousands of items, of course, some differences exist in breadth and quality; discrimination may be necessary in the use of such an extensive tool.

Similarly, Fred Blum's bibliography on Sibelius[24] lists books and articles in both music and nonmusic periodicals. The bibliography is classified and annotated.

*A Guide to the Music of Latin America* by Gilbert Chase[25] is a large bibliography of books and periodical articles on the music of Central and South America and the West Indies, including colonial, popular, folk, and theater materials. The work is classified and annotated, with entries grouped by countries and arranged under subheadings. It concludes with a supplement, a key to periodicals, and an index of authors.

Bruno Nettl's *Reference Materials in Ethnomusicology*[26] is a bibliography compiled by an expert as a guide to works worth consulting for research purposes. Likewise in ethnomusicology, Darius L. Thieme's *African Music*[27] has a good book section listing 84 works dealing with sub-Saharan African music and topics related to music. It is an extension and continuation of Varley's *African Native Music*[28] and Merriam's *An-*

[21]Harold D. Rutan, *An Annotated Bibliography of Written Material Pertinent to the Performance of Brass and Percussion Chamber Music* (Ann Arbor: University Microfilms, Inc., 1960). Doctoral dissertation submitted to the University of Illinois for the Ed.D. degree, 1960.

[22]Alan P. Squire, *An Annotated Bibliography of Written Material Pertinent to the Performance of Woodwind Chamber Music* (Ann Arbor: University Microfilms, Inc., 1960). Doctoral dissertation submitted to the University of Illinois for the Ed.D. degree, 1960.

[23]Otto Schneider and Anton Algatzy, *Mozart-Handbuch, Chronik, Werke, Bibliographie* (Vienna: Verlag Brüder Hollinek, 1962).

[24]Fred Blum, *Jean Sibelius: An International Bibliography of Books and Articles on the Occasion of the Centennial Celebrations, 1965*, Detroit Studies in Music Bibliography No. 8 (Detroit: Information Service, Inc., 1965).

[25]Gilbert Chase, *A Guide to the Music of Latin America* (2nd ed., rev. and enl.), (Washington: Pan American Union and Library of Congress, 1962).

[26]Bruno Nettl, *Reference Materials in Ethnomusicology*, Detroit Studies in Music Bibliography No. 1 (Detroit: Information Service, Inc., 1961).

[27]Darius L. Thieme, *African Music: A Briefly Annotated Bibliography* (Washington: Library of Congress, 1964).

[28]Douglas H. Varley, *African Native Music: An Annotated Bibliography* (London: Royal Empire Society, 1936).

*notated Bibliography of African and African-Derived Music.*[29] The Varley bibliography includes works up to 1936, Merriam's list goes to 1950, and Thieme's compilation to 1963. The Haywood bibliography of North American folk material[30] is another list for ethnic studies.

For the theorist, musicologist, or historian working with Renaissance sources, Davidsson's bibliography of sixteenth-century prints on theory[31] may be important. For the student of hymnology, Messenger and Pfatteicher's bibliography[32] and the lists in the *Jahrbuch für Liturgik und Hymnologie* (see above p. 69) are useful.

Current bibliographies in such journals as *Ethnomusicology* and the *Journal of Music Theory* give insight into the periodical's subject specialty. Large compilations, such as the "Bibliography of Asiatic Musics," appearing in *Notes*,[33] are unfortunately rare, but those few which are available are truly an aid to the investigator.

# Pamphlets

While pamphlets[34] may not generally be considered a major source of scholarly information, many of them have been so helpful that libraries maintain a pamphlet file approached through a finding list or, in a few cases, through the card catalog. Particularly valuable for some types of research are leaflets issued to describe curricula or educational resources, pamphlets distributed by publishers and containing biographical sketches and lists of works by contemporary composers, and booklets advertising new publications and instruments. Such miscellaneous smaller materials are often listed in a bibliography as "book" items, and in some libraries pamphlets which are considered to be of research value are bound in hard covers and treated as books, with complete cataloging and classification. Because policies differ with each library, it is advisable to ask a member of the staff about available pamphlet files.

[29]Alan P. Merriam, "An Annotated Bibliography of African and African-Derived Music since 1936," *Africa, Journal of the International African Institute*, XXI (October, 1951), 319–329.

[30]Charles Haywood, *A Bibliography of North American Folklore and Folksong* (2nd rev. ed.), (New York: Dover Publications, Inc., 1961).

[31]Åke Davidsson, *Bibliographie der musiktheoretischen Drucke des 16. Jahrhunderts*, Bibliotheca Bibliographica Aureliana IX (Baden-Baden: Verlag Heitz, 1962).

[32]Ruth Messenger and Helen Pfatteicher, *A Short Bibliography for the Study of Hymns* (New York: The Hymn Society of America, 1964).

[33]Richard A. Waterman, William Lichtenwanger, Virginia Hitchcock Hermann, Horace I. Poleman, Cecil Hobbs, comps., "Bibliography of Asiatic Musics," *Notes*, V (1947–1948), 21–35, 178–186, 354–362, 549–562; VI (1948–1949), 122–136, 281–296; 419–436, 570–583.

[34]Pamphlets are small booklets, usually having paper covers and consisting of a few pages.

## Theses and Dissertations

The theses and dissertations which the student has investigated in his search for his topic and has found to have some bearing upon his subject constitute another type of book material. The bibliographical tools mentioned in Chapter 8 in connection with surveys of research done in various universities may be used as sources of information. These lists often prove valuable in certain types of projects for which written material is mostly in the form of dissertations. Regardless of format,[35] theses and dissertations may be considered to be books.

## Evaluation

A carefully selected bibliography is a hallmark of a fine researcher. One must be discriminating as well as thorough. The most useful bibliographies —and scholastically the strongest—consist of items which are serviceable to the research problem at hand. Padding by the inclusion of unnecessary ephemera and/or books of questionable value is not honest. It is doubtful whether a professor or a graduate committee will be impressed by a bibliography merely because of its length. Moreover, an inflated bibliography may be misleading to the reader who, taking it at face value, uses it for further research.

Books selected from an annotated bibliography have been evaluated by the compiler and the notes may at least serve as a guide. But evaluation of other items involves consultation of reviews and critical writings. Such publications as *The New York Times*, *The London Times*, *The Saturday Review*, *Notes*, and *Musical Quarterly* are available in almost every library. They contain reviews, usually by scholars with ample knowledge of the subject of the book to be considered authoritative. Since 1949 many reviews have been indexed in the *Music Index* (see below, pp. 95–96), and they may be traced to the proper issues of the journals in which they appear. The special subject booklists in periodicals like the *Journal of Music Theory* also include critical reviews, some of them extensive and analytical.

Reviews are suggested because they provide some criteria for judging a book. In all fairness, however, one must remember that a review, even by

---

[35]Even when a thesis is read from microcards or microfilm, the entry for it in the bibliography is with books. The microcard or microfilm is merely a form of reproduction, and the original thesis is still a book.

the best-known authority, represents but a single opinion which may be strongly biased by the critic's background or point of view. Words of extravagant praise or of severe condemnation must be read with reservation. Perhaps the greatest value of a critique is to assist the student in summing up the author's accomplishment; it is still necessary for the reader to evaluate the work for himself.

A few rules of thumb may be applied to the evaluation of books. Usually, if a writer is a subject specialist,[36] his books are reliable. The references included in his bibliographical notes are probably carefully selected. Similarly, the books listed in bibliographies accompanying articles in the leading encyclopedias and dictionaries are generally to be recommended, for such studies are usually written by authorities.

A less reliable criterion, but one which sometimes proves valid, is that books produced for the musician should be given preference over those aimed at the layman and the best-seller market. Because personalities and events may be distorted in fictionalized biographies and popular histories, such books cannot be trusted for facts. They may be read for a general background or atmosphere of the times in which a person lived, but even then one must beware of exaggeration.

Books written with a strong subjective bias, although offering interesting points of view, may not be trustworthy for research in which objective accuracy is desired.[37] Likewise, statements based upon conjecture should not be given credence. Such declarations as, "While Beethoven was writing this music, he must have been thinking of his youth in Bonn," are made with no proof that such thoughts crossed Beethoven's mind. It is safer, if one wishes to know the circumstances of composition, to depend upon quotations from letters or diaries of the composer or his intimates.

An author may reveal the scope of his book, his attitude toward the subject, his aim, and something of his research methods in a preface or introduction. If he has tried to prove a theory or to promote a favorite bias—if he is extraordinarily eager to win the reader over to his side— this persuasive quality may be detected and the student may use the book with some reservation.

Scanning the table of contents and the index (if there is one), and sampling portions of the text are also aids in evaluation.

Length alone is not a reliable criterion, but may have some bearing on a book's value. Excluding the difference made by an expansive literary

[36]E.g., Curt Sachs on Oriental music and musical instruments; Alfred Einstein on Mozart and the Italian madrigal; Karl Geiringer on the Bach family and Haydn; Marc Pincherle on Corelli and Vivaldi.

[37]This is not to exclude strong personal preferences and convictions on controversial subjects or individual reactions to little-known or new works which may be valuable for some types of study.

style, a large tome containing illustrations, examples, footnotes, bibliographies, and appendixes, probably represents a fuller treatment of a subject than a small volume with few research aids. This is not to state categorically that the slimmer book is of lesser value; it may be a masterful presentation, but its brevity may preclude full documentation. An otherwise ordinary work may contain illustrations, charts, analyses, or examples which may be of value.

The timeliness of a subject may be an influencing factor. While one seeks objectivity in gathering data, it is understandable that an author, no matter how disciplined, is likely to be more excited, subjective, stubborn, or complimentary (or the reverse) in writing about contemporary events than in dealing with things of the past. A student of new music may encounter more heated and conflicting opinions than one studying a subject that has had the advantage of a cooling historical perspective.

One realizes that evaluation, though desirable, is a relative matter and may not always be possible. Some bibliographies may be easily evaluated, while others defy evaluation. There are subjects for which sources are so scarce that one must accept anything he can find until he himself is in a position to become an authority. If evaluation is possible, the resulting booklist becomes easier to use and forms a reliable adjunct to the research product.

# BIBLIOGRAPHY

Apel, Willi, *Harvard Dictionary of Music.* Cambridge, Mass.: Harvard University Press, 1956.

Baker, Theodore, *Baker's Biographical Dictionary of Musicians* (5th ed.), rev. by Nicolas Slonimsky. New York: G. Schirmer, Inc., 1958.

Basart, Ann Phillips, *Serial Music: A Classified Bibliography of Writings on Twelve-Tone and Electronic Music.* Berkeley: University of California Press, 1961.

*Bibliographie des Musikschrifttums.* Leipzig: F. Hofmeister, 1936–1941; 1954– .

Bibliothèque Nationale, *Catalogue général des livres imprimés: Auteurs.* Paris: Imprimerie Nationale, 1897– .

Blum, Fred, *Jean Sibelius: An International Bibliography of Books and Articles on the Occasion of the Centennial Celebrations, 1965,* Detroit Studies in Music Bibliography No. 8. Detroit: Information Service, Inc., 1965.

Blume, Friedrich, ed., *Die Musik in Geschichte und Gegenwart: Allgemeine Enzyklopädie der Musik.* Kassel: Bärenreiter-Verlag, 1949– .

*Books in Print: An Index to the Publishers' Trade List Annual.* New York: R. R. Bowker Company, 1948– ; *Subject Guide to Books in Print.* 1957– .

*The British Catalogue of Music.* London: The Council of the British National Bibliography, Ltd., 1957–    .

British Museum, Department of Printed Books, *Catalogue of Printed Books.* London: Clowes, 1881–1900; supplements, 1900–1905.

————, *General Catalogue of Printed Books.* London: [various publishers], 1931–    .

Bull, Storm, *Index to Biographies of Contemporary Composers.* New York: Scarecrow Press, 1964.

Chase, Gilbert, *A Guide to the Music of Latin America* (2nd ed., rev. and enl.). Washington: Pan American Union and Library of Congress, 1962.

*Cumulative Book Index: A World List of Books in the English Language.* New York: The H. W. Wilson Company, 1938–    .

Davidsson, Åke, *Bibliographie der musiktheoretischen Drucke des 16. Jahrhunderts,* Bibliotheca Bibliographica Aureliana IX. Baden-Baden: Verlag Heitz, 1962.

Duckles, Vincent, *Music Reference and Research Materials.* New York: The Free Press of Glencoe, 1964.

Edmunds, John, and Gordon Boelzner, *Some Twentieth-Century American Composers.* New York: The New York Public Library, 1959–1960.

*Ethnomusicology: Journal of the Society for Ethnomusicology.* Middletown, Conn.: Wesleyan University Press, 1953–    .

*Fontes artis musicae.* Paris: International Association of Music Libraries, 1954–    .

Garretson, Homer E., *An Annotated Bibliography of Written Material Pertinent to the Performance of Chamber Music for Stringed Instruments.* Ann Arbor: University Microfilms, Inc., 1961.

Grove, Sir George, *Grove's Dictionary of Music and Musicians* (5th ed.), ed. Eric Blom. London: Macmillan & Co., Ltd., 1954; supplement, 1961.

Haywood, Charles, *A Bibliography of North American Folklore and Folksong* (2nd rev. ed.). New York: Dover Publications, Inc., 1961.

"Index novorum librorum," *Acta musicologica.* [Various places]: International Musicological Society, 1928–    . "Index" runs from 1930 to 1952.

*Jahrbuch für Liturgik und Hymnologie.* Kassel: J. Stauda-Verlag, 1955–    .

*Journal of Music Theory.* New Haven, Conn.: Yale School of Music, 1957–    .

Krummel, Donald W., and James B. Coover, "Current National Bibliographies; Their Music Coverage," *Notes,* XVII (1960), 375–388.

Leguy, Jean, *Catalogue bibliographique des livres de langue française sur la musique.* Paris: Ploix, 1954; *Fascicule complémentaire . . . et supplément, 1954–1959,* 1959.

*Library of Congress Catalog . . . Books: Subjects.* Ann Arbor: J. W. Edwards, Inc., 1965.

Mecklenburg, Carl Gregor, Herzog von, *Bibliographie einiger Grenzgebiete der Musikwissenschaft.* Baden-Baden: Verlag Heitz, 1962.

Merriam, Alan P., "An Annotated Bibliography of African and African-Derived Music since 1936," *Africa, Journal of the International African Institute,* XXI (October, 1951), 319–329.

Messenger, Ruth, and Helen Pfatteicher, *A Short Bibliography for the Study of Hymns*. New York: The Hymn Society of America, 1964.

Mixter, Keith E., *General Bibliography for Music Research*, Detroit Studies in Music Bibliography No. 4. Detroit: Information Service, Inc., 1962.

Nettl, Bruno, *Reference Materials in Ethnomusicology*, Detroit Studies in Music Bibliography No. 1. Detroit: Information Service, Inc., 1961.

*Neuerwerbungen ausländischer Musikliteratur (1954–1955)*, Deutsche Staatsbibliothek bibliographische Mitteilungen 12. Berlin: Deutsche Staatsbibliothek, 1956.

*Notes*. Ithaca, N. Y.: Music Library Association, 1943–    .

*Paperbound Books in Print*. New York: R. R. Bowker Company, 1956–    .

"The Quarterly Book-List," *Musical Quarterly*. New York: G. Schirmer, Inc., 1915–    . "Book-List" has appeared since 1936.

Riemann, Hugo, *Musik Lexikon*. Mainz: B. Schott's Söhne, 1959.

Rutan, Harold D., *An Annotated Bibliography of Written Material Pertinent to the Performance of Brass and Percussion Chamber Music*. Ann Arbor: University Microfilms, Inc., 1960.

Schneider, Otto, and Anton Algatzy, *Mozart-Handbuch, Chronik, Werke, Bibliographie*. Vienna: Verlag Brüder Hollinek, 1962.

Squire, Alan P., *An Annotated Bibliography of Written Material Pertinent to the Performance of Woodwind Chamber Music*. Ann Arbor: University Microfilms, Inc., 1960.

Thieme, Darius L., *African Music: A Briefly Annotated Bibliography*. Washington: Library of Congress, 1964.

Varley, Douglas H., *African Native Music: An Annotated Bibliography*. London: Royal Empire Society, 1936.

Waterman, Richard A., *et al.*, "Bibliography of Asiatic Musics," *Notes*, V (1947–1948), 21–35, 178–186, 354–362, 549–562; VI (1948–1949), 122–136, 281–296, 419–436, 570–583.

# *10*

## *Bibliography: Periodicals*

### Importance of Periodical Literature

Hand in hand with the search for book material goes the investigation of periodical literature, without which most studies are incomplete. Articles in learned journals may represent the last word in research on a subject, an important factor in dealing with any topic but especially significant in studying a contemporary one. Accounts of many interesting discoveries have first appeared in periodicals, later being incorporated into books and monographs. Articles important enough to be of permanent value but too brief to be published as a book are presented successfully in journals, sometimes constituting the only form in which the information is available.

### Some Bibliographical Studies of Music Periodicals

In addition to the periodical indexes mentioned below, some references exist which deal with the history and developments of journals devoted to music. Such background studies are useful for understanding the nature of periodical literature and for discovering possibilities for research purposes. They indicate the scope of musical journalism, a field which every student should investigate as part of his training.

Immediately available to almost everyone is Alexander Hyatt King's article in *Grove's Dictionary*,[1] containing a history of music periodicals, a

[1]Alexander Hyatt King, "Periodicals," *Grove's Dictionary of Music and Musicians* (1954), VI, 637–672; supplement, 344–347.

bibliography of source materials about them, and a list of journals arranged chronologically by country of origin, concluded by a summary. Although some items may have been omitted, the article is the best general reference in English on music periodicals from the earliest publications to the early 1950's. Among the most recently founded journals to be listed is *Music and Musicians*, begun in 1952.

King's article is one of the bases for Eckert Rohlf's *Die deutschsprachigen Musikperiodika, 1945–1957*.[2] A guide to magazines in the German language regardless of place of origin, Rohlf's work also contains a study of musical journalism, a history of German periodicals, and a discussion of the various types of publications issued in German and dealing with music. (The classifications of journals included are Allgemeine Musikgeschichten, Musikforschung, Musikgeschichte, Kirchenmusik.) All sections have systematic bibliographies. Appendixes contain a chronological index, an index of titles, an index of names, and other lists. Although the compiler does not analyze the journals article by article, he indicates the nature of the publications and gives bibliographical data.

For decades Wilhelm Freystätter's *Die musikalischen Zeitschriften seit ihrer Entstehung bis zur Gegenwart* (originally issued in Munich in 1884; reprinted in 1963)[3] was considered the most important source of information on the history of music periodicals. The journals are listed in chronological order from their beginnings through 1883–1884, and the list is followed by a summary of their contents. Due partly to the age of the book (which outdates it) and to difficulties in communication at the time of its compilation (which made some periodicals unavailable to the bibliographer) the coverage is uneven. For example, most American periodicals are either omitted entirely or are merely mentioned at the end of the volume as having been founded; it is apparent that the compiler did not see the issues. On the other hand, the *American Musical Times* and the *American Art Journal* are accorded some attention, and it is safe to assume that at least a few issues were in the hands of Freystätter or that he had received a full description of them. In spite of the omissions, this book is still a useful tool in tracing early German sources.

Charles Wunderlich's *History and Bibliography of Early American Musical Periodicals, 1782–1852*[4] is a comprehensive study containing a description of the journals; their history; lists of publishers, printers, en-

---

[2]Eckert Rohlf, *Die deutschsprachigen Musikperiodika, 1945–1957*, Forschungsbeiträge zur Musikwissenschaft, Vol. XI (Regensburg: Gustav Bosse Verlag, 1961).

[3]Wilhelm Freystätter, *Die musikalischen Zeitschriften seit ihrer Entstehung bis zur Gegenwart* (Amsterdam: Frits A. M. Knuf, 1963).

[4]Charles E. Wunderlich, *A History and Bibliography of Early American Musical Periodicals, 1782–1852* (Ann Arbor: University Microfilms, Inc., 1962). Doctoral dissertation submitted to the University of Michigan for the Ph.D. degree, 1962.

gravers, editors, composers, and authors connected with them; and lists of musical compositions included either as supplements or as integral parts of the publications. An account is given of American periodical literature, which had hitherto not been adequately treated.

Although at the moment a history of East European music periodicals comparable to the aforementioned works is nonexistent in English, James B. Coover has provided a valuable bibliography of the music journals of the Middle and East European nations. The list appears in installments in various issues of *Fontes artis musicae* as follows:

> Vol. III, No. 2 (1956), 219–226: Introduction; Bulgaria
> Vol. IV, No. 2 (1957), 97–102: Czechoslovakia
> Vol. V, No. 1 (1958), 44–45: Estonia; Finland
> Vol. V, No. 2 (1958), 93–99: Hungary
> Vol. VI, No. 1 (1959), 27–28: Latvia, Lithuania
> Vol. VII, No. 1 (1960), 16–21: Poland
> Vol. VII, No. 2 (1960), 69–70: Rumania
> Vol. VIII, No. 2 (1961), 75–90: USSR
> Vol. IX, No. 2 (1962), 78–80: Yugoslavia

The bibliography was compiled from a variety of reference tools, listed in a section on sources for each country and including secondary as well as primary materials. Although containing no detailed analysis of individual publications, the Coover lists steer the student to appropriate periodicals.

## Some Basic Procedures

The procedure for compiling the file of periodicals is essentially the same as for books, with some additional information included for identification. A separate card for each entry should be used to note the name of the author, last name first; the title of the article; the full name of the journal, no matter how long (to insure accurate identification of the periodical in case there may be others with similar names); its volume number and date; and the pages on which the article is to be found. The library call number should also be given. A sample card for an article appears in Figure 10–1 and is self-explanatory.

Most of the bibliographical sources consulted in locating book material contain information about periodicals as well. Some special tools also exist. In some major libraries (e.g., the Music Division of the New York Public Library) data on significant articles are entered on cards and filed in the public catalog. Some university libraries and larger music libraries main-

Figure 10-1    A Card for an Article in a Journal.

```
Dahlhaus, Carl
"Innere Dynamik in Bachs Fugen"
Neue Zeitschrift für Musik 123 (1962), 498-
501
In Library X: ML5 N4819




                        ◯
```

tain a card file of principal articles from selected journals, either as a separate unit or as part of a larger bibliographic system. Unfortunately, however, they are the exception rather than the rule. Because indexing is taxing work, requiring not only an expert's knowledge of the subject but also many hours of valuable staff time, these convenient periodical files can be kept up by only the best-equipped, fully staffed institutions. Most college librarians are more concerned about getting new books onto the shelves and maintaining the reference and circulation services in good operation than about indexing the ever-growing number of journals. Even the special periodicals librarian in university and public libraries is too busy to analyze publications, no matter how valuable he considers periodical indexes to be. Therefore, the researcher must rely upon professionally prepared and printed periodical guides.

## Current Periodical Indexes

If one is working in a general library (rather than in a specialized music collection) he may first consult the *Readers' Guide to Periodical Literature*[5] and the *International Index*,[6] which contain references to some significant articles on musical subjects, together with articles on related

[5]*Readers' Guide to Periodical Literature: An Index to Selected General and Non-Technical Periodicals of Reference Value in Libraries* (New York: The H. W. Wilson Company, 1905–    ). Entries start with 1900; articles on music in periodicals of general interest are entered since 1949.

[6]*International Index: A Quarterly Guide to Periodical Literature in the Social Sciences and Humanities* (New York: The H. W. Wilson Company, 1907–    ).

fields. He may then proceed to the various national periodical indexes, both current and retrospective, which are described by Keith Mixter in his *General Bibliography for Music Research.*[7]

In the specific field of music the *Music Index*[8] is useful. It is published monthly, and at the end of each twelve-month period an annual cumulative volume appears. Covering the time from 1949 to the present, *Music Index* is an international periodical bibliography, accounting for articles in a large percentage of the musical journals currently in print. Because the publications to be indexed were chosen with the advice of music librarians who were familiar with the demands made upon periodical literature and because the work has been done by a staff of professional indexers, the *Music Index* has been serviceable. Each item is listed by author and by subject(s), with data on the page(s) and volume(s) in which it is located. In the first annual cumulation (1949) 41 selected periodicals were indexed, including such publications as the *Journal* of the American Musicological Society, *The Chesterian, Dansk Musiktidsskrift, Educational Music Magazine, English Church Music*, and *Music and Letters* (these represent a random sample of titles). Also indexed were periodicals of a more popular sort, such as *Billboard* and *Variety.* Such musical current-events publications as *Musical America* and *Musical Courier* were accounted for, along with a few program-note series: the Chicago Symphony Orchestra Notes, the New York Philharmonic Orchestra Notes, and the Philadelphia Orchestra Notes. Ten years later, in the cumulative volume for 1959, the number of periodicals indexed had increased to about 170 and the subject headings had multiplied in proportion. Subjects now run into the thousands, and in addition to purely musical topics they also include bibliographies, discographies, book reviews, thematic catalogs, and first performances. Such combinations as literature and music, poetry and music, and politics and music are also found.[9] They represent but a few picked from the cumulative volume for 1959.

The *Music Index* is available in most libraries of reasonable size and in periodical or reference departments of large public and college libraries. If the local library does not subscribe to it, the student should try to visit a library which does. *Music Index* is the only widely circulated index published in the United States that is devoted to current articles on music

Begun in 1907 as a supplement to *Readers' Guide,* it was changed to the *International Index* in 1920. Articles on musical subjects in such journals as *Music and Letters, Musical Quarterly, Music Review*, and *Notes*, as well as those in social science and humanities publications are listed.

[7]Mixter, *op. cit.*, pp. 22–24.

[8]*Music Index* (Detroit: Information Service, Inc., 1949–     ).

[9]The first volume of subject headings was issued in 1960; subsequent volumes have followed.

on an international basis. The coverage is wide. By bringing the many articles in print together in one reference, it becomes a time-saver.

✓ The aforementioned *Bibliographie des Musikschrifttums* (see pp. 81–82) is another international index useful in investigating periodical literature. Although much time elapses between the publication of the journals and the appearance of the index,[10] the coverage is wide and the indexing thorough. For example, in the volume devoted to 1956–1957 (published in 1961) articles from some 250 periodicals and *Festschriften*[11] are listed, including many writings on musical subjects appearing in nonmusical journals (e.g., American Library Association *Bulletin*, *American-German Review*, *Anthropos*, and *Archiv für Philosophie*). It may be easier for an American student to use the *Music Index*, but he should have little difficulty in consulting the *Bibliographie*. For a thorough investigation he should look into both references. In spite of overlapping entries, each contains a considerable amount of material not found in the other. The *Bibliographie*, of course, gives an impressive listing of German sources and presents a German bias. The *Music Index*, on the other hand, is naturally slanted toward American sources.

Another tool, useful if one is searching for fairly recent articles and pictures of the dance and the theater as well as music, is *Guide to the Musical Arts*, an analytical index to articles and illustrations for the period 1953–1956, compiled by S. Yancey Belknap.[12] Divided into two parts, the *Guide* contains a list of some 15,000 articles and 6,000 illustrations appearing in the various periodicals dealing with music, opera, the dance, and the theater. The articles, comprising Part I, are indexed by author and by broad subject areas. The illustrations, comprising Part II, are designated by type (photograph or portrait), and the name of the photographer is indicated when known.

Since the issue for material appearing in 1957, when *Guide to the Musical Arts* was renamed *Guide to the Performing Arts* and the coverage was broadened accordingly, annual compilations have continued to be published.[13] The volumes are divided into a main portion containing lists of articles and illustrative materials in the musical arts and a subsidiary portion devoted to the television arts. Because the *Guide* is designed to assist editors, producers, and students, including those on the high school level, some of the items may be unimportant or ephemeral in the eyes of

[10]The average is four years. Such an interval may be more serious in the case of articles from periodicals than in the case of books.

[11]A *Festschrift* is a volume of essays issued to commemorate an event or to honor a person. When published in honor of a noted scholar, the volume often contains articles by various authorities in the person's specialty.

[12]S. Yancey Belknap, *Guide to the Musical Arts* (New York: Scarecrow Press, 1957–1959).

[13]S. Yancey Belknap, *Guide to the Performing Arts* (New York: Scarecrow Press, 1960–    ).

the serious graduate student. But many of the articles are worthwhile. Under such headings as broadcasting research, censorship, copyright, and criticism are items which may be important for contemporary studies.

S. Yancey Belknap has also compiled an index to the performing arts of Latin America.[14] Appearing as No. 17 of the *Inter-American Music Bulletin*, the index lists articles in eight journals devoted to studies in Latin American culture.

The *Art Index*,[15] covering the period from 1929, and the *Education Index*,[16] covering the same time span, may be useful for some peripheral areas of musical research. Both publications are available in most general libraries. The *Guide to Dance Periodicals*[17] is another source for articles dealing with music found in nonmusical journals. The several volumes of this *Guide* are most practical for ballet, ballet music, and ballet perform-ance, including conducting of the music. Entries for folk dance and folk song also are found. Among the publications indexed are *Ballet Today, Ballroom Dancing Times, Country Dancer, Dance Observer, Dance Per-spectives, English Folk Dance and Song*, and the *Times Educational Sup-plement*.

Such bibliographies as those in the *Journal of Music Theory, Ethno-musicology, Musica disciplina* (articles on early music), and *Svensk Tidskrift för Musikforskning* (articles in Swedish journals) are examples of periodical indexes included in scholarly serials. They are devoted to either specialized subjects or to articles in journals published in a given country. Although some of the entries may naturally be found in larger, more general indexes, it is best to check or recheck the special lists to insure complete bibliographical coverage. Likewise, such published indexes as the Basart, Garretson, and Nettl bibliographies (see Chapter 9) con-tain notations on articles from current and recent periodicals as well as books.

## Retrospective Periodical Indexes

For a short research paper requiring a few weeks of preparation or a thesis for which only recent references are necessary, the bibliography of periodical literature thus far compiled may be adequate. But if the research

---

[14]S. Yancey Belknap, *Latin-American Performing Arts: An Analytical Index, 1957–1958*, appearing as *Inter-American Music Bulletin* No. 17 (May, 1960).

[15]*Art Index* (New York: The H. W. Wilson Company, 1933–    ).

[16]*Education Index* (New York: The H. W. Wilson Company, 1932–    ).

[17]S. Yancey Belknap, *Guide to Dance Periodicals*, Vols. I–VII (1931–1956), (various places, publishers, and dates); Vols. VIII–X (New York: Scarecrow Press, 1960–1963). From 1966, this bibliography is incorporated in *Guide to the Perform-ing Arts*.

is to be historical or retrospective or of greater magnitude and depth than a term paper, the investigator should probe into the wealth of material published before such present-day indexes as the *Music Index* and the *Schmieder Bibliographie* became available.

Retrospective periodical indexing, long considered an important bibliographical need, has been fully discussed by learned societies, but the task is so monumental that a wholehearted attempt has not been made since the 1930's. During the "depression years" of the thirties, a large WPA project resulted in the preparation of hundreds of thousands of cards for a gigantic periodical index. Unfortunately so much confusion arose from lack of uniformity in methods of entry, from differences of opinion among indexers engaged in the project, and from the incompleteness of some periodical series that it has been impossible to coordinate the cards into a practical bibliographical tool. Many experts have considered the revision of the cards but the consensus is that revision is not practical.

Some libraries maintain periodical files antedating the *Music Index*, but in most cases they are far from complete, and uniformity of items may be lacking. Consequently, there exists no publication like the *Music Index* to account systematically for articles in music before 1949. Although the *Bibliographie des Musikschrifttums* began with materials issued as early as 1936, it was suspended during the 1940's, leaving a large gap between the prewar and postwar publications.

The *Readers' Guide* and the *International Index* (see above, p. 94), which fortunately go back many years, are of considerable value. *Poole's Index*[18] is useful for periodical entries for the nineteenth century. Other retrospective indexes, although selective, also exist, so that with some searching one may achieve a fairly complete survey of his field. A few representative tools, conveniently available to most music students, are given brief comment below.

Ernst C. Krohn's *The History of Music: An Index to the Literature Available in a Selected Group of Musicological Publications*[19] is aptly described by its title. Thirty-nine journals, yearbooks, and congress proceedings, the majority in either English or German, have been analyzed for articles appearing up to January, 1952. The entries are arranged by conventional historical periods (prehistoric, primitive, medieval, and so on) and subdivided into subject headings appropriate to each era. Although purposely limited in scope and presumably devoted only to the history of music, the index is useful for other aspects of music: theory, pedagogy,

---

[18]*Poole's Index to Periodical Literature, 1802–1881* (rev. ed.), (Boston: Houghton Mifflin Company, 1891); supplements, 1882–1887, 1887–1892, 1892–1896, 1897–1902, 1902–1907.

[19]Ernst C. Krohn, *The History of Music: An Index to the Literature Available in a Selected Group of Musicological Publications* (St. Louis: Baton Music Co., 1958). A reissue, with emendations, of No. 3 of the Washington University Library Series.

drama, correlation between music and other arts, and the writing of musical treatises. With the exception of the *Revue belge de musicologie* and the *Bulletin de la Société "Union Musicologique,"* publications in French, Italian, and Spanish are not indexed.

For a selection of books and articles in periodicals appearing between 1915 and 1926, one may consult Eric Blom's *A General Index to Modern Musical Literature in the English Language, Including Periodicals for the Years 1915–1926.*[20] All entries, for subjects as well as for authors, are arranged in a single alphabet. The book is limited in scope and out of print but is in the collection of many libraries and is useful for topics in English music history.

The advisability of consulting dictionaries and encyclopedias has already been suggested in connection with books, as has the necessity for investigating bibliographical notes in books of history and biography. References to articles, both current and retrospective, in periodicals with international coverage are usually included in these sources.

Some journals, notably *Musical Quarterly* and *Music and Letters,* have been professionally indexed, and cumulative lists are available in print. Herbert K. Goodkind's *Cumulative Index to the Musical Quarterly*[21] consists of two alphabetical lists, one by author and the other by subject, including articles, book reviews, record reviews, and "Current Chronicle," which appeared in the periodical from 1915 to 1959. Hazel Gertrude Kinscella has prepared a second index to the same publication: the *Americana Index to the Musical Quarterly,*[22] a list of articles dealing with music in the United States and the Americas appearing during the period 1915 to 1957. The entries are elaborately cross-indexed and arranged in a single alphabet. Rapid access to reviews of individual compositions is one of its features.

The index to Volumes 1 to 40 (1920–1959) of *Music and Letters* was nearly completed by Eric Blom before his death in April, 1959. Jack Westrup finished the compilation, edited and cross-indexed it, and wrote the preface. The completed work appeared in 1962.[23] One section contains entries by author and subject in an alphabetical sequence; the second contains reviews by author and subject in another alphabetical sequence. In the latter the language of the book reviewed is given in brackets imme-

[20]Eric Blom, *A General Index to Modern Musical Literature in the English Language, Including Periodicals for the Years 1915–1926* (London: J. Curwen and Sons, Ltd., 1927).

[21]Herbert K. Goodkind, *Cumulative Index to the Musical Quarterly* (New York: Goodkind Indexes, 1960), Supplement, 1963.

[22]Hazel Gertrude Kinscella, *Americana Index to the Musical Quarterly* (Washington: Music Educators' National Conference, 1958). This constitutes Vol. VI, No. 2 of the *Journal of Research in Music Education.*

[23]Eric Blom, *Music and Letters: Index to Volumes I–XL,* ed. Jack Westrup (London: Oxford University Press, 1962).

diately following the title. An alphabetical list of reviewers appears on the last two pages. The cumulative indexes to both the *Musical Quarterly* and *Music and Letters* are useful in proportion to the excellence of the two journals.

In the absence of a cumulative index for a periodical, an annual index is useful.[24] Some publications, the *Musical Times* for example, contain such indexes which are usually bound with the yearly volume and may be consulted easily, especially in libraries granting stack privileges to graduate students. By taking the bound journals off the shelves and systematically reading through the appropriate sections, one may know their contents. The annual list is far easier to scan than individual tables of contents for each monthly or quarterly issue. Regardless of the number of volumes which may have to be consulted, the results of scanning annual indexes may prove fruitful enough to justify the effort. In some cases this is the only method of getting at materials if one's library has few bibliographical tools.

Some special indexes of articles on music subjects appearing in non-musical or general journals are being prepared. Wolff's *Speculum* index[25] and Ciurczak's index of the *Journal of Aesthetics and Art Criticism*[26] are examples.

Specially prepared bibliographies of periodical literature exist for some research subjects. The two volumes of *Some Twentieth Century American Composers* by Edmunds and Boelzner (see above, p. 83) are examples, the first containing fifteen composers, the second, seventeen. Articles by the composers, articles about them, and articles dealing with their works are listed, covering the period from 1940 to 1959. In quite another field, the Varley-Merriam-Thieme sequence of African bibliographies (see above, pp. 84–85) covers periodical literature from the beginnings to July 15, 1963, presenting a useful retrospective index.

## Pseudoperiodical Sources

Daily newspapers, although issued at regular time intervals, are not considered in some quarters to be proper periodicals. Obviously, they belong with periodicals rather than with books, no matter what their

[24]Many such annual indexes exist. See Chapter 17 for names of periodicals containing an annual or volume index.

[25]Arthur Sheldon Wolff, *Speculum: A Journal of Mediaeval Studies, 1926–1962 (with addenda, 1963–1964)* . . . *A Check-list of Articles and Book Reviews Pertaining to Music, Including a Selection of Articles on Related Subjects* (Denton, Tex.: North Texas State University, 1965).

[26]Peter Louis Ciurczak, *The Journal of Aesthetics and Art Criticism, 1941–1964* . . . *An Index of Articles and Book Reviews Pertaining to Music* . . . (Emporia: Kansas State Teachers College, 1965).

classification may be. In making a source file, articles from newspapers may be included. For contemporary compositions whose first performances and the attendant critical reaction may be important, or for new movements in music education which may create controversy or give rise to lively discussion in the press, newspaper accounts are surely valid references. Most large libraries simplify matters for the student by subscribing to *The New York Times* and *The New York Times Index*.[27] Retrospective research in the *Times* and several other important newspapers has been implemented in some institutions through microfilm files of papers. Most public libraries and some college collections keep clippings from local newspapers or make an attempt at partial coverage of articles by an index, a scrapbook of articles, or some other device.

Program annotations in major symphony orchestra booklets (which are periodical during the concert season) are indexed in *Music Index* because they often yield valuable information. Program notes may provide analyses of compositions being played for the first time or those so new that explanatory comments are helpful. For a retrospective evaluation of certain older works as well, notes by outstanding annotators may be both interesting and informative. When a composer has supplied his own program notes, a new insight into his work may be gained if he is articulate about his music.

## Evaluation

Systematic evaluation of a list of periodical articles is neither as practical nor as necessary as the evaluation of a booklist. Being shorter than books and monographs, essays in journals can be read in a correspondingly brief time. Unwanted items can be eliminated as the student takes notes. Moreover, except in cases in which an article has provoked such controversy as to call for a rebuttal, critical comments on articles do not exist.

The same rules of thumb applied in the evaluation of books may be applied in an assessment of a periodical list. Articles written by authorities are more likely to contain valuable data than chatty essays designed for popular consumption. Likewise, studies in learned journals are probably more fruitful of research material than those printed in ordinary magazines. As a matter of policy the scholarly periodicals maintain a high standard of editorial excellence which, at least in part, protects the reader.

Unfortunately, an author in an institution subscribing to the "publish or perish" philosophy may feel compelled to produce articles in rapid succession. He may repeat himself or sparingly dole out material among several essays, which the student must read to glean a few bits of essential data. The writer's statements may have to be checked for accuracy in case

[27]*The New York Times Index* (New York: The New York Times, 1913–     ).

he has allowed errors to slip into his work in his anxiety to break into print. In spite of such hazards, periodical literature is an important research source. Under the best conditions journals can supply the latest information on a subject in the most expedient fashion.

# BIBLIOGRAPHY

*Art Index*. New York: The H. W. Wilson Company, 1933–    .

Belknap, S. Yancey, *Guide to Dance Periodicals*. Vols. I–VII (1931–1956), various places, publishers, and dates; Vols. VIII–X. New York: Scarecrow Press, 1960–1963.

————, *Guide to the Musical Arts*. New York: Scarecrow Press, 1957–1959.

————, *Guide to the Performing Arts*. New York: Scarecrow Press, 1960–    .

————, *Latin-American Performing Arts: An Analytical Index, 1957–1958* (*Inter-American Music Bulletin* No. 17 [May, 1960]).

*Bibliographie des Musikschrifttums*. Leipzig: F. Hofmeister, 1936–1941; 1954–    .

Blom, Eric, *A General Index to Modern Musical Literature in the English Language, Including Periodicals for the Years 1915–1926*. London: J. Curwen and Sons, Ltd., 1927.

————, *Music and Letters: Index to Volumes I–XL*, ed. Jack Westrup. London: Oxford University Press, 1962.

Ciurczak, Peter Louis, *The Journal of Aesthetics and Art Criticism, 1941–1964 . . . An Index of Articles and Book Reviews Pertaining to Music. . . .* Emporia: Kansas State Teachers College, 1965.

Coover, James B., "A Bibliography of East European Music Periodicals," *Fontes artis musicae*, III (1956), 219–226; IV (1957), 97–102; V (1958), 44–45, 93–99; VI (1959), 27–28; VII (1960), 16–21, 69–70; VIII (1961), 75–90; IX (1962), 78–80.

Edmunds, John, and Gordon Boelzner. *Some Twentieth Century American Composers*. New York: The New York Public Library, 1959–1960.

*Education Index*. New York: The H. W. Wilson Company, 1932–    .

*Ethnomusicology: Journal of the Society for Ethnomusicology*. Middletown, Conn.: Wesleyan University Press, 1953–    .

Freystätter, Wilhelm, *Die musikalischen Zeitschriften seit ihrer Entstehung bis zur Gegenwart*. Amsterdam: Frits A. M. Knuf, 1963. Originally published in Munich by Riedel, 1872.

Goodkind, Herbert K., *Cumulative Index to the Musical Quarterly*. New York: Goodkind Indexes, 1960; *Supplement, 1960–62*, 1963.

*International Index: A Quarterly Guide to Periodical Literature in the Social Sciences and Humanities*. New York: The H. W. Wilson Company, 1907–    .

*Journal of Music Theory.* New Haven, Conn.: Yale School of Music, 1957– .

King, Alexander Hyatt, "Periodicals," *Grove's Dictionary of Music and Musicians* (1954), VI, 637–672; supplement (1961), 344–347.

Kinscella, Hazel Gertrude, *Americana Index to the Musical Quarterly.* Washington: Music Educators' National Conference, 1958. (*Journal of Research in Music Education*, Vol. VI, No. 2.)

Krohn, Ernst C., *The History of Music: An Index to the Literature Available in a Selected Group of Musicological Publications.* St. Louis: Baton Music Co., 1958.

Merriam, Alan P., "An Annotated Bibliography of African and African-Derived Music since 1936," *Africa, Journal of the International African Insitute,* XXI (October, 1951), 319–329.

Mixter, Keith E., *General Bibliography for Music Research,* Detroit Studies in Music Bibliography No. 4. Detroit: Information Service, Inc., 1962.

*Music Index: The Key to Current Music Periodical Literature.* Detroit: Information Service, Inc., 1949– .

*The New York Times Index.* New York: The New York Times, 1913– .

*Poole's Index to Periodical Literature, 1802–1881* (rev. ed.). Boston: Houghton Mifflin Company, 1891; supplements, 1882–1887, 1887–1892, 1892–1896, 1897–1902, 1902–1907.

*Readers' Guide to Periodical Literature: An Index to Selected General and Non-Technical Periodicals of Reference Value in Libraries.* New York: The H. W. Wilson Company, 1905– .

Rohlf, Eckert, *Die deutschprachigen Musikperiodika, 1945–1957.* Regensburg: Gustav Bosse Verlag, 1961.

*Svensk Tidskrift för Musikforskning.* Stockholm, 1919– .

Thieme, Darius L., *African Music: A Briefly Annotated Bibliography.* Washington: Library of Congress, 1964.

Varley, Douglas H., *African Native Music: An Annotated Bibliography.* London: Royal Empire Society, 1936.

Wolff, Arthur Sheldon, *Speculum: A Journal of Mediaeval Studies, 1926–1962 (with addenda, 1963–1964) . . . A Check-list of Articles and Book Reviews Pertaining to Music, Including a Selection of Articles on Related Subjects.* Denton, Tex.: North Texas State University, 1965.

Wunderlich, Charles E., *A History and Bibliography of Early American Musical Periodicals, 1782–1852.* Ann Arbor: University Microfilms, Inc., 1962.

# 11

## Bibliography: Music

Compiling a list of music to be used in a research project may be an easy process, depending upon the nature of the topic. There is no problem, for example, if one is to analyze the Sibelius violin concerto for which the score is available in the local library, nor is there a problem other than the mechanical one of collecting the items if one requires only those compositions currently in print and obtainable in a library or a music store. Moreover, in libraries in which scores and sheet music are carefully classified and cataloged, the search for available materials becomes the simple matter of consulting the card catalog. Results may be rewarding if the library is rich in its holdings of works pertaining to the student's topic.

Unfortunately, such happy circumstances may not be universal. Problems arise in cases calling for (1) investigation of music from some previous era; (2) comparison of various editions of a single work or group of works; (3) perusal of many different compositions; or (4) analysis of pieces to be found only in anthologies and historical sets.

## The Publication Date

Depending upon the type of research in which he is engaged, one may be confronted by the knotty problem of assigning approximate dates to printed music from which the year of publication is omitted. Such very early printings as part-books from the sixteenth and seventeenth centuries usually bear some indication of the time of issue: the date on the title page, the date affixed to the composer's dedicatory letter,[1] or the date in the colophon.[2] Most music published in the twentieth century bears either a printing date or a copyright date, and while the year of copyright may not necessarily coincide with the year of publication, the two are close enough to assign the work to its place in the chronology of a composer's creative career or in the general historic period. But in the printed music of the late eighteenth and nineteenth centuries questions of dating arise because publishers did not always indicate the year of issue. This problem is sometimes solved by the publisher's plate numbers, the numbers and letters found in small print at the bottom of a page of music. Plate numbers, which ascend numerically in chronological order of preparation of the printing plates, may be used by catalogers to determine the approximate date of publication.[3] If plate numbers appear on the library catalog card, they should be noted on the student's bibliographical card, for they constitute a method of dating a work.

Information contained in an entry for music may include: the composer's name; the title of the composition; opus number, if any; the imprint, using publication date, copyright date, preface date, colophon date, or publisher's plate number; and the call number in the library in which the particular work is found. A description of the format may be useful. Such terms as "miniature score," "full score," and "separate instrumental parts" may help a researcher to choose the appropriate type of publication. The Antheil score in Figure 11–1 is of fairly recent issue, and bibliographical information is easily located.

Figure 11–2, on the other hand, shows a card for a quartet which was published probably in the 1820's, but the exact date is not known (or at least it was unknown to the cataloger at the time it was being processed in the library). A probable date of issue is indicated in brackets in the imprint, and the publisher's plate number is added.

The notations "Miniature score" in Figure 11–1 and "Separate parts" in Figure 11–2 indicate the format of the music. If contrapuntal or har-

---

[1]Renaissance and Baroque composers customarily dedicated their works to a patron, setting forth their sentiments in a letter printed immediately following the title page. This practice was later abandoned.

[2]A colophon is a printer's inscription at the end of a book, providing information on the production of the book and sometimes worked in with the printer's insignia.

[3]Plate numbers are used to keep the plates in order as they are stored in a publishing house. They are numbers and letters put on the plates for each page of a given work for identification; thus every page of a publication bears the same number. Chronological identifications of numbers used by such firms as Artaria, Sieber, and Imbault have been compiled by catalogers, and some libraries maintain a plate-number file. Oliver W. Neighbour, *English Music Publishers' Plate Numbers in the First Half of the Nineteenth Century* (London: Faber & Faber, Ltd., 1965) is a useful reference.

Figure 11-1   A Card for Music, Simple Entry.

```
Antheil, George
Over The Plains
New York: Weintraub, 1950
Miniature score
In Library X: M 1045 A6270m


              ◯
```

Figure 11-2   A Card Using Plate Numbers.

```
Spech, Johann
Quatuor pour 2 violons, viola et violon-
celle, Oeuvre 22
Vienne: Mechetti [182-]
Pub. pl. no. 425
Separate parts
In Library X: M 452 S742


              ◯
```

monic analysis must be made, the score rather than the separate parts should be used.

## Music in Collected Works and Anthologies

Searching a card catalog for pieces published separately is a comparatively simple procedure, but delving for works buried in anthologies and monuments of music is another matter. To some extent the difficulties attending the search have been minimized by Anna Harriet Heyer's

*Historical Sets, Collected Editions and Monuments of Music: A Guide to their Contents.*[4] In the title, the term "Collected editions" (or *Gesamtausgaben* in German) refers to the "complete works" or authoritative collections of music by one composer.[5] Examples are *Oeuvres complètes de François Couperin*, published by the Oiseau Lyre Editions; the *Complete Works of Purcell*, published by the Purcell Society; the *J. S. Bach Werke*, published by the Bach-Gesellschaft. "Historical sets," exemplified by *Publikationen älterer Musik* and Prunières' *Les maîtres du chant*, are collections of works by several or many composers, illustrating an aspect of the history of music, tracing a musical style, or representing a given creative period. "Monuments of music" (or *Denkmäler*) are collections of the best or the most representative music of a national group or country.[6] The *Denkmäler der Tonkunst in Oesterreich* (Austria), *Das Erbe deutscher Musik* (Germany), and *Musica Britannica* (Britain) are representative monuments.

In addition, the Heyer list includes publishers' series, which, like *Nagels Musik Archiv* and *Hortus musicus*, are publications of compositions not necessarily intended for any specific medium or representing any one historical period but selected for issue because they meet a certain high standard of musicality. Individual compositions appear from time to time, generally in a uniform format—same size, cover design, and printing—and bearing serial numbers. Finally, Heyer analyzes anthologies like the *Historical Anthology of Music* and books of examples like Gleason's *Examples of Music before 1400* or Soderlund's *Examples of Gregorian Chant*.

The coverage in Heyer extends to completed sets and projected sets in which any volumes were in print by July, 1956, as well as to some collections containing both music and nonmusic materials. Bibliographical data are given for identification of the sets, and the contents of each are listed by types (sonatas, madrigals, motets) rather than by titles of individual compositions. The list may be useful in locating many kinds of music. It covers a long historical span, from the earliest works printed in collections to sets now being published.

Following are some uses to which the Heyer work may be put: (1) A student seeking a collected edition of a composer's works may look for his name in its alphabetical position. If an edition exists, its title, editor, place and date of publication, and the name of the publishers will be given, together with the general contents of each volume. (2) One wishing names of the composers represented in a collection such as the *Denkmäler*

[4]Anna Harriet Heyer, *Historical Sets, Collected Editions and Monuments of Music: A Guide to their Contents* (Chicago: American Library Association, 1957).
[5]See Wolfgang Schmieder, "Gesamtausgaben," *Musik in Geschichte und Gegenwart*, IV, cols. 1850–1876.
[6]See Wolfgang Schmieder, "Denkmäler der Tonkunst," *Musik in Geschichte und Gegenwart*, III, cols. 164–191.

*deutscher Tonkunst* or *I classici della musica italiana* will find them under the title of the collection. (3) A researcher may wish to find volumes containing a specific type of music (e.g., church cantatas) in the collected edition of a composer's works. For example, by looking under the heading of Bach, subheading *Werke*, he may locate the volumes devoted to the church cantatas of Bach.

The composer and subject index to the list provides additional approaches to a subject. In investigating the vocal works of William Byrd, one learns from the main portion of the book that several volumes of his collected works contain pieces for voice. But there may be vocal pieces in other collections that one might wish to see for comparison, or perhaps the library does not possess the collected edition and the student needs another source. Looking under Byrd's name in the index, he finds several other sets containing Byrd's vocal music. A person searching for keyboard pieces of Antonio de Cabezón may not find a collected edition mentioned in the main list, but Cabezón's name does appear in the index, where information is given on the several historical sets including his music. Finally, if one is assigned the analysis of some *frottole*, the index shows collections in which these Italian songs may be found. By providing a simple approach to music which is concealed in hundreds of collections, the Heyer work fills a need in implementing some types of research.

Until the revised and updated second edition of the Heyer list appears in print, the student must look elsewhere for information on sets which have been started and on volumes added to existing collections since June, 1956. One source is the contents notes included on catalog cards in some libraries. Also, catalogers may have analyzed the contents of large collections and prepared *analytics* or separate sets of cards for the works contained therein; such entries are usually filed under the name of the collection.

For the contents of some collected editions one may consult leaflets issued as prospectuses for new sets. Admittedly they are primarily advertising matter, but may serve a bibliographical purpose as well.

The Music Library Association Index Series includes some practical lists. Two examples are the alphabetical indexes to the volumes of the Berlioz *Werke*[7] and the Monteverdi *Opere*.[8] In the case of Monteverdi, each set of pieces (e.g., *Primo libro di madrigali à cinque voci*) is analyzed alphabetically by title or *incipit*, the initial measures of a composition or of movements of a multimovement composition.

The thousands of individual songs published in miscellaneous collections and anthologies present a serious bibliographical problem. To analyze the

[7]*An Alphabetical Index to Hector Berlioz Werke*, MLA Index Series No. 2 (New York: Music Library Association, n.d.).

[8]*An Alphabetical Index to Claudio Monteverdi, Tutte le Opere*, MLA Index Series No. 1 (New York: Music Library Association, n.d.).

dozens of volumes found in even the smallest music libraries would consume more time than librarians can afford. The *Song Index* (1926) and its supplement (1934), edited by Minnie Earl Sears, account for almost 20,000 songs in 366 volumes and are valuable in locating music issued up to 1932.[9] Since the death of the editor in 1933, the index has not been continued. In the meantime many song collections have been issued, but no organized, printed approach to their contents existed until the publication of *Songs in Collections*, compiled by Desiree De Charms and Paul Breed,[10] which brings the indexing up to date as far as the early 1960's.

Most librarians cannot take time to prepare extensive indexes to materials in their collections. Like the periodical files, such indexes require more effort and many more hours than the staff can afford. Although some libraries do maintain checklists of songs by the composers whose works are in greatest demand by their patrons, few have complete files. Excellent song catalogs, like those in the Music Divisions of the New York Public Library at Lincoln Center and the Buffalo and Erie County Library, are exceptional and can be continued only by the best-staffed libraries or by those whose song collections form a significant part of their holdings.

The same problem of "hidden" compositions exists also for miscellaneous keyboard pieces, especially the short works which are published in collections rather than issued separately. To a serious but perhaps lesser degree, the same may be said of works for almost all media. There are not enough tools like the section in *Music for the Piano* by Friskin and Freundlich in which anthologies of early keyboard music are analyzed by volume.[11]

For other indexes to collections and anthologies which may be maintained by the local library, the student may consult the librarian. Some libraries have checklists or files listing operatic arias, pieces found in methods books, or other material considered buried with no other easy manner of approach.

## Miscellaneous Lists of Music

Because no one library, no matter how extensive its collection, can own all the pieces of music published, it may be necessary for the investigator to look into current lists to supplement his music bibliography. The same

[9]Minnie Earl Sears, ed., *Song Index: An Index to More than 12,000 Songs in 177 Song Collections Comprising 262 Volumes* (New York: The H. W. Wilson Company, 1926); *Supplement: An Index to More than 7000 Songs in 104 Collections Comprising 124 Volumes* (1934).

[10]Desiree De Charms and Paul Breed, comps., *Songs in Collections* (Detroit: Information Service, Inc., 1965).

[11]James Friskin and Irwin Freundlich, *Music for the Piano* (New York: Holt, Rinehart and Winston, Inc., 1954), pp. 113–122.

tools used by the librarian for the selection of compositions may be employed by the researcher.

The Library of Congress provides printed cards representing the works cataloged for the Library. Any library may obtain cards or reproductions thereof in several different forms: (1) Many libraries subscribe to proof sheets, which are long strips of paper on which are printed the proofs for cards representing items cataloged by the Library of Congress. They are available for specific subjects and are issued periodically. Libraries sometimes cut them into card-sized slips and file them by main entry for bibliographical, book-selection, or cataloging purposes. (2) Some libraries order a single Library of Congress card for each work in a specific subject. Cards, being of stiff, durable stock, are easier to handle and to file than the more fragile proof sheets and are preferred by some librarians. (3) Cumulative lists of works represented by the printed cards of the Library of Congress have been issued in book form since 1953, the lists for music being entitled: *Library of Congress Catalog, Music and Phonorecords.*[12] Each volume contains much reduced reproductions of the cards, arranged alphabetically on the page, and the entries are listed in a subject index. Some librarians prefer to keep proof sheets or a card file because the small print resulting from the reduced image in the cumulative volumes is difficult to read. Moreover, the fact that each volume covers a limited time period makes it necessary to consult several issues to find all the desired entries. On the other hand, many librarians prefer the convenience of the portable, tidy, cumulative volumes. Regardless of the format of the Library of Congress catalog available in the local library, it is extremely useful. Because it is kept in different departments in different libraries, one should inquire about its location and availability.

National catalogs, exemplified by *The British Catalogue of Music,*[13] serve essentially the same bibliographical purpose as the Library of Congress catalog. Since 1957, music (excepting dance music and some popular music) and books about music which have been deposited with the Copyright Receipt Office of the British Museum have been listed in the *Catalogue,* arranged both alphabetically and by subject.

Many periodicals contain sections on new music, in some cases coupled with reviews. For example, each issue of *Fontes artis musicae,* the afore-

[12]*Library of Congress Catalog, Music and Phonorecords: A Cumulative List of Works Represented by Library of Congress Printed Cards* (Washington: Library of Congress, 1953–    ). For cards before 1953 see the numbers of the *Library of Congress Author Catalog.*

[13]*The British Catalogue of Music* (London: The Council of the British National Bibliography, Ltd., 1958–    ). Annual volumes, supplemented by interim issues (January-March, April-June, July-September). Material begins with 1957.

mentioned journal of the International Association of Music Libraries, includes a list of music publications by country, and the *Notes* of the Music Library Association has two bibliographical aids. Under the heading, "Music Received," *Notes* contains a selected but fairly extensive list of recent music received by the Association from all countries. *Notes* also carries detailed, analytical reviews of the most important recent publications and new editions and reprints of older music.

The entire issue of the *Journal of Research in Music Education* for Spring, 1959, is devoted to a selected bibliography of music education materials, including classified and annotated lists of music for a variety of teaching purposes.[14] *The School Musician* for December, 1962, contains a good example of a list coupled with reviews: "Music for Solo and Band," with reviews by Ben Vitto and David Kaplan.[15] A list with annotations of new music for piano teaching appears in the December, 1962, issue of *Clavier,* under the title, "George Anson Recommends—Review of New Piano Music."[16] These examples, picked at random, are but a sampling of lists of a nonmusicological nature.

Margaret K. Farish's *Violin Music in Print,*[17] valuable for locating published violin compositions, contains bibliographical data to facilitate identification for purchase or reference. The material in it has been expanded into *String Music in Print,*[18] including all types of music (solo, ensemble, and orchestral) for all stringed instruments, in addition to study materials and literature about strings. *String Music in Print* is divided into major areas (music for one instrument, two instruments, and so on through ten; chamber music scores; music for solo stringed instruments with orchestra; study scores; study materials; and literature), each subdivided under appropriate subheadings, with composers and their works arranged in alphabetical order, and with publication data given in brief entries.

James J. Pellerite's *A Handbook of Literature for the Flute*[19] is a graded and annotated list of flute music. A selected bibliography, it includes flute methods, studies, solos, and ensemble works, with publication data and an index of composers.

[14]"Music Education Materials: A Selected Bibliography," *Journal of Research in Music Education*, VII (Spring, 1959).

[15]Ben Vitto and David Kaplan, "Music for Solo and Band," *The School Musician*, XXXIV (December, 1962), 16–19.

[16]George Anson, "George Anson Recommends—Review of New Piano Music," *Clavier*, I (November-December, 1962), 34–40.

[17]Margaret K. Farish, *Violin Music in Print* (New York: R. R. Bowker Company, 1963).

[18]Margaret K. Farish, *String Music in Print* (New York: R. R. Bowker Company, 1965).

[19]James J. Pellerite, *A Handbook of Literature for the Flute* (2nd ed.), (Bloomington, Ind.: Zalo Publications, 1965).

The Satorius list of organ concertos[20] is arranged alphabetically by composer and includes brief biographical sketches, and for each concerto the title, publication data, duration, and instrumentation. Though possibly more useful for the performer, it may be practical also for the researcher. The Zeyringer *Litertur für Viola*[21] is similar.

The Prosniz *Handbuch der Klavier-Literatur bis 1904*[22] and the many Altmann lists[23] are examples of music bibliographies of older compositions. Although many of the items given in them may be out of print, it is possible at least to determine their existence and their publisher.

Publishers' annual catalogs are another important source of information. C. F. Peters's classified lists, for example, are to be recommended. Some European firms issue excellent catalogs of their music. The Suvini-Zerboni catalog, containing thumbnail sketches of the composers and a list of their works, is a fine example. A classified index enables one to locate music by medium and by publication format (pocket score, full score). Other publishers, both European and American, also distribute catalogs. The "Catalogs Received" section of *Notes* is a list of catalogs received by the Music Library Association and serves as an international guide to available lists. Most publishers are willing to send copies of their trade lists without charge to interested persons.

Among foreign bibliographies of some scope one may also mention the *Deutsche Musikbibliographie*, started in 1829 by the firm of Hofmeister as the *Hofmeister musikalisch-literarischer Monatsbericht*, listing works issued by Swiss, German, and Austrian publishers. Issued in monthly installments, the *Musikbibliographie* has been cumulated into annual volumes, entitled *Hofmeisters Jahresverzeichnis der Musikalien und Musikschriften*, begun in 1852. Another useful list, representing offerings of some 65 publishers from Germany, Austria, Switzerland, Czechoslovakia, and Hungary, is *Musik und Musikbücher*, with brief accounts of all varieties of music publications.

[20]Richard H. Satorius, *Bibliography of Concertos for Organ and Orchestra* (Evanston, Ill.: The Instrumentalist Co., 1961).

[21]Franz Zeyringer, *Literatur für Viola: Verzeichnis der Werke für Viola* (Hartberg: J. Schönwetter, 1963).

[22]Adolf Prosniz, *Handbuch der Klavier-Literatur bis 1904* (Leipzig: L. Doblinger, 1907).

[23]Wilhelm Altmann, *Handbuch für Klaviertriospieler* (Wolfenbüttel: Verlag für musikalische Kultur, 1934); *Handbuch für Streichquartettspieler* (Berlin: M. Hesse, 1928–1931); *Kammermusik-Katalog* (6th ed.), (Leipzig: F. Hofmeister, 1945); *Katalog der seit 1861 in den Handel gekommenen theatralischen Musik* (Wolfenbüttel: Verlag für musikalische Kultur, 1935); *Literaturverzeichnis für Bratsche und Viola d'amore* (Wolfenbüttel: Verlag für musikalische Kultur, 1937); *Orchester-Literatur-Katalog* (Leipzig: F. E. C. Leuckart, 1919). There are other similar lists.

# Bibliographies of Early Music

Early music may be variously defined. In general, the term designates music written or published before 1800, although in some cases, as in American music, it may also include works produced before the mid-nineteenth century. Early manuscripts and printed music books are found in many libraries, and some excellent lists provide information about them.

At present the most important and monumental bibliographical tool is the *International Inventory of Musical Sources,* commonly called *RISM* after its French title, *Répertoire international des sources musicales.*[24] A world-wide survey of resources of libraries, the vast inventory is still in progress, and when it is completed, it will supersede two earlier tools, the Eitner *Quellen-Lexikon*[25] and the Eitner-Haberl *Bibliographie der Musik-Sammelwerke,*[26] as a means of access to early music. At the end of 1966 four volumes devoted to early music bibliography (and not counting the volume on theoretical works) had been published:

> Vol. I. A chronological list of collections printed in the sixteenth and seventeenth centuries, with a summary of their contents and two indexes: one to publishers, the other to authors and titles.
>
> Vol. B-II (the volumes were renumbered after 1962 to achieve accurate designation of the several projected series). An alphabetical list of collections printed in the eighteenth century, with an index to publishers and another to composers.
>
> Vol. B-IV¹. A catalog of manuscripts containing polyphonic music from the eleventh to the early fourteenth century,

[24]*International Inventory of Musical Sources (RISM).* Vol. I. *Recueils imprimés: XVIe–XVIIe siècles,* ed., François Lesure (München-Duisburg: G. Henle Verlag, 1960); Vol. B–II. *Recueils imprimés: XVIIIe siècle,* ed. François Lesure (München-Duisburg: G. Henle Verlag, 1964); Vol. B–IV¹. *Manuscripts of Polyphonic Music, 11th-Early 14th Century,* ed. Gilbert Reaney (München-Duisburg: G. Henle Verlag, 1966); Vol. B–V¹. *Tropen und Sequenzenhandschriften,* ed. Heinrich Husmann (München-Duisburg: G. Henle Verlag, 1964); though perhaps not entirely pertinent to the search for compositions, there is also a volume on theoretical works: *The Theory of Music From the Carolingian Era up to 1400,* ed. Joseph Smits van Waesberghe (München-Duisburg: G. Henle Verlag, 1961).

[25]Robert Eitner, *Biographisch-bibliographisches Quellen-Lexikon der Musiker und Musikgelehrten der christlichen Zeitrechnung bis zur Mitte des neunzehnten Jahrhunderts* (Leipzig: Breitkopf und Härtel, 1900–1904).

[26]Robert Eitner and F. X. Haberl, *Bibliographie der Musik-Sammelwerke des XVI. und XVII. Jahrhunderts* (Berlin: L. Liepmannssohn, 1877).

arranged by country and followed by an index of composers and an index of text *incipits*.

Vol. B-V¹. A list by country of manuscripts containing tropes
and sequences, with a variety of indexes.

The Eitner-Haberl *Bibliographie der Musik-Sammelwerke des XVI. und
XVII. Jahrhunderts*, which has been replaced by the first two volumes of
*RISM*, is still useful if one is working in a library which does not own
*RISM*. Almost 800 printed collections are listed chronologically, with
bibliographical data, summary of contents, and list of composers.

The Eitner *Quellen-Lexikon*,[27] to be superseded eventually by *RISM*,
is a bio-bibliography of music up to the mid-nineteenth century. Both the
Eitner works and the volumes of *RISM* give location of copies; the library
coverage of *RISM* is, of course, wider and more up-to-date than that of
Eitner.

The large output of Italian music during the Renaissance has been listed
in several bibliographies, of which a few are given here as examples. The
Vogel *Bibliothek der gedruckten weltlichen Vocalmusik Italiens*[28] is a
two-volume work giving data on Italian secular vocal music from 1500
to 1700. The first volume is an alphabetical list of printed works by individual composers; the second is a chronological list of collections. Location of copies in European libraries is given, although losses and changes
due to the two World Wars have invalidated some of the information.
The Einstein revisions pertain to Volume II.

The printed instrumental music of the same period has been treated in
the Sartori *Bibliografia della musica strumentale italiana*[29] which lists
instrumental music, vocal music with instrumental accompaniment, and
vocal collections containing instrumental pieces. Sartori's *Bibliografia delle
opere musicali stampate da Ottaviano Petrucci*[30] is a catalog of works
printed by one of the outstanding Italian publishers of the Renaissance.

The publications of the sixteenth-century French Adrian Le Roy and
Robert Ballard are listed in Lesure and Thibault's *Bibliographie*,[31] where
they are given in chronological order, analyzed by first line or *incipit* and

[27]Some corrections and additions have been made in *Miscellanea musicae bio-
bibliographica*, ed. by H. Springer, M. Schneider, and W. Wolffheim (Leipzig:
Breitkopf und Härtel, 1912–1916); reprint (New York: Musurgia, 1947).

[28]Emil Vogel, *Bibliothek der gedruckten weltlichen Vocalmusik Italiens* (Berlin:
A. Haack, 1892); reprint (Hildesheim: Olms, 1962); Alfred Einstein's revision in
*Notes*, II–V (1945–1948), *passim*.

[29]Claudio Sartori, *Bibliografia della musica strumentale italiana stampata in Italia
fino al 1700* (Florence: L. S. Olschki, 1952).

[30]Claudio Sartori, *Bibliografia delle opere musicali stampate da Ottaviano Petrucci*
(Florence: L. S. Olschki, 1948).

[31]François Lesure and G. Thibault, *Bibliographie des éditions d'Adrian Le Roy et
Robert Ballard (1551–1598)* (Paris: Société Française de Musicologie, 1955).

composer, and indexed. Location of copies in European libraries is given.

Typical of bibliographies of early church music are the Schreiber lists, *Kirchenmusik von 1500–1600* and *Kirchenmusik von 1600–1700*,[32] listing both published and manuscript sources in alphabetical order by composer under the year of issue, and indexed by composer and by form. Locations (though some are no longer accurate because of loss during World War II) are given for copies in European libraries.

Dichter's *Handbook of American Sheet Music*[33] and the Sonneck-Upton *Bibliography of Early Secular American Music*[34] are examples of Americana lists. Others may be found in Duckles's *Musical Reference and Research Materials*.

## Works of Individual Composers

In addition to standard bibliographies mentioned above, there are other approaches to the music of individual composers. Usually issued by their principal publisher in commemoration of birthdays or as part of celebrations in their honor are printed catalogs of complete works to date of such well-known contemporary figures as Stravinsky, Copland, and Britten.[35] The Sibelius centennial catalog is another example.[36] As a rule the lists are carefully compiled, with useful information included about individual compositions. Publishers also issue catalogs of individual composers' works for advertising; some of them (e.g., those for Persichetti, Alain, and Walton[37]) are useful to the researcher as well as to the prospective purchaser.

Publications of composers' associations, cultural organizations, and national documentation centers are likewise practical for tracing music of contemporary composers. The quarterly *Bulletin* of the American Composers' Alliance (ACA)[38] is an example, each issue containing a biog-

[32]Max Schreiber, *Kirchenmusik von 1500–1600* (Regensburg: Druckerei St. Georgsheim Birkeneck, 1932); *Kirchenmusik von 1600–1700* (1934).

[33]Harry Dichter, *Handbook of American Sheet Music, 1st Series* (Philadelphia: Dichter, 1947); *2nd Series* (1953).

[34]Oscar G. T. Sonneck, *A Bibliography of Early Secular American Music*, rev. and enl. by W. T. Upton (Washington: Library of Congress, 1945).

[35]*Igor Stravinsky: A Complete Catalogue of His Published Works* (London: Boosey and Hawkes, 1957); *Aaron Copland: A Complete Catalogue of His Works* (London: Boosey and Hawkes, 1960); *Benjamin Britten: A Complete Catalogue of His Works* (London: Boosey and Hawkes, 1963).

[36]Lauri Solanterä, *The Works of Jean Sibelius* (Helsinki: Westerlund, 1965).

[37]*The Music of Vincent Persichetti* (Philadelphia: Elkan-Vogel, n.d.); *Jehan Alain* (Paris: A. Leduc, n.d.); *The Music of William Walton* (London: Oxford University Press, n.d.).

[38]*Bulletin* (New York: American Composers' Alliance, 1951–    ).

raphy, commentary, and catalog complete to date of works by one or more writers selected from the ACA membership. Some of them are young and comparatively little known, although most are well established, having worldwide recognition; thus the quantity of information given in the *Bulletin* varies with the individual. The Pan American Union's *Composers of the Americas*[39] is another example. The several volumes are annual compilations of individual catalogs appearing in the *Boletín de música y artes visuales*,[40] in which a portrait, biographical sketch, and a chronologically arranged classified list of works are given for each composer.

The Swiss Composers' League has issued a volume of similar intent, *40 Contemporary Swiss Composers*,[41] giving commentaries and lists of selected works, with some notes on the most important compositions. The *Catalogue of Canadian Composers*[42] uses a dictionary arrangement of composers to give a biographical outline and a list of compositions, including title, type, performing time, and publisher. Its organization is similar to that of Clair Reis's *Composers in America*,[43] which lists works up to the mid-forties.

National documentation centers, exemplified by Donemus and CeBeDeM, publish some important booklets with notes on individual composers. Centre Belge de Documentation Musicale (CeBeDeM) has a series of small volumes under the general title of *Catalogue des oeuvres de compositeurs belges*,[44] each consisting of a biographical sketch and a classified catalog of works to date, with performance times and publishers. The Documentatie in Nederland voor Muziek (Donemus) is the music documentation center for Holland, and it has issued catalogs bearing the general title of *Catalogue van Werken van Nederlandse Componisten*.[45]

Broadcast Music, Inc. (BMI) continues to issue leaflets on composers associated with the organization. More than a hundred recent and contemporary writers, both American and European, have pamphlets consisting of a short biography and a list of works with annotations.

In searching for such lists, catalogs, leaflets, and pamphlets, it is best to

[39]*Composers of the Americas: Biographical Data and Catalogs of Their Works* (Washington: Music Division, Pan American Union, 1955–    ).

[40]*Boletín de música y artes visuales* (Washington: Pan American Union, 1950–1956). Continued as *Boletín interamericano de música*.

[41]Swiss Composers' League, *40 Contemporary Swiss Composers* (Amriswil: Bodensee-Verlag, 1956).

[42]Helmut Kallmann, ed., *Catalogue of Canadian Composers* (Toronto: Canadian Broadcasting Corp., 1953).

[43]Clair E. Reis, *Composers in America* (rev. and enl. ed.), (New York: The Macmillan Company, 1947).

[44]*Catalogue des oeuvres de compositeurs belges* (Bruxelles: Fonds Daniele Cohen-Deswarts, 1953–    ).

[45]*Catalogue van Werken van Nederlandse Componisten* (Amsterdam: Donemus, 1954–    ).

consult the librarian. Being of small format, they may be treated in varying ways, ranging from full cataloging and binding to haphazard filing.

## Choice of Editions

After amassing the cards for the music to be used in the study, it is advisable, especially if one is working in a retrospective or historical field, to check the entries against thematic catalogs or lists of works given in biographical sources to make sure that the proper compositions have been chosen and correct identification has been made. Thematic catalogs (or thematic indexes) are bibliographical tools in which the known works of a composer or group of composers are listed in some systematic order, with *incipits* or beginning measures of each piece of music (or movements of larger works). For each work they give title(s), opus number, key(s), first performance, format, publication, and location of manuscript. Well-known examples are the Köchel index of Mozart's works[46] and the Schmieder index of the music of Bach.[47] In the case of a composer who has written several symphonies in the same key or several works with similar titles, the thematic index is indispensable for accuracy of identification. The Music Library Association's *A Check List of Thematic Catalogues*[48] lists available items up to 1953.

As a rule, one should compare various editions of the same work to determine their accuracy. Works which have gone through the hands of different editors (no matter how scholarly they may be) may display varying degrees of excellence, differences of editorial opinion, and variance of musical taste. Such details as phrasing, bowing, fingering, and dynamic markings are as important to the music as the notes themselves. In older compositions the realization of the figured bass and the addition of *musica ficta* must also be considered. If possible, pieces should be compared with a collected edition of the composer's music to guard against discrepancies and errors which might have crept in through the steps of editing and re-editing. To study a work of Bach without reference to the Bach-Gesellschaft edition or the newer Bach *Werke* issued by Bärenreiter[49] is to run a risk.

[46]Ludwig von Köchel, *Chronologisch-thematisches Verzeichnis der Werke W. A. Mozarts* (5th ed.), ed. Alfred Einstein (Leipzig: Breitkopf und Härtel, 1961); (6th ed.), ed. F. Giegling, A. Weinman, and G. Sievers (New York: C. F. Peters Corp., 1964).

[47]Wolfgang Schmeider, *Thematisch-systematisches Verzeichnis der Werke Johann Sebastian Bachs* (Leipzig: Breitkopf und Härtel, 1950).

[48]*A Check List of Thematic Catalogues* (New York: The New York Public Library for the Music Library Association, 1954).

[49]Johann Sebastian Bach, *Werke* (Leipzig: Bach-Gesellschaft, 1851–1926); reprint

Likewise, *Urtext* ("original text") publications like the Henle Urtext Editions[50] or the Vienna Urtext Editions[51] are valuable. Although careful checking may not be deemed necessary for a superficial or general treatment of a work, it becomes an absolute prerequisite to advanced research.

# BIBLIOGRAPHY

*Aaron Copland: A Complete Catalogue of His Works.* London: Boosey and Hawkes, 1960.

Altmann, Wilhelm, *Handbuch für Klaviertriospieler.* Wolfenbüttel: Verlag für musikalische Kultur, 1934.

———, *Handbuch für Streichquartettspieler.* Berlin: M. Hesse, 1928–1931.

———, *Kammermusik-Katalog* (6th ed.). Leipzig: F. Hofmeister, 1945.

———, *Katalog der seit 1861 in den Handel gekommenen theatralischen Musik.* Wolfenbüttel: Verlag für musikalische Kultur, 1935.

———, *Literaturverzeichnis für Bratsche und Viola d'amore.* Wolfenbüttel: Verlag für musikalische Kultur, 1937.

———, *Orchester-Literatur-Katalog.* Leipzig: F. E. C. Leuckart, 1919.

*An Alphabetical Index to Claudio Monteverdi, Tutte le Opere*, MLA Index Series No. 1. New York: Music Library Association, n.d.

*An Alphabetical Index to Hector Berlioz Werke*, MLA Index Series No. 2. New York: Music Library Association, n.d.

Anson, George, "George Anson Recommends—Review of New Piano Music," *Clavier*, I (November-December, 1962), 34–40. This is a regular feature of the journal.

*Benjamin Britten: A Complete Catalogue of His Works.* London: Boosey and Hawkes, 1963.

*Boletín de música y artes visuales.* Washington: Pan American Union, 1950–1956. Continued as *Boletín interamericano de música.*

*The British Catalogue of Music.* London: Council of the British National Bibliography, Ltd., 1958–   .

*Bulletin.* New York: American Composers' Alliance, 1951–

*Catalogue des oeuvres de compositeurs belges.* Bruxelles: Fonds Daniele-Cohen-Deswarts, 1953–   .

*Catalogue van Werken van Nederlandse Componisten.* Amsterdam: Donemus, 1954–   .

*A Check List of Thematic Catalogues.* New York: The New York Public Library, 1954.

(Ann Arbor: J. W. Edwards, 1947); *Neue Ausgabe sämtlicher Werke* (Kassel: Bärenreiter-Verlag, 1954–   ).

[50]Published by G. Henle, München-Duisburg.

[51]*Wiener Urtext Ausgabe* (Vienna: Universal-Edition).

*Composers of the Americas: Biographical Data and Catalogs of Their Works.* Washington: Music Division, Pan American Union, 1955–    .

De Charms, Desiree, and Paul Breed, comps., *Songs in Collections.* Detroit: Information Service, Inc., 1965.

*Deutsche Musikbibliographie.* Leipzig: F. Hofmeister, 1829–    . Began as *Holmeisters musikalisch-literarischer Monatsbericht*; annual cumulations in *Hofmeisters Jahresverzeichnis der Musikalien und Musikschriften* since 1952.

Dichter, Harry, *Handbook of American Sheet Music, 1st series.* Philadelphia: Dichter, 1947. *2nd series*, 1953.

Eitner, Robert, *Biographisch-bibliographisches Quellen-Lexikon der Musiker und Musikgelehrten der christlichen Zeitrechnung bis zur Mitte des neunzehnten Jahrhunderts.* Leipzig: Breitkopf und Härtel, 1900–1904.

————, and F. X. Haberl, *Bibliographie der Musik-Sammelwerke des XVI. und XVII. Jahrhunderts.* Berlin: L. Liepmannssohn, 1877.

Farish, Margaret K., *String Music in Print.* New York: R. R. Bowker Company, 1965.

————, *Violin Music in Print.* New York: R. R. Bowker Company, 1963.

Friskin, James, and Irwin Freundlich, *Music for the Piano.* New York: Holt, Rinehart and Winston, Inc., 1954.

Heyer, Anna Harriet, *Historical Sets, Collected Editions and Monuments of Music: A Guide to Their Contents.* Chicago: American Library Association, 1957.

*Igor Stravinsky: A Complete Catalogue of His Published Works.* London: Boosey and Hawkes, 1957.

*International Inventory of Musical Sources (RISM).* München-Duisburg: G. Henle Verlag, 1960–    .

*Jehan Alain.* Paris: A. Leduc, n.d.

Kallmann, Helmut, ed., *Catalogue of Canadian Composers.* Toronto: Canadian Broadcasting Corporation, 1953.

Köchel, Ludwig von, *Chronologisch-thematisches Verzeichnis der Werke W. A. Mozarts* (5th ed.). Leipzig: Breitkopf und Härtel, 1961. 6th ed., New York: C. F. Peters Corp., 1964.

Lesure, François, and G. Thibault, *Bibliographie des éditions d'Adrian Le Roy et Robert Ballard (1551–1598).* Paris: Société Française de Musicologie, 1955.

*Library of Congress Catalog, Music and Phonorecords.* Washington: Library of Congress, 1953–    .

"Music Education Materials: A Selected Bibliography," *Journal of Research in Music Education,* VII (Spring, 1959).

*The Music of Vincent Persichetti.* Philadelphia: Elkan-Vogel, n.d.

*The Music of William Walton.* London: Oxford University Press, n.d.

Neighbour, Oliver W., *English Music Publishers' Plate Numbers in the First Half of the Nineteenth Century.* London: Faber & Faber, Ltd., 1965.

Pellerite, James J., *A Handbook of Literature for the Flute* (2nd ed.). Bloomington, Ind.: Zalo Publications, 1965.

Prosniz, Adolf, *Handbuch der Klavier-Literatur bis 1904.* Leipzig: L. Doblinger, 1907.

Reis, Clair E., *Composers in America* (rev. and enl. ed.). New York: The Macmillan Company, 1947.

Sartori, Claudio, *Bibliografia della musica strumentale italiana stampata in Italia fino al 1700*. Florence: L. S. Olschki, 1952.

———, *Bibliografia delle opere musicali stampate da Ottaviano Petrucci*. Florence: L. S. Olschki, 1948.

Satorius, Richard H., *Bibliography of Concertos for Organ and Orchestra*. Evanston, Ill.: The Instrumentalist Co., 1961.

Schmieder, Wolfgang, "Denkmäler der Tonkunst," *Musik in Geschichte und Gegenwart*, III, cols. 164–191.

———, "Gesamtausgaben," *Musik in Geschichte und Gegenwart*, IV, cols. 1850–1876.

———, *Thematisch-systematisches Verzeichnis der Werke Johann Sebastian Bachs*. Leipzig: Breitkopf und Härtel, 1950.

Schreiber, Max, *Kirchenmusik von 1500–1600*. Regensburg: Druckerei St. Georgsheim Birkeneck, 1932.

———, *Kirchenmusik von 1600–1700*. Regensburg: Druckerei St. Georgsheim Birkeneck, 1934.

Sears, Minnie Earl, ed., *Song Index*. New York: The H. W. Wilson Company, 1926; supplement, 1934.

Solanterä, Lauri, *The Works of Jean Sibelius*. Helsinki: Westerlund, 1965.

Sonneck, Oscar, G. T., *A Bibliography of Early Secular American Music*, rev. and enl. by W. T. Upton. Washington: Library of Congress, 1945.

Springer, H., M. Schneider, and W. Wolffheim, eds., *Miscellanea musicae bio-bibliographica*. Leipzig: Breitkopf und Härtel, 1912–1916. Reprint, New York: Musurgia, 1947.

Swiss Composers' League, *40 Contemporary Swiss Composers*. Amriswil: Bodensee-Verlag, 1956.

Vitto, Ben, and David Kaplan, "Music for Solo and Band," *The School Musician*, XXXIV (December, 1962), 16–19.

Vogel, Emil, *Bibliothek der gedruckten weltlichen Vocalmusik Italiens*. Berlin: A. Haack, 1892. Reprint, Hildesheim: Olms, 1962. Revision by Alfred Einstein in *Notes*, II–V (1945–1948), *passim*.

Zeyringer, Franz, *Literatur für Viola: Verzeichnis der Werke für Viola*. Hartberg: J. Schönwetter, 1963.

# 12

## Discography

As a result of technical advancement in sound reproduction, recordings are important for many artistic fields, and particularly so for music. So diverse have the ramifications of the record industry become that sound research has assumed proportions and complexities unforeseen a score of years ago. Both the number and the quality of recordings have increased to the degree that some studies are incomplete without their use. Indeed, the only approach to some compositions may be through a recording. A case in point is Lester Trimble's symphony, the recording of which was available in libraries in 1964, before its first public "live" performance was given in 1965 and the score issued.

Records in disc or tape form are found in many libraries. Some record collections are independent units, others are part of the audio-visual department, and still others are integrated into the music division. Regardless of their location, record libraries may be either one of two types: (1) the archive, (2) the listening collection. Both types may be maintained in some institutions. The aim of the archive is the preservation of recordings in mint condition (or in a condition as nearly perfect as possible) for technical or historical reasons. Such records are generally not available for student listening except when one is engaged in technical research. The functional collection, on the other hand, exists to be heard. No archival purpose is considered, and the privilege of home use is often extended, thus facilitating study for one who needs to hear a work repeatedly.

If an appreciable number of records is to be used in a research project, a discography may be compiled. To locate the recordings available in a given library is a simple matter. Most catalogers prepare a detailed and even elaborate catalog, which, if the collection is large, may be maintained separately from the book and music catalog. Compositions on discs are usually represented by entries under the composer, title, medium and form (ORCHESTRAL MUSIC—SYMPHONIES; PIANO MUSIC—SONATAS), and performer(s). In less detailed catalogs the entries may be limited to composer and title and may be interfiled with the music catalog.

In a typed discography which is a part of the research paper, the data should include composer, title, performer, issuing company, and the company's serial number for the record. An indication of the type of recording (monaural or stereophonic) may also be noted. A discography card used by the student in locating the record should also bear the call number in the library owning the disc.

**Figure 12-1    A Card for Discography.**

```
Ives, Charles

Symphony No. 2
New York Philharmonic Orchestra
Leonard Bernstein, Conductor
Columbia MS6889
Stereophonic

In Library X: 7371


            ◯
```

## Discographies in Print

In searching for recordings not owned by the local library one may consult printed discographies. The Lippincott Keystone Books in Music include a series of paperback discographies, each representing recorded works of a composer or a group of related composers:[1]

[1]Keystone Books in Music (Philadelphia: J. B. Lippincott Company, 1958–    ).

Briggs, John, *The Collector's Beethoven*, 1962.

————, *The Collector's Tschaikovsky and The Five*, 1959.

Broder, Nathan, *The Collector's Bach*, 1958.

Burke, C. G., *The Collector's Haydn*, 1959.

Cohn, Arthur, *The Collector's Twentieth Century Music in the Western Hemisphere*, 1961.[2]

Schauensee, Maximilian de, *The Collector's Verdi and Puccini*, 1962.

Schoenberg, Harold C., *The Collector's Chopin and Schumann*, 1959.

Wilson, John S., *The Collector's Jazz: Modern*, 1959.

————, *The Collector's Jazz: Traditional and Swing*, 1958.

Most of the volumes are revised and updated versions of lists which had previously appeared in the issues of *High Fidelity*. In the books devoted to one composer or a few composers, biographical sketches are given, and the compositions are listed by medium (works for piano, works for orchestra, chamber music), with short notes and indication of recommended recordings. In the books on jazz, the composers are given in alphabetical order, with information about their works and recordings incorporated into their biographical sketch.

*Records in Review*,[3] issued as an annual since the mid-fifties, is a good discographical tool. Another reference is the Library of Congress Catalog, *Music and Phonorecords*,[4] consisting of Library of Congress cards reproduced in reduced size, over 20 to a page, and representing recordings and music cataloged by the library.

Since 1935 the *Musical Quarterly* has included a section on recordings. At first it was a quarterly list. In June, 1952, an extensive compilation of record reviews was begun, with articles contributed by competent critics. Other journals, among them *Audio, HiFi/Stereo Review, New Records*, and the *Saturday Review*, are likewise sources of information. The Italian *Discoteca* and the French *Musique et radio* are among representative European periodicals with discographies.

Published discographies are available for individual composers and for special types of music. An example of a composer discography is Johnson's discography of Sibelius,[5] while an example of a discography by medium

[2]See also Arthur Cohn, *Twentieth-Century Music in Western Europe* (Philadelphia: J. B. Lippincott Company, 1965).

[3]*Records in Review* (Great Barrington, Mass.: Wyeth Press, 1955–    ).

[4]*Library of Congress Catalog, Music and Phonorecords* (Washington: Library of Congress, 1953–    ).

[5]Harold E. Johnson, *Jean Sibelius: The Recorded Music* (Helsinki: Westerlund, 1965).

is Schonberg's list of chamber music and solo instrumental music.[6] Coover and Colvig's classified discography of medieval and Renaissance works[7] is representative of the period discography. Ethnic and national recordings are listed in several sources, including books and periodicals, some typical lists being:

> Duran, Gustavo, *Recordings of Latin American Songs and Dances: An Annotated Selected List of Popular and Folk Music.* Washington: Pan American Union, 1942.
>
> *Folk Music: A Catalog of Folk Songs, Ballads, Dances, Instrumental Pieces, and Folk Tales of the United States and Latin America on Phonograph Records.* Washington: Library of Congress Recording Laboratory, 1959.
>
> *The UNESCO Archives of Recorded Music*: Series B (Oriental Music); Series C (Ethnographical and Folk Music). Various places, various publishers, 1952–    .

Special discographies prepared by subject experts are a feature of *Recorded Sound*, the bulletin of the British Institute of Recorded Sound.[8] Volume I alone contains the following lists:

> Enrique J. Muttoni, "Uruguayan Music and Poetry on 78s" (June, 1961), 57–58.
>
> Marie Slocombe and Patrick Saul, "Dylan Thomas Discography" (Summer, 1961), 80–89.
>
> Harold Barnes, "Jane Bathori Discography" (Autumn, 1961), 109–110.
>
> Desmond Shawe-Taylor and Eric Hughes, "Nikisch Discography" (Autumn, 1961), 114–115.
>
> Harold Craxton, "Tobias Matthay Discography" appended to a biographical study (Winter, 1961/62), 143.
>
> Eric Hughes, "Edwin Fischer Discography" (Winter, 1961/62), 158–163.
>
> H. L. Anderson, "Harold Samuel Discography" (Spring, 1962), 191–192.
>
> ———— and Patrick Saul, "Moriz Rosenthal Discography" (Summer, 1962), 217–220.
>
> Derek Aylward, "Martinelli on LP" (Autumn, 1962), 239–240.
>
> Patrick Saul, "Isidore Philipp Discography" (Autumn, 1962), 248.

[6]Harold C. Schonberg, *Chamber and Solo Instrument Music: A Discography* (New York: Alfred A. Knopf, Inc., 1955).
[7]James Coover and Richard Colvig, *Medieval and Renaissance Music on Long-Playing Records,* Detroit Studies in Music Bibliography No. 6 (Detroit: Information Service, Inc., 1964).
[8]*Recorded Sound* (London: British Institute of Recorded Sound, 1961–    ).

The entire issue for January, 1963, is devoted to an Elgar study by Jerrold N. Moore, Curator of Historical Sound Recordings at Yale University. It includes a lengthy annotated Elgar discography, a catalog of Elgar's compositions, and an index of recordings. For the ethnomusicologist there is the valuable "International Catalogue of Records of the Folk and Classical Music of the Orient Commercially Available on 31 December, 1962" by Peter Crossley-Holland (April/July, 1963), pp. 75–105, which provides annotated entries, giving contents and instrumentation of each disc, as well as source, record number, and title. In the same issue is "International Directory of Folk Music Record Archives" (pp. 106–114).

Discographies, which are becoming as important as bibliographies, are being printed as appendixes to many books, especially those of a biographical or historical nature (Paul Nettl's *Beethoven und seine Zeit*,[9] Donald Mitchell's *Benjamin Britten*,[10] David Ewen's *A Journey to Greatness: The Life and Music of George Gershwin*,[11] Serge Moreux's *Béla Bartók: Leben, Werk, Stil*;[12] Wilfred H. Mellers' *Music in a New Found Land*[13]). Recently published college textbooks and references on music appreciation also contain extensive discographies (Joseph Machlis's *Introduction to Contemporary Music*,[14] William Hugh Miller's *Introduction to Music Appreciation*[15]). The notes on the library catalog card for these books will indicate the inclusion of such lists.

## Trade Lists

Trade lists and discographies printed for the marketing of phonorecords and tapes are useful for locating items currently available. Such a list is the *Schwann Long-Playing Record Catalog*, published monthly and found in almost any music library or music store.[16] For tapes currently available, one may see the *Harrison Catalog of Stereophonic Tapes*.[17] Similar cata-

---

[9]Paul Nettl, *Beethoven und seine Zeit* (Frankfurt-am-Main: S. Fischer Verlag GmbH, 1958).

[10]Donald Mitchell, *Benjamin Britten: A Commentary on His Works* (New York: Philosophical Library, Inc., 1953).

[11]David Ewen, *A Journey to Greatness: The Life and Music of George Gershwin* (New York: Holt, Rinehart and Winston, Inc., 1956).

[12]Serge Moreux, *Béla Bartók: Leben, Werk, Stil* (Zürich: Atlantis Verlag, 1952).

[13]Wilfred H. Mellers, *Music in a New Found Land* (London: Barrie and Rockliff, 1964).

[14]Joseph Machlis, *Introduction to Contemporary Music* (New York: W. W. Norton & Company, Inc., 1961).

[15]William Hugh Miller, *Introduction to Music Appreciation* (Philadelphia: Chilton Company—Book Division, 1961).

[16]*Schwann Long-Playing Record Catalog* (Boston: W. Schwann, 1949–    ).

[17]*Harrison Catalog of Stereophonic Tapes*, ed. by V. Rangel-Ribeira (New York: Record and Radio-Phonograph Research, Inc.).

logs are issued in Europe. The *Bielefelder Katalog* is an example.[18] Begun in 1952, it is an international list arranged by composer and indexed by title, with special sections for folklore and for collections. A useful booklet found in many libraries is *Der Bärenreiter-Bote*,[19] a trade catalog of music and phonorecords issued jointly by eight companies in Germany, Austria, Czechoslovakia, and Switzerland. In a section entitled "Neue Schallplatten" are reviews of new recordings produced by the companies represented. Catalogs of individual recording firms are also useful.

Recordings are of increasing importance as a study source. Although questions arise concerning the validity of certain types of performance (such as the playing of Baroque music on twentieth-century instruments), and scholars disagree on the value of the recording as a research tool, there are instances in which no score is available for a piece, and the only approach to the music may be through a sound reproduction. Records may likewise be necessary when a student lacks resources to implement a live performance of a composition for a large ensemble and his sole resource for hearing the music is the phonorecord.

# Evaluation

In considering questions as to the quality and validity of performance, the student may welcome a guide to the selection of good recordings, especially in cases of multiple releases. Although record reviews are helpful, one sometimes becomes confused by both the number of critiques and the diversity of opinion expressed in them. To assist listeners, each issue of *Notes* contains a section, "Index to Record Reviews," in which the several reviews of a single recording are tabulated for comparison. A cumulative volume of installments of this index that appeared in *Notes* from March, 1948, to 1956 was published as *Record Ratings*.[20] For indexes after 1956 one must see the individual issues of the journal. The purpose of *Record Ratings* and the Index is to present several different opinions for the investigator to compare and contrast in his effort to arrive at something like the objective truth about a recording.

Although it has no rating scheme, *Music Index* provides a way to find record reviews in a large number of periodicals. Darrell's *Tapes in Review*, an annual, is a good approach to tapes.[21]

---

[18]*Bielefelder Katalog: Katalog der Schallplatten klassischer Musik* (Bielefeld: Bielefelder Verlagsanstalt, 1953–    ).

[19]*Der Bärenreiter-Bote* (Kassel: Bärenreiter-Verlag, *et al.*).

[20]Kurtz Myers, comp., *Record Ratings: The Music Library Association's Index of Record Reviews*, ed. by Richard S. Hill (New York: Crown Publishers, Inc., 1956).

[21]R. D. Darrell, *Tapes in Review* (Great Barrington, Mass.: Wyeth Press, 1963–    ).

# BIBLIOGRAPHY

*Der Bärenreiter-Bote*. Kassel: Bärenreiter-Verlag, *et al.*

*Bielefelder Katalog: Katalog der Schallplatten klassischer Musik*. Bielefeld: Bielefelder Verlagsanstalt, 1953–    .

Cohn, Arthur, *Twentieth-Century Music in Western Europe*. Phildelphia: J. B. Lippincott Company, 1965.

Coover, James, and Richard Colvig, *Medieval and Renaissance Music on Long-Playing Records*, Detroit Studies in Music Bibliography No. 6. Detroit: Information Service, Inc., 1964.

Darrell, R. D., *Tapes in Review*. Great Barrington, Mass.: Wyeth Press, 1963–    .

Duran, Gustavo, *Recordings of Latin American Songs and Dances: An Annotated Selected List of Popular and Folk Music*. Washington: Pan American Union, 1942.

Ewen, David, *A Journey to Greatness: The Life and Music of George Gershwin*. New York: Holt, Rinehart and Winston, Inc., 1956.

*Folk Music: A Catalog of Folk Songs, Ballads, Dances, Instrumental Pieces, and Folk Tales of the United States and Latin America on Phonograph Records*. Washington: Library of Congress Recording Laboratory, 1959.

*Harrison Catalog of Stereophonic Tapes*, ed. by V. Rangel-Ribeira. New York: Record and Radio-Phonograph Research, Inc.

Johnson, Harold E., *Jean Sibelius: The Recorded Music*. Helsinki: Westerlund, 1965.

Keystone Books in Music. Philadelphia: J. B. Lippincott Company, 1958–    .

*Library of Congress Catalog, Music and Phonorecords*. Washington: Library of Congress, 1953–    .

Machlis, Joseph, *Introduction to Contemporary Music*. New York: W. W. Norton & Company, Inc., 1961.

Mellers, Wilfred H., *Music in a New Found Land*. London: Barrie and Rockliff, 1964.

Miller, William Hugh, *Introduction to Music Appreciation*. Philadelphia: Chilton Company—Book Division, 1961.

Mitchell, Donald, *Benjamin Britten: A Commentary on His Works*. New York: Philosophical Library, Inc., 1953.

Moreux, Serge, *Béla Bartók: Leben, Werk, Stil*. Zürich: Atlantis Verlag, 1952.

Myers, Kurtz, *et al*, "Index to Record Reviews," *Notes*, V (1948)–    .

Myers, Kurtz, comp., *Record Ratings: The Music Library Association's Index of Record Reviews*. New York: Crown Publishers, Inc., 1956.

Nettl, Paul, *Beethoven und seine Zeit*. Frankfurt-am-Main: S. Fischer Verlag GmbH, 1958.

*Recorded Sound*. London: British Institute of Recorded Sound, 1961–   .

*Records in Review (High Fidelity Record Annual)*. Great Barrington, Mass.: Wyeth Press, 1955–   .

Schonberg, Harold C., *Chamber and Solo Instrument Music: A Discography*. New York: Alfred A. Knopf, Inc., 1955.

*Schwann Long-Playing Record Catalog*. Boston: W. Schwann, 1949–   .

*The UNESCO Archives of Recorded Music*: Series B (Oriental Music); Series C (Ethnographical and Folk Music). Various places and various publishers, 1952–   .

# 13

## Organization

### Organization of the Bibliography

When the investigator has amassed all the cards for the many items to be included in his bibliography and discography and has evaluated the materials, he may organize them into the sort of working order recommended by his professor. Although the type of research largely determines the disposition of the bibliography, one of two basic procedures is generally followed. (1) In some cases the preferred organization is the listing of items in one long, unbroken sequence, so that all types of sources— books, periodicals, scores, and recordings—appear in a single alphabet. (2) In other cases, a subdivided bibliography is desirable. Separate alphabetical lists are made for each type of source: one for books, another for periodicals, another for scores. As a rule, the former procedure is practical for a short bibliography, while the latter is more useful for a long one. Also possible is a partially subdivided list in which books and periodicals are interfiled in an alphabetical sequence, and scores and sheet music, and possibly records, are combined into another sequence. In any case, the form of bibliography ideally should be determined by its ultimate uses; the arrangement should insure the greatest convenience to the reader by being the most meaningful to him. After organizing his bibliography the student may go on with his outline or his reading unless required to submit a preliminary typed copy of his proposed references.

In many institutions a candidate for an advanced degree is expected to submit a preliminary bibliography, together with a statement of the nature, scope, and methods of his research, for approval by the graduate committee. In all probability he has been assigned a thesis manual or a style-sheet to follow, outlining the rules for the form of his presentation. Details of procedure may vary according to the institution in which the investigator is working. Essentially, however, the information required in the bibliography remains the same. Moreover, the form is identical whether the bibliography is one submitted for preliminary approval or the final list accompanying the completed thesis or dissertation. Briefly, the basic principles of arranging a bibliography are:

1. The entries are listed in alphabetical order by the last name of the author. If no author is given, the name of the editor, the compiler, or the organization sponsoring the work may be used with the appropriate designation. If no such agency is given, the title is used to assign the book its proper place in the list. (Alphabetizing by title usually means by the initial of the first word following the article, i.e., the word following such words as "the," "a," "an" in English; "der," "die," "das," "ein," "eine" in German; "le," "la," "les," "un," "une" in French. A title reading *A Short History of Opera* is placed under "S.")

2. The title of the work follows the author's name in the entry and is usually underlined in typing (italicized in printing). Several correct rules of capitalization of titles exist, but ordinarily in English either (1) the first word and all other words except conjunctions and prepositions are capitalized or (2) the first word and proper nouns and proper adjectives are capitalized. In Romance languages the first word and all proper nouns are capitalized, while in German titles usually the first word and all nouns (as well as words used as nouns) are capitalized.

3. If the book in question has been edited, revised, or translated by a person other than the author, his name should also appear with his proper designation. This follows the title.

4. The imprint appears next, including the place of publication, the name of the publisher, and the date. If an edition number is known, it should be given. Some departments also ask that the collation or the number of pages contained in the book be noted.

Although this handbook is not a thesis manual, and the student should consult his own style-sheet, a few simple examples are given below for guidance. An entry by author of a book with an English title may appear thus:

Parrish, Carl, *The Notation of Medieval Music.* New York: W. W. Norton & Company, Inc., 1957. 288 pp.

or, depending upon the capitalization practice adopted, thus:

Parrish, Carl, *The notation of medieval music.* New York: W. W. Norton & Co., Inc., 1957. 288 pp.

If proper adjectives or proper nouns are used in the title, the entry may read:

Howard, John Tasker, *Our American music; three hundred years of it.* New York: Thomas Y. Crowell Company, 1931. 713 pp.

or:

Redlich, Hans Ferdinand, *Alban Berg, the man and his music.* New York: Abelard-Schuman, Limited, 1957. 316 pp.

An entry by editor may be made as follows:

Reeser, Eduard, ed., *Music in Holland: a review of contemporary music in the Netherlands.* Trans. by Ian F. Finlay. Amsterdam: J. M. Meulenhoff, 1959. 247 pp.

It will be noted in the entry just given that the name of the translator, with proper designation, appears immediately following the title.

Titles in French appearing in a simple entry are illustrated below:

Leibowitz, René, *Schoenberg, et son école: l'étape contemporaine du langage musical.* Paris: J. B. Janin, 1947. 302 pp.
Romain, Louis de, *Essais de critique musicale.* Paris: A. Lemerre, 1890. 319 pp.

German titles in simple entries may read as follows:

Leupold, Ulrich, *Die liturgischen Gesänge der evangelische Kirche im Zeitalter der Aufklärung und der Romantik.* Kassel: Bärenreiter-Verlag, 1933. 169 pp.
Schiedermayr, Ludwig, *Deutsche Musik im europäischen Raum: geschichtliche Grundlinien.* Münster: Böhlau, 1954. 272 pp.

An edition number should be included in the entry, especially if a new edition represents significant changes in the text. The third edition of Ferguson's history text may be listed in this way:

Ferguson, Donald Nivison, *A history of musical thought* (3rd ed.). New York: Appleton-Century-Crofts, Inc., 1959. 675 pp.

In preparing entries for articles from periodicals it is necessary to give the name of the author, the title of the article, the name of the periodical, its volume number and date, and the pages on which the article is to be found:

*Periodicals*

Porter, Hugh, "Sing unto the Lord a new song," *Journal of church music*, IV (December, 1962), 5–6.

Wellek, Albert, "The relationship between music and poetry," *Journal of aesthetics and art criticism*, XXI (Winter, 1962), 149–156.

An article published in a volume of proceedings may be treated in the same manner as an article from a periodical:

Anderson, Emily, "Beethoven's operatic plans," Royal Musical Association *Proceedings*, Vol. 88 (1961/62), pp. 61–71.

In dealing with musical compositions in a bibliography, the following information should be given: the name of the composer, the title of the work, the opus number (if any), the place of publication, publisher, and date. If the publisher's plate number is to be used for an approximate dating, it should be noted:

Jongen, Joseph. *Rhapsodie, pour piano, flûte, hautbois, clarinette, cor, et basson*, Op. 70. Brussels: CeBeDeM, 1962.

Soergel, F. W. *Quatuor pour deux violons, viola et violoncelle*, Oeuv. 11. Leipzig: Breitkopf und Härtel [183–?] Pub. pl. no. 3655.

Recordings must be identified in a bibliographical (i.e., discographical) list by the name of the composer, title of the work, opus number (if any), performer, recording company, and company serial number:

Stravinsky, Igor. *Agon ballet*. Südwestdeutsches Orchester, Hans Rosbaud, cond. Westminster, XWN 18807.

Some graduate departments prefer to have the bibliography divided into several sections by type of material. Two of the common divisions are (1) books, periodicals, music, and records, each in a separate section; and (2) books and periodicals together in one alphabetical list, with music and records in a second list. Division of the bibliography is generally recommended when the number of items becomes too large to handle comfortably. It is easier for the reader to scan several shorter lists in some classified arrangement than to read through an unclassified succession of sources taking up many pages. Some departments favor an undivided listing in which all items, regardless of their number and the types of material, are given in one large alphabetical organization; in such a case the form of entry varies with the type of source, and several forms may be found together in the same list:

Abraham, Gerald. "The Bartók of the quartets," *Music and letters*, XXVI (October, 1945), 185–194.

Bartók, Béla. *Quartet No. 1*, Op. 7. Vegh string quartet. Angel, ANG 35240.

Bartók, Béla. *Quatuor à cordes*, Op. 7. Budapest: Rózsavölgyi, 1911.

Moreux, Serge. *Béla Bartók, sa vie, ses oeuvres, son langage*. Paris: Richard-Masse, 1949.

Stevens, Halsey. *The life and music of Béla Bartók*. New York: Oxford University Press, 1953.

The first item above is an article from a periodical, the second is a recording, the third a score, and the last two are books, with appropriate forms of entry for each type of source.

As the student prepares his bibliography, he must keep in mind that all such lists and files are out of date as soon as they are compiled, because of the heavy schedules for publishing books, periodicals, and music, and for pressing recordings. This might strike the young researcher as alarming. Likewise alarming is the rate at which many items go out of print. But all research scholars must face reality: however conscientious one may be, he must draw the line somewhere. The sensible thing to do is to bring the study as much up to date as possible immediately before the paper is to be put into its final form. Beyond that point one can hardly be held responsible for new publications.

The investigator must also bear in mind that, in spite of preliminary evaluation of materials, it will not always be possible to use all of the items given in his tentative bibliography, and in the final presentation of his thesis or dissertation his bibliography may have to be considerably pared down. In some types of research the bibliography may be quite short, although in others it may cover many pages. The length per se of the reading list is neither an index to its practicability nor an indication of its excellence. It is obvious, therefore, that one's bibliography must be rearranged from time to time as his work progresses, and that such change is normal.

## Outline

In the process of compiling his list of books, periodicals, music, and recordings, the student has gained a great deal of knowledge, even before he has begun his serious reading. By the time he has completed his bibliography he has probably reached some decision as to how he will approach his subject. At this point, if he does not have sufficient previous background to guide him in making his tentative outline, he should take time to do some reading in those books or periodicals which will provide subject orientation.

Before approving the student's research topic for a thesis or dissertation, most graduate committees ask for a written statement of the purpose and scope of the study, as well as an account of the general methods to be employed in reaching a successful conclusion. At some institutions the candidate is required to submit an outline of his proposed work, with a preface or expository essay and his proposed reading list. Some departments call for an outline or an exposition without a tentative bibliography. Regardless of the form it takes, the statement serves the graduate committee as (1) a preview of the study, (2) a basis for judging the value of the subject, and (3) a method of controlling the standard of research carried on in the department. It gives the student an opportunity to investigate his subject, get his bearings, and decide upon a method of approach.

In spite of variations (for no two research topics are the same), the rules for submitting an outline are governed by a few universal principles. Since each piece of research is undertaken to find out something about a subject or to prove something, the student must determine his goal. As a prerequisite he must establish the background of his study. He must set the stage, so to speak, for what he is about to do. This naturally opens the way to a general treatment of his subject, which in turn leads to an investigation of the topic in its various aspects. After developing the information as far as he is able, the researcher arrives at conclusions and finally summarizes his findings. In this manner the plan of research starts at a given point, proceeds along a well-defined path, and arrives at its destination.

The best research papers are those which, in addition to meaningful content, have orderly structural form. As in all things, there must naturally be a beginning, a middle, and an end. Meanderings about a subject are a poor excuse for research. Just as a large musical composition must have a plan of organization—a type of architectural structure—so must a piece of research, especially one of considerable proportions, like a thesis or a dissertation. In such works an arrangement often evolves similar to that of a sonata form, in which the introduction and general statement of the subject are equivalent to the exposition; the treatment of the various aspects of the topic, with some attention given to detail, is like the development; and the conclusions and summary are similar to the recapitulation. At the risk of belaboring the analogy, one may envision an outline as having a skeletal form something like the following:

I. Exposition

    A. Statement and definition of the subject
       1. Background
       2. Scope

    B. Statement of the procedure, or what one plans to do with the subject

II. Development

    A. Presentation of accumulated information in some logical sequence, on the various aspects or phases of the subject

    B. Presentation of any new ideas evolved or generated from the information

III. Recapitulation

    A. Restatement of the problem

    B. Arrival at conclusions and evaluation of the findings

    C. Coda: summary and/or concluding remarks

Although no example is adequate to demonstrate procedures in a field with as many possibilities of variation as musical research, a short outline for an essay is presented here. The outline was for a master's essay in the area of piano performance in which the writer analyzed the pianist's approach to the problems attendant upon playing the Second Sonata by Paul Hindemith:

### OUTLINE

PREFACE: The need for an analysis of the sonata for interpretation of the work

I. INTRODUCTION

    A. The composition: a general structural description

    B. Brief account of the style

II. PROBLEMS OF PERFORMANCE ARISING FROM CERTAIN ASPECTS OF THE STYLE

    A. Linear motion

    B. Rhythm

    C. Vertical sonorities

    D. Phrasing

    E. Dynamics

III. SUMMARY AND CONCLUSIONS

    A. The synthesis

    B. The performer's conclusions

    C. Summary

BIBLIOGRAPHY

The above example, a simple outline for a brief essay, shows the introduction, development, and results of the study. For longer papers involving a broader subject, the outline will of necessity be enlarged and elaborated. Outlines for topics in areas other than music repertory (historical research, theoretical studies, analyses of pedagogical practice) may differ considerably from the example.

The outline, which is merely a skeletal plan for the research, is subject to change as the student proceeds with his reading. It will undergo a number of modifications before the completion of the study and thus appear considerably altered before the paper is submitted in its final form. In spite of this, it does serve as a stabilizing factor as the work progresses.

# The Preface
## and Expository Statement

A preface is a clear, brief statement preceding a work. It defines the scope and goals of the study and gives an account of the methods used in research. A preface may include data on the resources tapped for information and the editions of scores used. In some cases the preface which is submitted to the graduate committee for preliminary approval may be used with minor changes as the preface to the completed thesis, provided the writer has had the foresight to plot his course accurately. A note of acknowledgment to persons who have assisted in the preparation of the work may be added to the preface.

An expository statement is a short essay whose purpose is to explain the extent of the research problem and the methods to be used to work out a solution. Being an essay rather than an introductory statement, its various items (although similar to those in a preface) may be more fully described or explained. Because of the fuller explanation, some institutions prefer to use the exposition as the basis for judging the prospective thesis topic. After the study plan has been approved and the research completed, this statement may be used as the basis for writing a preface. Sometimes slight revisions and some condensation are the only alterations necessary.

# Reading and Note-Taking

In reading one's books and periodicals it is theoretically best to follow the plan of the outline, beginning with those sources which contain general information necessary to the study. For example, in investigating the origin of a technical device in composition or the evolution of a style, the student must first establish the background against which the subject is to be placed and developed; or in evaluating some principle of teaching, he must learn about its forerunners and the conditions which gave rise to it; or in tracing the stylistic development of a composer, he should place him in his chronological and cultural setting. This accomplished, the investigator should next read the sources dealing with the specific work, period, style, principle, or technique with which he is particularly concerned. As he does this reading he may analyze his scores and listen to his recordings. He may draft and send out questionnaires to make a poll of current opinion or current practices for statistical purposes. He may plan charts and methods of tabulating his data. This detailed information should fit nicely into the general background which he has already established.

If all the information gathered were to fit in as neatly and logically as described above, the accumulation of data would be comparatively simple and completely sensible. Unfortunately, many complications arise from the obvious fact that books and articles are not necessarily written with the student researcher in mind, and the data required are sometimes not available in the sort of workable sequence that seems appropriate to the thesis. It may be wise from time to time at least to review the reading or go over the analysis or recheck the details of one's study. In the average case it is advisable to shuffle notes around, arranging and rearranging the information as the reading progresses. Thus the success of a piece of research often rests upon the success of note-taking.

In amassing data for his proposed paper the student may choose one of several methods of note-taking. The purpose of taking notes is, of course, to collect information from as many sources as possible in a fashion designed for accuracy and ease of arrangement and assimilation. The student is sometimes advised to use cards for this purpose. Thesis advisers often recommend a 3″ x 5″ card, since it is the same size as the bibliography cards and it is easy to handle. Others suggest a slightly larger card to insure sufficient room for full notes. Still others favor slips of paper or notebooks. Actually, each person has his own work habits, so it is difficult to designate any one system as the best. No matter what method is chosen by the student, he should remain with it. His method should make provision for shifting, adding, or deleting items without disrupting the body of his data. Uniformity of format for all notes taken for a given project makes such rearrangement practical.

Having selected the format for his notes, the reader should indicate carefully on each unit (card, page in notebook) the exact location of every piece of information. Whenever he comes upon evidence useful to his research, he should write a statement or two about it. The word-for-word copying of material from an article or a book is not recommended, for it is not only mechanical but often a waste of time. To get at the heart of the matter in order to record the significant facts or ideas is more important, requiring real skill and demanding mental effort.

In the event, however, that the student considers a source so valuable that he wishes to use the author's own words in his finished paper, he must copy the pertinent sections verbatim, carefully reproducing every detail: the writer's exact spelling, punctuation, capitalization, and all the idiosyncrasies of his literary style. He must note the exact place from which he has quoted. As a matter of scholarly ethics he should give credit to the author upon using his work, and the complete bibliographical reference establishes the identity of the source.

In reading from periodicals, one should likewise make sure of positive identification by recording the complete bibliographical data: the author and title of the article, the name of the journal, the volume number and date, and page reference. Noting sources with utmost care is far from being a waste of time and energy. How often has one commiserated with his classmates as they have desperately searched for identification of a quotation important to their paper among the dozens of notes they have made in preparation of their work! Such crises at the eleventh hour can easily be avoided by checking and double-checking the material while the sources are at hand.

As one progresses with his reading and note-taking, it may be advisable to apply subject headings to each card or each page of the notebook on which notes are made. For some topics one may be able to assign a subject to each note from the very beginning, but for others one must wait until he has done some background reading to arrive at workable headings. After several references have been read, it may profit one to survey his findings and to arrange the cards in some order—cards on background in one pile, cards on biographical data in another, and so on. The outline headings previously prepared may be useful in sorting information.[1]

In the preparation of seminar or course papers, the student has but a limited time for his work. He is apt to do his research all at once; even if continuous effort is not possible, he rarely allows any more than a few days to elapse between sessions of reading and note-taking. But in the preparation of a graduate thesis, and especially of a dissertation, several years often elapse between the commencement of the project and the final accounting of data. A doctoral candidate may find that professional commitments, such as teaching and concert appearances, interfere with research for an extended period. If one must work on a dissertation for a

---

[1]An excellent treatment of the note-taking and rearranging process appears in Jacques Barzun and Henry F. Graff, *The Modern Researcher* (New York: Harcourt, Brace & World, Inc., 1957), pp. 25–31, 237ff.

number of years, he can save himself much trouble with a few mechanical devices, such as a file of subjects on which notes have already been taken, a list of sources already read, and a file of references relegated to secondary importance. Such specific indexes of work accomplished and work to be done are an aid to memory which. however accurate it may be, has a tendency to play tricks on one. They also help to reorient the student before active resumption of note-taking.

When as last all the data are gathered, the scores analyzed, the answers to questionnaires collected and tabulated, and the recordings heard, one may start to plan the final presentation of his study. If the presentation is to be oral, as in a seminar report, the style is governed by the professor's assignment. The style of the written product—the term paper, the essay, thesis, or dissertation—generally is governed by the style-sheets and thesis manuals prescribed by the various individual departments.

# BIBLIOGRAPHY

Barzun, Jacques, and Henry F. Graff, *The Modern Researcher.* New York: Harcourt, Brace & World, Inc., 1957.

# 14

## The Finished Research Paper

### Term Paper and Thesis Manuals

Most graduate departments issue their own style-sheets or recommend thesis manuals outlining the basic procedures for preparing the final draft of the research paper. The mechanics of thesis writing not only vary from one college to another, but are also somewhat modified by the nature of the topic. Because the present book is not a writing manual but a guide to research, the general treatment of mechanics is left to other texts, and only a few problems peculiar to the presentation of music research are discussed. If the student's college does not provide a thesis manual, books listed at the end of this chapter may be used. The books noted treat such subjects as the format of the paper, the front matter (title page, preface, table of contents, lists of charts), the text, footnotes, tables and illustrations, appendix, and bibliography. Some include sample pages; some give rules of punctuation; others give suggestions on literary style.

As for the actual style of writing, so many handbooks are available as to cause an embarrassment of riches. If a suggestion may be offered, a compact book by William Strunk, Jr., and E. B. White, *The Elements of Style* (New York: The Macmillan Company, 1959), is a good choice, for it is not only instructive but a delight to read.

Most college manuals contain detailed specifications for such physical properties as the weight and grade of paper, the size of type, the width of the margins, and the number of copies required, and the method of submitting the finished work. Although such requirements may appear unimportant, for the student is naturally more concerned with the contents of his thesis than with its appearance, a valid reason for enforcing regulations exists which is especially pertinent to papers submitted for advanced degrees. The master's thesis or the doctoral dissertation, once it is handed in and approved, is a bona fide publication. The copies which are retained by the university serve the following functions: (1) The original (or "ribbon") copy is part of the research archive of the institution granting the degree. (If the dissertation is to be microfilmed for the University Microfilm project, the original is photographed, after which it is put into the university archive.) (2) A carbon or Xerox copy, presented to the library for circulation, is used by other readers and may be available for interlibrary loan.[1] (3) Sometimes a third copy is retained for reference in the department directly concerned with the research. Some uniformity of format and a well-organized appearance is necessary.

Generous margins are requested to allow for binding, a process necessary for preservation of the paper. Whether the binding is done by the library staff or by a commercial bindery, about half an inch on the left margin is taken up in sewing, and the resulting tightness of the binding takes up another half-inch. To insure complete legibility of the text, a left-hand margin of an inch and a half is usually recommended. A right-hand margin of at least three-quarters of an inch is requested because trimming may be desirable in the binding process to make the pages uniform, and precautions must be taken to prevent the text from being sliced off the page.

Clear typing is always desirable. Dissertations to be microfilmed for the University Microfilms project require clear type to insure good film reproduction. Institutions may ask for pica rather than elite type for ease in reading both the typescript and the microfilm. Because a worn ribbon and unclean type result in a faint, fuzzy copy, advisers insist upon use of a new ribbon and frequent cleaning of the type face. For legible, neat copies, they ask for a change of carbon every few pages to avoid smudging and unevenness of impression.

## Musical Examples

Musical examples are as important in some theses as the text. They must be considered an integral part of the work, to be selected and presented with the same care as every other aspect of the research. Naturally, overloading or padding a dissertation with extraneous examples is discouraged.

For the best results, both in permanence and neatness, musical quota-

[1]Some institutions do not send dissertations on interlibrary loan if a microfilm copy is available for purchase.

tions should be written directly on the page in India ink. But because the preparation of handwritten examples in all of the required copies of a dissertation poses an almost insurmountable problem of time, especially if the citations are lengthy or are in full score, most universities allow the pasting in of ozalid or Xerox copies of examples. For the ozalid process a transparency is made on special opaque paper, using India ink or black ink with heavy carbon content, and copies are made from it. In the Xerox process no master sheet is required; copies can be made directly from the printed or written page. No matter what duplicating technique has been used, the examples must be trimmed and pasted on the typed page in the space left blank for that purpose. Margins allowed for music should be the same as those for the typed text.[2]

To prevent warping, wrinkling, and curling of the paper, use either rubber cement or paper cement in preference to ordinary glue or paste. If the adhesive is of good quality and is carefully applied to both the page and the example, the bond is permanent and the examples will remain intact indefinitely. If the cement is stintingly applied, or of a type that dries, the examples fail to adhere properly and may soon become detached. Conversely, if the adhesive is too copiously used or is allowed to "bleed," it may cause serious discoloration or even disappearance of the typed copy with which it comes into contact. The use of plastic tape to secure examples is discouraged because of discoloration.

In most manuals on music theses, some procedure is described for labeling the musical examples, which should be identified as accurately as a quotation from a book. The composer's name, the title of the composition, designation of the movement in a multimovement work, the page, and measure number(s) are usually to be given. Indication of the edition from which the music is cited also is important, and if two different scores are used for the same composition, they should be differentiated.

## Xerox versus Carbon Copies

Multiple copies usually are required in submitting a thesis for a graduate degree. Duplicates are necessary for the convenience of the several members of the student's advisory or examining committee who must read it. Later, after approval, the duplicates are needed for archival and library purposes, as described above. Until recently the copies conventionally were made by using carbon, but the tendency of carbon copies to smudge even

[2]For a discussion of details of music preparation, see Anthony Donato, *Preparing Music Manuscript* (Englewood Cliffs, N. J.: Prentice-Hall, Inc., 1963).

under the best of circumstances has led some universities to turn to other methods to obtain clear, permanent copies. If the college possesses a duplication center with a Xerox machine, it is possible that Xerox duplicates will be accepted, thus eliminating the necessity for making numerous carbon copies and simultaneously doing away with the need for pasting musical examples into many copies. One clear original, typed on the proper grade of bond paper, with musical examples either written or pasted in, serves as the master for the required number of Xerox copies. Copying may be done on any grade of paper; the weight and quality prescribed for the thesis is entirely practical. Because most of the other duplicating processes produce copies on chemically treated paper which may change color or in some other way fail to meet the requirements of graduate departments, Xerox is recommended for its permanence and its adaptability as well as its clarity. Actually, any process which results in a good, legible, permanent copy should be acceptable.

## Microfilming

If the student's graduate department subscribes to the University Microfilms project of filming and Xeroxing dissertations, the original is sent to Ann Arbor for filming. It must be letter-perfect, for all errors are naturally reproduced on film. The intensity of the type should be as uniform as possible, so that all pages will photograph clearly and evenly. Careful collation is recommended in order to avoid misplaced and lost pages.

A nominal fee is charged by University Microfilms for the service, with an additional fee if collation by the company staff is requested. Depending upon the policy of the school, the charges may be paid by either the university or the student, with the latter practice being by far the more usual one. At the time of microfilming, the writer may have his work copyrighted, and although the copyright application forms may be provided by the graduate department, the fee is borne by the student. Some doctoral candidates feel that the amount of research involved in a successful dissertation warrants protection of their work by copyright, especially since the availability of the thesis for purchase makes it a publication.

From the master microfilm on file at Ann Arbor, any number of copies may be made on either film or Xerox paper. Authors and titles of works thus available are listed in *Dissertation Abstracts* and *Masters Abstracts*, each followed by a concise statement of the research processes and results. Individuals and institutions may purchase copies from University Microfilms.

# BIBLIOGRAPHY

Albaugh, Ralph M., *Thesis Writing: A Guide to Scholarly Style*. Ames, Iowa: Littlefield, Adams, and Co., 1957.

Campbell, William Giles, *Form and Style in Thesis Writing*. Boston: Houghton Mifflin Company, 1954.

Cordasco, Francesco, and Elliott S. M. Gatner, *Research and Report Writing*, College Outline Series No. 72. New York: Barnes & Noble, Inc., 1964.

Donato, Anthony, *Preparing Music Manuscript*. Englewood Cliffs, N. J.: Prentice-Hall, Inc., 1963.

Hook, Lucyle, and Mary Gaver, *The Research Paper* (3rd ed.). Englewood Cliffs, N. J.: Prentice-Hall, Inc., 1962.

Hubbell, George Shelton, *Writing Term Papers and Reports*, College Outline Series No. 37. New York: Barnes & Noble, Inc., 1962.

Kahn, Gilbert, and Donald J. D. Mulkerne, *The Term Paper: Step by Step*. Garden City, N. Y.: Doubleday & Company, Inc., 1964.

*A Manual of Style, Containing Typographical and Other Rules for Authors, Printers and Publishers*. Chicago: University of Chicago Press, 1959.

Schmitz, Robert M., *Preparing the Research Paper* (4th ed.). New York: Holt, Rinehart and Winston, Inc., 1957.

Strunk, William, Jr., and E. B. White, *The Elements of Style*. New York: The Macmillan Company, 1959.

Turabian, Kate L., *A Manual for Writers of Term Papers, Theses and Dissertations*. Chicago: University of Chicago Press, 1955.

————, *Student's Guide for Writing College Papers*. Chicago: University of Chicago Press, 1963.

# 15

## Research Etiquette

Because a student engaged in research must come in contact with many people and must work in rather close cooperation with several, he must be constantly aware of the rules of research etiquette. Every graduate student has probably been told more than once that his study should show some independent effort. It is true that he receives guidance in classes and seminars, and his thesis adviser gives him suggestions at conferences. Fundamentally, however, the difference between an immature student and an adult scholar lies in the latter's manifestation of originality and self-reliance. This concept of independence is basic to graduate study. The ability to use one's ingenuity in searching for material, in evaluating the data collected through reading and analysis, and in arriving at conclusions is a *sine qua non* to research.

But paradoxically, as much as a person may wish to be self-reliant, he cannot get along by himself. Much of the etiquette of research is based upon the awareness of what one owes, for the scholar constantly borrows from others—he borrows knowledge, he borrows time, and he borrows goodwill. The congenial and friendly exchange of ideas between the student and his adviser forms a foundation for some important aspects of research etiquette.

## The Faculty Adviser

The student-adviser relationship is a most important one, based on mutual obligation and mutual respect. A professor, whether he acts as a classroom instructor, a seminar discussion leader, or a thesis adviser, is a professional man who is available on the campus to assist the student with his work. He is thoroughly trained, has a wide knowledge of his subject field, and has had some experience with research of his own. His duty to the student is to guide him in his work by sharing his knowledge with him. Although the adviser may know a great deal about the subject, he expects also to learn from the findings of his student. He owes it to his advisee to be available for consultation at appointed hours and to give unselfishly of his time and knowledge.

The student's obligation to his adviser is to follow his suggestions to the best of his ability. He should remember that the professor is hired by the university not to do his work for him but rather to teach him how to do it, and he must be willing to develop some of his own ideas before going to the adviser for assistance. Having received instructions for research, the student should accomplish some tangible work and have the results clearly written or typed in legible form before he asks for more assistance. Constructive advice may easily be given when one can see what has been done, but it is well-nigh impossible to comment upon something which exists only as a nebulous notion in another's mind.

As the work progresses and the investigator has more and more of his research to show, he should present his adviser with a legible copy, preferably neatly typed, with enough margin on each page for corrections and suggestions. It is unkind to try the adviser's patience by submitting a pencil copy or one which has been crossed out, marked up, or is generally difficult to decipher. When the adviser offers his suggestions, they should be seriously considered no matter how inappropriate they may seem at the moment. As a rule, an adviser, who has had the advantage of greater experience in research than the student and who at the same time retains a more objective point of view on the work, finds opportunities for improvement even where the student least expects to encounter them. If the adviser asks for a retyping of the draft at any point in the research, the student should comply, making an effort to keep every page as neat as possible, and incorporating corrections recommended by the professor.

One should bear in mind that no person, no matter how learned, can possibly carry the burden of total knowledge within even a small subject field. Since a professor expects a researcher to discover new facts or formulate new ideas, the student should not interpret willingness on the teacher's part to accept new ideas from him as a sign of ignorance or of incompetence. The best advisers are those who not only give freely of their knowledge to their students but are willing to learn from them. No greater measure of respect can be given a younger person by an older one than this very receptiveness.

## The Librarian

The librarian, like the faculty adviser, is a professional person, who is appointed by the university to procure and make available the materials of study. If he is hired by the city or the county to preside over a public library, his function is the same. He is trained in both a subject field and in library science—the technical processes of giving bibliographical service. Often he is himself a research scholar.

The obligation of the librarian is to supply as many of the research materials as is possible with the financial, temporal, and personnel resources allotted to him. These resources vary from place to place. The degree of service per capita is dependent upon the nature and size of the institution, which also influence the type of clientele to be served. But no matter what type of patron he may have, the librarian must be ready to give aid to the fullest extent of his ability. This means giving advice on the material that is locally available, guiding the patron through the bibliographical maze, assisting him in locating items not only in his own library but also in other collections, and negotiating interlibrary loans and sending requests for photocopy.

Although many librarians do teach, the librarian is not ordinarily a full-time classroom teacher, and it is understandable that the student-librarian relationship in a college or university may be a little difficult to define. In actuality the relationship is similar to that existing between the student and his adviser, the only difference being that the librarian is the bibliographical adviser and is not usually on the student's thesis or examining committee. To ask for the expert counsel of a librarian is just as appropriate as to seek the professional advice of a professor, although here again the element of self-reliance must be borne in mind. It is, for example, quite proper to ask the librarian for instruction in the use of the catalog, but it is improper to expect him to compile one's bibliography. In like manner, a librarian fully expects to be questioned on the use of certain reference tools but does not feel called upon to look up material for the student.

There are times when one becomes completely exasperated with libraries. Most particularly does a student become impatient when it takes an assistant half an hour to find a book which should be on the shelves, or, worse still, when the book cannot be found at all. This situation exasperates the librarian as much as it does the student. It simply cannot be helped. No matter how well-ordered the library stacks may be, there are bound to be such losses, both temporary and permanent. The proportion of loss seems to grow in direct ratio to the size and complexity of the collection. If, after a reasonable search, the item cannot be found, most librarians are willing to ask for it on interlibrary loan.

# Interlibrary Loan

Interlibrary loans are negotiated for the purpose of serious research, and most lending libraries are hesitant about sending books for an undergraduate paper. Because of the large number of requests for interlibrary loan, each librarian (both the lending and the borrowing agent) feels more responsibility toward the research project of greater proportions. If one needs materials for a thesis or a dissertation, he should by all means have the librarian send for them on loan, but if one is preparing a class report or a term paper, he must not be offended if the librarian asks him to be content with the resources available in the local library.

In asking for interlibrary loans it is best to request only a few items at a time. Often a lending library is not willing to send anything to a person who requests what might appear to be more than his share of books. The usual period of loan being two weeks or a month, it stands to reason that one cannot do justice to dozens of books within the prescribed time. One's own librarian becomes embarrassed at having to ask for renewals, and the lending librarian may consider the student to have become an unwelcome interlibrary loan client. The sensible thing is to request a limited number of books at a time, waiting until one has finished with the first group of sources before sending for the second.

Parenthetically, the same thing holds true in the local library. A student may be strongly tempted to take out all the material pertaining to his subject at one time. This is a dubious practice. To be sure, it is one method of accumulating everything one wishes to use for his work, but surely he cannot expect to read all of it within the loan period allotted to him. More important, some other researcher or faculty member might need the same sources for a purpose just as honorable and urgent. The philosophy that playing dog-in-the-manger is justified merely by paying fines on overdue books is hardly reasonable or tenable.

A library book does not belong to any one person; it is borrowed property, a cultural asset to be shared by many people, whether the owner happens to be a local institution or a library hundreds of miles away. One would not dream of mutilating other people's property. He should likewise refrain from marking and dog-earing pages of library books. And no one has the right to inflict his marginalia upon others.

# Courtesy by Mail

In working on research projects some types of information are obtainable only through questions put to institutions or persons outside the investigator's own college. Librarians in particular expect to receive questions by mail, for many bibliographical problems concerning the holdings of their libraries arise. (Each library has material which is slightly different in both content and arrangement from every other.) Staff members of reference and service departments are willing to go to some measure of trouble to furnish data, provided that there is reasonable need for them and that the time involved in supplying the information does not become excessive.

A common and certainly legitimate question which a scholar must ask a librarian is the extent of the library's holdings related to his research and the amount of cooperation he may expect from the institution. Most American libraries do not publish a printed catalog; catalogs of special collections, such as the Backus catalog of music before 1801 at the Huntington Library, are exceptions. In this day of rapidly growing libraries, many with subject specialties, answering direct questions is often the only method of making desired bibliographical information available.

But it works a hardship upon the library staff when a student, in all innocence, makes unreasonable demands. To receive a letter asking for the author and title of every book on sixteenth-century theory owned by the library, for example, is not only disheartening but may present serious problems. Depending upon the size of the collection, such a list might easily run into dozens or even hundreds of items. With the shortage of clerical assistance characteristic of most libraries, it may be necessary to refuse such a request. To make matters easier for all concerned, the researcher may send a legible copy of his bibliography as far as he has been able to compile it with the tools he has on hand. He may ask the librarian to check the listed items available for loan in his collection and to add other sources found in his library. Another simple method is merely to ask for a microfilm copy of the catalog cards representing works on the subject in question. While one must pay a few cents per frame for such copy, he is almost certain to receive a quick reply.

The student writing for information must make certain that his request is clearly stated. Recently, when the librarian of a music school received a request for a "bibliography on the scope of music education," he found it difficult to answer. The student had failed to define his subject. He had not given any idea of the extent to which he had gone in compiling his bibliography (and in this case, some clue to the writer's intentions might have been discernable if a partial bibliography had been presented). Moreover, if the student actually expected the librarian to compile his entire bibliography for him, he was mistaken. On the other hand, when the same librarian received a list of Lully's operas, with a request that he check those for which contemporary scores were available for photocopy, he was able to send the reply within an hour of receipt of the letter. Clarity of definition and simplicity of demand can truly be an open sesame to the services of a librarian.

Students understandably become time-conscious when they request information by mail. It is needless, however, to admonish the librarian that time is of the essence and that the answer is needed immediately. As a rule, the librarian fully realizes the urgency of any request having to do with a thesis or dissertation. Indeed, the necessity for speed is taken for granted. It is likewise impolite to declare that the answer must be as complete as possible. Completeness of detail, like the need for speed, is taken for granted by the library staff.

In trying to do the correct thing in requesting bibliographical service, some well-meaning students err by offering to pay for the work. While the offer is surely made in good faith, it may cause embarrassment. Librarians are appointed to answer bibliographical and reference questions without commission. If payment of a fee commensurate with the value of professional advice were required, the student would be obliged to pay some staggeringly large bills. Moreover, the extraordinary cases in which special clerical help must be hired to compile lengthy reports do not fall within the scope of service for a graduate student. A thesis writer needs only to ask for bibliographical assistance, and a clearly written or typed letter, bearing a well-defined and reasonable request, will normally be given immediate and undivided attention. Only an acknowledgment of the aid is expected.

If the librarian believes the question put to him involves so many hours of staff time as to be impossible to answer by mail, or if his library contains an outstanding collection helpful to the research, he may suggest that the writer visit his library to study the materials at first hand. Far from indicating a lack of interest in the project, this invitation is an offer of hospitality for the student's greatest benefit.

Questionnaires may be used to obtain data for statistical projects in which one polls opinions or takes a census of current practices. No matter who the respondent is—a secretary, a classroom teacher, a supervisor, or an administrator—he sacrifices valuable time to answer the queries. It is best to keep the questionnaire brief and clear. The format should be attractive and legible. Space provision for answers should be ample, so that the cooperating person may write his replies quickly without having to use another sheet of paper, write on the reverse side of the sheet, or in other ways experience inconvenience. Multiple-choice questions, in which one checks appropriate items rather than writing out his answers, may be recommended. Although drafting such questions may cost the student more effort than drawing up some other variety, he may rest assured that they will be appreciated by the person answering the questions.

In writing to authorities in some subject field for their considered opinions or in asking a composer for information about a work, the investigator should not only be brief and respectful, but also, as a matter of policy, should refrain from requesting data available in a published source. It is presumptuous to expect the cooperating person to answer with a long exposition of a subject or with a complete analysis of a composition. When a prominent music educator was asked to send a complete list of the articles he had written for various periodicals (the list ran to over a hundred items), giving the exact location of each, together with a full statement of his philosophies at certain stages of his development as an educator, he was put to some disadvantage. As willing as he was to supply the information (for he realized that the student's intentions were serious) he found it impossible to do justice to the request. To make a list of his publications would have taken many hours and to account for his educational philosophies would have consumed weeks. A few leading questions calling for brief, specific answers would have been reasonable and the results would have been satisfactory.

One should send a first-copy typed letter when writing for any sort of information, no matter how many persons are to be canvassed for the project. To send a carbon copy of a letter or one with such a heading as "To whom it may concern" shows lack of respect. Each letter should be addressed to a specific person and signed by the writer.[1] It should be accompanied by a self-addressed and stamped envelope for the reply, for the student must not expect the cooperating person to pay return postage. When the answer has been received, the student should immediately acknowledge receipt in writing.

## Acknowledgments

Not only is it proper for one to acknowledge receipt of information but it is essential that he give expression of indebtedness when he quotes or paraphrases another person's work. A student is usually obliged at one point or another to base his research upon material previously written. He

---

[1]When questionnaires are mimeographed or otherwise duplicated, copies rather than originals are sent out. The student must be sure that the copies are clearly legible, and he should accompany the questionnaire with a letter requesting the favor of a reply.

must in all honesty give credit where it is due when he gleans facts and opinions from someone's research. Whether he quotes a passage verbatim from a book or journal, or paraphrases it, he should indicate by footnote the author, title, and page reference of the work he has used as his source. Naturally, in addition to the footnote, he must list the item in his bibliography.

When a thesis writer quotes materials from copyrighted music and books, he is expected to ask permission of the copyright owner (whose name clearly appears in the copyright notice) to use the quotations. This is essential if a dissertation is to be microfilmed and copies are to be sold, and if the quotations are of appreciable length. In any case, it is the polite thing to do. In asking for permission, which will be granted gladly in almost every case, one should state the purpose of the quotation and include specific page and measure references as well as the name of the author or composer and title of the work. In the rare instances in which permission is refused, the writer must understand that refusal is usually for a good reason and that other examples or citations must be found to replace the original choice.

## The Typist

A student who does not type his own thesis but calls upon the services of a professional typist has some obligations. A neatly typed or written draft—*not* a pencil copy—should be submitted to the typist. The form, punctuation, spelling, and grammar should be in good order. Although some typists, especially those who have specialized in dissertations, are also capable editors, their duty is simply to copy what appears in the writer's draft.

When the finished thesis is received from the typist, the writer must assume complete responsibility for proofreading. Although typographical errors may be the typist's fault, the author bears the obligation of having them corrected. In the final analysis it is the student's place to see that a perfect typescript is submitted.

## Some Rights and Privileges

When a thesis or dissertation topic has been approved by the proper agency in the college, the student may consider the subject to be his own. Although approval does not necessarily prevent someone else from working on a similar project at another university, the student may rightfully expect that the approval of the graduate committee is his guarantee of having the subject to himself within his own institution.[2] He may assume that such endorsement is given because the committee members consider the proposed work to be worthy of the school and the writer to be capable of doing it justice.

While he is engaged in the research, the student is entitled to a certain amount of assistance from both the faculty and the library staff. These professional people have been appointed to give their suggestions and to direct the investigator's work, provided that he requests their help in a courteous manner and his demands are reasonable.

When the research is finished and the findings have been presented in writing, the research paper is theoretically the property of the writer. By common law, it may not be copied or paraphrased without his consent. However, if the research is a thesis or a dissertation submitted and accepted in partial fulfillment of degree requirements, its final disposition may be determined by university policies with which the student must comply. Although the work may be "his," the thesis may become the property of the graduate department, the college, or the library. If one wishes to publish something from his dissertation, therefore, it is courteous to inform the degree-granting institution of his intentions. Conversely, if the college wishes to publish any part of the work, the authorities should ask the writer's permission. The thesis writer has the privilege of copyrighting his work, although this is not at all mandatory.

To have written successfully a thesis or a dissertation is an accomplishment of which the student may be justly proud. He has learned a great deal more than he has been able to incorporate into his writing. He has been privileged to work with many interested persons. He has been obliged to organize his thoughts. Above all, he has had an opportunity to add something, no matter how small, to the sum total of human knowledge and experience.

[2]Topics of doctoral dissertations in progress are reported for inclusion in the Hewitt list of doctoral dissertations (discussed in Chapter 8), which serves as a clearing house for subjects and helps to prevent duplication of effort. Scholarly ethics prohibit one from working on a topic known to be taken by another scholar. If two graduate students unknowingly work on the same subject, the one who submits his thesis first "wins" the topic, and the other writer should modify his field of research. Duplication has caused many a heartache among thesis writers.

*Part Three*

# *SURVEY*
# *OF RESEARCH*
# *MATERIALS*

# 16

## Types of
## Research Materials

### General Music Research Aids

Resources for music research continue to increase rapidly with the never-ending appearance of new works. As an aid to their location and evaluation, several helpful guides to materials have been prepared, some representative ones being:

> Vincent Duckles, *Music Reference and Research Materials.* New York: The Free Press of Glencoe, 1964. A classified and annotated list of 1106 sources for musical investigation, with location of reviews.
>
> Glen Haydon, *Introduction to Musicology.* Englewood Cliffs, N. J.: Prentice-Hall, Inc., 1941. A useful early reference defining the areas of serious music study; includes bibliographical aids.
>
> Lincoln B. Spiess, *Historical Musicology.* Brooklyn, N. Y.: The Institute of Mediaeval Music, 1962. A handbook for historical research; includes bibliography.
>
> Constance Winchell, *Guide to Reference Books*, and supplements. Chicago: American Library Association, 1951–     . An extensive guide to general reference books, including those in music.

This chapter presents a definition and brief summary of basic types of materials useful in music research and available in many public and college libraries.[1] The books have been divided arbitrarily into the following

[1] The titles mentioned are for the most part those owned by institutions represented at the six workshops for music librarians held at the Eastman School of Music during the summers of 1957, 1958, 1959, 1961, 1963, and 1965, and offering a cross-section of library resources in the United States and Canada.

simplified bibliographical categories for ease of discussion:

1. Works for quick reference: encyclopedias and dictionaries
2. Lists of items available or recommended: bibliographies, discographies, catalogs, and indexes
3. Works dealing with background, developments, and personalities: histories, biographies, and autobiographies
4. Analyses of compositions and styles: analytical guides
5. Miscellaneous: commemorative volumes and materials issued by documentation centers

## Works for Quick Reference: Encyclopedias and Dictionaries

Strictly speaking, an encyclopedia (or cyclopedia) is an alphabetically arranged reference giving data on a wide field of knowledge; a dictionary is a similarly arranged reference containing definitions of words. But such titles as *Dictionary of Music and Musicians, Cyclopedic Survey of Chamber Music*, and *Biographical Dictionary of Musicians* which suggest overlapping functions, make it expedient to deal with encyclopedias and dictionaries as a single category, especially since their arrangement and the technique of use are similar.

Music dictionaries (of the sort we envision as dictionaries) began late in the fifteenth century with Tinctorus's *Terminorum musicae diffinitorium.*[2] The sixteenth and seventeenth centuries produced little in lexicography, but in the eighteenth century such notable works as those of Brossard[3] and Walther[4] appeared. The following century produced the Choron and Fayolle biographical dictionary,[5] the Fétis *Biographie universelle,*[6] the first edition of *Grove's Dictionary* (1879–1889), and the early editions of Riemann's *Musik Lexikon* (1882–    ). So many works have been published in the twentieth century as to cause an embarrassment of riches. For a detailed study of musical lexicography, together with bibliographies of dictionaries and encyclopedias, one may consult:

[2]Johannes Tinctorus, *Terminorum musicae diffinitorium* (late 15th century); Latin-English ed. (New York: The Free Press of Glencoe, 1963).

[3]Sébastien de Brossard, *Dictionnaire de musique* (Paris: Ballard, 1703); fascimile of first folio ed. (Hilversum, The Netherlands: Frits A. M. Knuf, 1964).

[4]Johann G. Walther, *Musicalisches Lexicon* (Leipzig: W. Deer, 1732); fascimile ed. (Kassel: Bärenreiter-Verlag, 1953).

[5]Alexandre E. Choron and F. J. M. Fayolle, *Dictionnaire historique des musiciens, artistes et amateurs* (Paris: Valade, 1810–1811).

[6]François J. Fétis, *Biographie universelle des musiciens et bibliographie générale de la musique* (Bruxelles: Meline, Cans et Cie., 1837–1844).

James Coover, *Music Lexicography, Including a Study of Lacunae in Music Lexicography and a Bibliography of Music Dictionaries*. Denver: Denver Public Library, 1958.

Hans Heinrich Eggebrecht, "Lexika der Musik," *Die Musik in Geschichte und Gegenwart: Allgemeine Enzyklopädie der Musik* (1960), VIII, cols. 685–699.

Alexander Hyatt King, "Dictionaries and Encyclopedias," *Grove's Dictionary of Music and Musicians* (1954), II, 691–700.

Richard Schaal, "The Fore-runners of the Grove-Blom: A Bibliography of Musical Dictionaries in Chronological Order," *Hinrichsen's Musical Year Book*, VII (1952), 594–601.

Ranging in length from a single volume to multivolume sets, the general music dictionaries and encyclopedias contain definitions of terms, biographical data, and explanations and descriptions of forms and media. They may also include bibliographies. In some, the entries are signed by their respective authors; in others they bear no indication of authorship other than the name of the editor or compiler, who may or may not be responsible for the articles. Some representative general music dictionaries and encyclopedias found in most libraries include:

Sir George Grove, *Grove's Dictionary of Music and Musicians* (5th ed.), ed. Eric Blom. London: Macmillan & Co., Ltd., 1954; supplement, 1961. 9 vols. and supplement.

*Larousse de la musique*, under the direction of Norbert Dufourcq, with the collaboration of Félix Raugel and Armand Machabey. Paris: Librairie Larousse, 1957. 2 vols.

*Encyclopédie de la musique*, under the direction of François Michel in collaboration with François Lesure and Vladimir Fédorov. Paris: Fasquelle, 1958–1961. 3 vols.

Friedrich Blume, ed., *Die Musik in Geschichte und Gegenwart: Allgemeine Enzyklopädie der Musik*. Kassel: Bärenreiter-Verlag, 1949–     . 12 vols. as of August, 1966; in progress.

Hugo Riemann, *Musik Lexikon* (12th ed.), ed. Willibald Gurlitt. Mainz: B. Schott's Söhne, 1959–     . 3 vols.: I and II, biographies; III, definitions.

Percy A. Scholes, *The Oxford Companion to Music* (9th ed.). London: Oxford University Press, 1955.

Oscar Thompson, *The International Cyclopedia of Music and Musicians* (9th ed.), ed. R. Sabin. New York: Dodd, Mead & Company, Inc., 1964.

Jack A. Westrup and F. L. Harrison, *The New College Encyclopedia of Music*. New York: W. W. Norton & Company, Inc., 1960.

Some dictionaries are truly dictionaries in the sense that they contain definitions of terms. The above-mentioned works by Tinctoris and Brossard are examples. Modern dictionaries most frequently found in American college and public libraries include:

> Willi Apel, *Harvard Dictionary of Music*. Cambridge, Mass.: Harvard University Press, 1956. First published in 1944.
>
> Willi Apel and Ralph T. Daniel, *The Harvard Brief Dictionary of Music*. Cambridge, Mass.: Harvard University Press, 1960.
>
> Theodore Baker, *Dictionary of Musical Terms*. New York: G. Schirmer, Inc., 1923.
>
> Marie Bobillier, (Michel Brenet, pseudonym), *Dictionnaire pratique et historique de la musique*. Paris: A. Colin, 1926. 2nd ed., 1930.
>
> W. J. Smith, *A Dictionary of Musical Terms in Four Languages*. London: Hutchinson & Co., Ltd., 1961. The languages are English, French, Italian, German.

Dictionaries may be biographical, giving accounts of musicians from many countries, or bio-bibliographical, including both vital and bibliographical data. Some may be nominally international in coverage but emphasize musicians of a given country or group of countries, while still others are specifically national. The following are examples of different types:

> Theodore Baker, *Baker's Biographical Dictionary of Music and Musicians* (5th ed.), rev. by Nicolas Slonimsky. New York: G. Schirmer, Inc., 1958. International biographical dictionary.
>
> *Dictionnaire des musiciens Français*. Paris: Seghers, 1961. Small biographical dictionary of French musicians.
>
> Robert Eitner, *Biographisch-bibliographisches Quellen-Lexikon der Musiker und Musikgelehrten der christlichen Zeitrechnung bis zur Mitte des neunzehnten Jahrhunderts*. Leipzig: Breitkopf und Härtel, 1900–1904. 10 vols. Bio-bibliographical dictionary.
>
> Carlo Schmidl, *Dizionario universale dei musicisti*. Milano: Sonzogno, 1926–1929; supplement, 1937. 2 vols. and supplement. International bio-bibliographical dictionary with emphasis upon Italian musicians.

Dictionaries may be prepared for individual forms of music, such as chamber music, hymnology, and opera. References also exist for historical periods and for musical instruments:

> Walter W. Cobbett, ed., *Cyclopedic Survey of Chamber Music* (2nd ed.). London: Oxford University Press, 1963. 3 vols.
>
> John Julian, *A Dictionary of Hymnology* (rev. ed. with sup-

plement). London: John Murray (Publishers), Ltd., 1908. Reprint, New York: Dover Publications, Inc., 1957.

Harold D. Rosenthal and John Warrack. *Concise Oxford Dictionary of Opera*. London, New York: Oxford University Press, 1964.

Jeffrey Pulver, *A Biographical Dictionary of Old English Music*. London: Routledge & Kegan Paul, Ltd., 1927.

Many other references may be found by consulting the library catalog, where entries are filed under DICTIONARIES or under specific subjects (MUSICAL INSTRUMENTS—DICTIONARIES), as well as under names of authors and compilers.

Whether they are general or specific, international or national, the particular usefulness of encyclopedias and dictionaries lies in their orderly presentation of data. The writers do not pretend to cultivate a literary style or create "atmosphere" but strive to be succinct, accurate, and informative. The typically neat exposition and the attempt to keep information as objective as possible have led thesis advisers to recommend consultation of dictionaries and encyclopedias as a preliminary step to research. One may expect three types of questions to be answered:

1. Who or what is it? (Identification and definition)
2. How, when, and where did it develop? (Historical)
3. How does it work? (Analytical and descriptive)

Thus, not only do these references aid in defining and limiting one's subject but they may also provide some assistance in pointing the way to further, more detailed study.

## Lists: Bibliographies, Discographies, Catalogs, and Indexes

A bibliography is a list of written materials. In music it may include works about the subject (books, monographs, articles in journals) and items representing the sounds of a composition (scores, sheet music, instrumental parts, vocal part-books). Music bibliography first developed as a discipline in musicology (*Musikwissenschaft*) in Germany, where systematic studies in music history, theory, philosophy and psychology, and acoustics were first undertaken on a large scale. Adlung's *Introduction*[7] was possibly the earliest of the scholarly, critical bibliographies, followed

---

[7]Jacob Adlung, *Anleitung zu der musikalischen Gelahrheit*, 1758; 2nd ed. (Leipzig and Dresden: Breitkopf, 1783); fascimile reprint of 2nd ed. (Hildesheim: Olms, 1953).

by such others as Forkel's *Allgemeine Litteratur*[8] and Becker's *Darstellung*.[9] Subsequent lists representing musicological interests were issued in large number. Only recently has bibliography been developed in music education and ethnomusicology, but lists, representing serious work in these fields are impressive (e.g., Kunst's bibliography of ethnomusicology,[10] which contains more than 4,500 items).

Bibliographies range in length from a few pages in a book or journal to large volumes. They refer to music in general, with many divisions and subdivisions; to one aspect or one style of music; or to an individual composer or group of composers. They may contain all pertinent sources regardless of their availability, or they may be limited to items in print, to items recommended (as are lists appended to encyclopedia articles, "selected" bibliographies, "recommended readings"), or to those actually consulted in a piece of research (bibliographies in theses and dissertations). In some textbooks an extensive bibliography may be appended to the principal text. Other bibliographies have been discussed above in Chapters 8 and 9.

In a bibliography each entry is identified by the author, title of the work, and date of publication. Most compilers also include the place of publication and name of the publisher. When a work cited is part of a multivolume set, the volume number is given. An article in a periodical is identified by author, title of the article, name of the journal, the volume number and date, and the page(s) on which it is found. In lists of musical compositions, each entry contains name of composer, title, opus number (if any), place, publisher, and date of publication or of copyright. Sometimes, if similar titles are used for several works, the performing medium or instrumentation is specified. Annotated bibliographies contain notes describing or evaluating the items.

Among contemporary phenomena are the development of sound-reproducing techniques and the mushrooming of the record industry. Recordings provide not only a source of pleasurable listening and entertainment but a medium of research as well. So numerous and varied have they become that encyclopedias and guides to recordings have been issued, among them the following:

> Francis F., Clough and G. J. Cuming, *The World's Encyclopedia of Recorded Music*. London: Sidgwick & Jackson, Ltd., 1952; supplements, 1952, 1957.

[8] Johann N. Forkel, *Allgemeine Litteratur der Musik* (Leipzig: Schwikert, 1792); reprint (Hildesheim: Olms, 1962).

[9] Carl F. Becker, *Allgemeine systematisch-chronologische Darstellung der musikalischen Literatur von der frühesten bis auf die neueste Zeit* (Leipzig: R. Friese, 1836–1839); fascimile reprint (Hilversum, The Netherlands: Frits A. M. Knuf, 1964).

[10] Jaap Kunst, *Ethnomusicology* (3rd ed.), (The Hague: Nijhoff, 1959).

R. D. Darrell, comp., *Gramophone Shop Encyclopedia of Recorded Music*. New York: Gramophone Shop, Inc., 1936. 2nd ed., New York: Simon and Schuster, Inc., 1942. 3rd ed., New York: Crown Publishers, Inc., 1948.

Edward Greenfield, Ivan March, and Denis Stevens, *Stereo Record Guide*. London: The Long-Playing Record Library, Ltd., 1960–1961.

The term "discography" was coined to denote a list of recordings, and as long as the records were on discs, the meaning was obvious. With the growing number of available tape recordings, another term may become necessary. Data customarily included in a discography are composer, title, opus number, performing artist(s), recording company, and serial number of the disc. Some technical discographies may also give the matrix number. Discographies serve the same purpose for recordings as bibliographies do for written material. They may be general or selective, current or retrospective. Some are classified (items arranged in related groups) and some are annotated. They are a feature of many textbooks, especially those on music appreciation, and are an important adjunct to histories, biographies, and articles in learned journals. A useful tool for further study of discographies is the bibliography by Bruun and Gray.[11] Discographies for various types of music have also been discussed in Chapter 12, while periodicals dealing with records will be summarized in Chapter 17.

Because recordings are generally more expendable than books, and because a single composition may be recorded by several different performers and issued by several different companies, the problem of compiling record lists and keeping them up to date is a serious one; hence the proliferation of discographies and the rapid shifting of their contents. The student must accept this condition. In spite of seeming instability and flux, the record industry is thriving and its products are increasing in importance to the researcher.

A catalog is a list, arranged in an orderly fashion, of names and/or objects, sometimes with a brief description of each. Types of catalogs generally useful in music research include:

1. Composers' catalogs: lists of works by a given composer or by a group of composers. Besides indicating what has been written, they are useful for proper identification of works, their chronology and their attribution.

2. Thematic catalogs: lists of musical *incipits* or first lines. Usually arranged in chronological order or numerical order by opus, these lists provide positive identification in case of questionable attribution, or in instances in which

[11]Carl L. Bruun and John Gray, "A Bibliography of Discographies," *Recorded Sound* (Summer, 1962), pp. 206–213.

two or more works bear similar titles or are in the same key. By noting thematic material one may come closer to true identification than would be otherwise possible.

3. Publishers' catalogs: lists of publications issued by a company or group of companies. Generally speaking, current catalogs are most valuable in locating books and music in print; retrospective catalogs are practical for historical tracing of items which have been published in the past.

4. Dealers' catalogs: lists of items available for purchase at a given music store or through an agency.

5. Library catalogs: lists of holdings of libraries. Whether they are on cards or in book form, they provide information on materials and state where they are available. If a catalog is a union catalog, it indicates availability in several locations and may be regional, national, or even international (see above, pp. 50ff.).

6. Museum catalogs: lists of items exhibited or owned by collections. For musical iconography, a history of instruments, or a study involving music and art, they are practical and may constitute the sole approach to certain types of resources.

7. Exhibition catalogs: lists of items shown at an exhibition, e.g., *Richard Strauss Ausstellung, Wien, 1964*, compiled by Franz Grasberger and Franz Hadamousky (Vienna: Oesterreichische Nationalbibliothek, 1964), listing material shown at a special commemorative exhibit. Such catalogs are valuable in revealing unusual associated items such as letters, souvenirs, and autographs which might otherwise remain unknown.

8. National catalogs: lists of works published in a given country. Their importance has been discussed in Chapter 8.

Catalogs are arranged in the order considered most practical from the standpoint of their contents. They may appear in alphabetical order, in chronological sequence, or in classified groupings. They may vary in physical make-up—the book form and the card form are the most common.

The thematic catalog (also known as thematic index) needs an additional word. Compositions are listed in some predetermined order and identified by an *incipit* or theme from each piece or from each movement of a multimovement work. A full title, date of composition (or of publication or first performance), opus number, location of manuscript, particulars of publication, editions, performance time, and instrumentation are provided. Thematic catalogs are prepared for music of an individual composer, works by a group of composers, manuscripts within a library, and on any other pieces that require identification, dating, or attribution. The entries may be in chronological order by date of composition,[12] in

[12]Köchel's Mozart *Verzeichnis* is an example of a thematic catalog arranged in

numerical order or opus-number sequence,[13] in alphabetical order by title or first line of text, or in classified order by form or medium.[14] As stated earlier, thematic catalogs are a valuable aid in identifying a work in case of doubt arising from lack of opus number, from duplication or similarity of title or key between two works, or from questionable authorship. At present the Music Library Association's checklist of thematic catalogs (see above, p. 117) is the only such guide easily available in libraries. A revision of this list is projected.

Closely allied in aim to thematic catalogs but often poles apart in nature are the booklets containing *incipits* of popular music, pieces for band, teaching pieces, and choral octavo works. They are often incorporated into dealers' and publishers' catalogs and may be useful in locating pieces of special styles or grades of difficulty.

An index is a list, usually in alphabetical order, of items contained in a book or a series of books. Its purpose is to facilitate location of specific articles or subjects by giving the volume and page(s) where they are found, thus eliminating the necessity for thumbing through entire books in the search. Publishers often place indexes at the end of a volume or a series; in the case of periodicals they usually appear at the end of an accumulated annual volume. An index may exist as a separate publication and may list items in several or many books or sets of volumes. An example is *Songs in Collections*, locating individual songs in many anthologies.[15]

Like catalogs, indexes may be one large unit containing all entries in alphabetical sequence, or they may be divided into units by category. A book may contain several indexes: an index of names and places mentioned in the text, an index of subjects discussed, an index of a composer's works, and so on. The index may cover a single book or it may be cumulative. In such compilations as the Goodkind index to the *Musical Quarterly*, the list makes an accounting of material appearing over a period of years (1915–1959). On the other hand, an index may be selective, as in Kinscella's Americana index to the *Musical Quarterly*, which lists only items pertaining to Americana.

The terms "catalog" and "index" are not always differentiated. They are often used interchangeably, as Thematic Catalog and Thematic Index. Obviously, then, they both designate lists.

chronological order by date of composition, with catalog numbers assigned to each item.

[13]Georg Kinsky, *Das Werk Beethovens* (Munich: G. Henle, 1955), is a thematic catalog arranged by opus number.

[14]Franklin B. Zimmerman, *Henry Purcell, 1659–1695: An Analytical Catalogue of His Music* (London: Macmillan, 1963) is an example of a thematic catalog arranged by type of composition.

[15]Compiled by De Charms and Breed. See above, Chapter 11.

# Histories

Music histories are accounts of the beginnings, development, and progress of styles, forms, media, practice, and theory of music, together with some consideration of the persons involved. They range from general histories of world music to histories of tonal developments within a limited geographic area, time-span, medium, or form. Their value differs widely from one book to the next on the basis of quality. The value of a volume also fluctuates from one generation to the next, for historical concepts are constantly being altered by new discoveries and re-evaluation of established facts in the light of changing tastes. Although the histories by Burney[16] and Hawkins,[17] published in 1776, remain today important writings, most of the early historical accounts have long since been superseded by more recent studies. Twentieth-century books, often written as textbooks for college courses, are even more vulnerable to replacement.

Some important histories of music enjoying relative permanence in the scholarly field have been issued in a series or in a large symposium form, in which various authorities in specialized areas have contributed one or more volumes to a multivolume set. Three German examples may be cited:

> Hermann Krezschmar, ed., *Kleine Handbücher der Musikgeschichte nach Gattungen.* Leipzig: Breitkopf und Härtel, 1905–1922. 14 vols.
>
> Ernst Bücken, ed., *Handbuch der Musikwissenschaft.* Wildpark-Potsdam: Akademische Verlagsgesellschaft Athenaion, 1927–1931. Reprint, New York: Musurgia, 1949. 13 vols. in 9.
>
> Guido Adler, ed., *Handbuch der Musikgeschichte* (2nd ed.). Berlin-Wilmersdorf: Keller, 1930. Reprint of 2nd ed., Tutzing: Schneider, 1961. 2 vols.

(In these titles *Handbuch* means more than a mere manual.) The two series of Oxford Histories[18] are British examples. In the United States W. W. Norton has issued The Norton History of Music Series,[19] and

---

[16]Charles Burney, *A General History of Music* (London, 1776–1789); reprint (London: Foulis, 1935).

[17]Sir John Hawkins, *A General History of the Science and Practice of Music* (London, 1776); reprint of 1853 edition (New York: Dover Publications, Inc., 1963).

[18]The Oxford History of Music (2nd ed.), (London: Oxford University Press, 1929–1938). The New Oxford History of Music (London: Oxford University Press, 1954–    ). There is no duplication of authors between the two series.

[19]The Norton History of Music Series (New York: W. W. Norton & Company, Inc., 1940–    ).

Prentice-Hall has begun its Prentice-Hall History of Music Series.[20]
Some valuable histories have been written as one-author works, three
American examples being:

> Paul H. Lang, *Music in Western Civilization*. New York: W.
> W. Norton & Company, Inc., 1941.
>
> Alfred Einstein, *A Short History of Music* (3rd American
> ed.). New York: Alfred A. Knopf, Inc., 1947.
>
> Donald J. Grout, *A History of Western Music*. New York:
> W. W. Norton & Co., Inc., 1960.

Pincherle's *Illustrated History of Music*[21] is representative of a study with
commentary and pictures. Histories may also be in outline or modified
outline form:

> Harold Gleason, *Music Literature Outlines*, Series 1–5.
> Rochester, N. Y.: Levis, 1949–1955.
>
> Karl Nef, *An Outline of the History of Music*, trans. Carl
> Pfatteicher. New York: Columbia University Press, 1935.

Each form of presentation has its strengths. The multivolume series, for
which several authors write one or two volumes apiece, has the advantage
of an authoritative approach. Each volume is by an acknowledged scholar
concentrating on his specialty without dissipating his energies upon aspects
of music which may hold little interest for him, and the reader may expect
maximum enthusiasm as well as depth of knowledge. On the other hand,
some lack of unity between individual volumes of a series may arise from
individual differences in viewpoint and in literary style. Although every
contributor may be an authority, the same degree of success is not necessarily achieved by all of them.

In a one-author work, the style is generally consistent and the point of
view clearly defined, but because no one can be equally knowledgeable in
all areas of a subject as vast as the history of music, some unevenness is
bound to occur in the coverage of material. The maximum interest is well-
nigh impossible to sustain throughout a large work; all periods of history
cannot equally stimulate the writer's imagination and enthusiasm.

Although the outline history is succinct and easily grasped, it is not
conducive to interpretation. Facts may be completely accurate but they
remain "cold." The fine literary style which one associates with the best
scholarly writing is rarely possible in skeletal form.

In writing a history, the author ideally should essay accuracy of statement and fairness of interpretation. It is not humanly possible, however,

[20]Prentice-Hall History of Music Series, edited by H. Wiley Hitchcock (Englewood Cliffs: Prentice-Hall, 1965–     ).
[21]Marc Pincherle, *An Illustrated History of Music*, trans. Rollo Myers (New
York: Harcourt, Brace & World, Inc., 1959).

to avoid some personal bias in even the most objective accounts; one perceives from his point of view and interprets accordingly. Indeed, such interpretation adds the human element which saves history from becoming merely a succession of facts and dates. Thesis directors encourage students to read as many historical accounts as possible and to consider many divergent opinions in order to arrive at something approximating the truth. They encourage the study of the most recently issued histories as well as standard works to obtain the newest interpretations and latest available data. In view of the new facts constantly being disclosed, it is generally better to look for them in recent publications, while simultaneously being careful not to neglect the fine older accounts.

Closely allied to histories are anthologies of musical examples tracing the development of music:

> Willi Apel and Archibald T. Davidson, *Historical Anthology of Music*. Cambridge, Mass.: Harvard University Press, 1946–1950, 1962. 2 vols.
>
> Harold Gleason, *Examples of Music before 1400*. New York: Appleton-Century-Crofts, Inc., 1942.
>
> Arnold Schering, *Geschichte der Musik in Beispielen*. Leipzig: Breitkopf und Härtel, 1931. Reprint, New York: Broude Bros., 1950.

They are not histories in the sense that they are written accounts, but rather are collections of music illustrating different styles, to be used in conjunction with texts.

# Biographical Materials

Biographies and autobiographies are accounts of a person's life and works. A researcher reads them to gain knowledge of a person, of the background of the society in which he functioned, and of his colleagues.

A biography may be written for various reasons, the most common being:

1. To document the subject's life by the presentation of known facts
2. To reveal a personality representative of some society
3. To prove or disprove a thesis about a person
4. To debunk

Several purposes are served simultaneously in most biographies. Depending upon the subject, the writer's ultimate aim, and his point of view, the presentation may vary greatly from one biography to another.

Because one's professional achievements are an integral part of his life, it is necessary in writing about a musician to write about his music. For example, Waters, in his life of Victor Herbert,[22] uses a straight narrative method, working chronologically from the beginning to the end of his subject's life. Because Herbert the man and Herbert the musician merge into a single personality, whose career was possible only in America and only in his generation, Waters has interwoven the music into the account in a way that presents an image of the whole man. The narrative is continuous up to the last chapter, which gives a critical summary and evaluation, and the biography is documented by a catalog of works, a discography, notes by chapters, and an index.

Alban Berg, the subject of a biography by Redlich,[23] was quite a different character from Herbert, far less peripatetic, having fewer involvements. Redlich's narrative therefore is a framework for extensive analysis (with musical examples) of Berg's style and methods, with some attention paid to certain important works. Both Waters and Redlich have produced informative, scholarly works, yet each biography is individual and distinctive, with differences not only in subject but also in literary style, emphasis, and end result.

If his subject is a complex character or has a large and varied output, the biographer may be obliged to view his subject's career from different angles. Einstein's treatment of Mozart[24] is an example. His book is divided into several large sections, the first dealing with the development of Mozart as a man. Although the music is mentioned, the emphasis is upon the life story. Later, Einstein considers him in the light of universality and in relation to his contemporaries. He dwells upon the processes and techniques of Mozart's composition. He devotes another portion of his book to an analytical and aesthetic discussion of Mozart's instrumental works, vocal music, and operas. The biography is thus sectionalized but the coordinated whole becomes a complete study.

In the symposium type of biography several authors, each contributing a section on some aspect of the subject's life and works, write a composite study. *Handel: A Symposium*, edited by Abraham,[25] is an example. Following a presentation of Handel as a man, there are sections by various writers dealing with large groups of compositions (such as oratorios, operas, church music), and the whole is unified by a summary of the Handelian style, a list of works, a chronology, and bibliography.

[22]Edward N. Waters, *Victor Herbert: A Life in Music* (New York: The Macmillan Company, 1955).

[23]H. F. Redlich, *Alban Berg: The Man and His Music* (New York: Abelard-Schuman Limited, 1947).

[24]Alfred Einstein, *Mozart, His Character, His Work*, trans. Arthur Mendel and Nathan Broder (London: Oxford University Press, 1945).

[25]Gerald E. H. Abraham, ed., *Handel: A Symposium* (London, New York: Oxford University Press, 1954).

An author may write about several people in a single book if the subjects are related by nationality, by style, or by school.[26] This method, allowing for a comparative exposition of the interrelations of style and mutual influence, is effective when applied to a small number of individuals. It loses its effectiveness when so many subjects are introduced that the book becomes a miniature biographical dictionary, and interpretation through comparison and contrast becomes difficult or even impossible.

The above-mentioned books strive for factual accuracy and a scholarly presentation. Documentation by the inclusion of records, correspondence, and other primary sources is part of the biographical method. Catalogs of works, bibliographies, and discographies are typical research aids included with the text. Interpretation, as well as chronology, is an important, integral part of the biography.

Similarly striving for accuracy are biographies re-evaluating a subject. Johnson's study of Sibelius[27] is a case in point. By revealing both the composer's greatness and his weakness, Johnson gives perhaps a truer, more human image of Sibelius than do some of the panegyrics of earlier writers. Written with a perspective unattainable 20 or 30 years ago, his book places the composer more accurately in the history of twentieth-century music. New assessments are a part of cultural evolution; it is reasonable to expect a researcher to read both early and recent biographies to gain perspective.

Biographers may interpret a person's life in the light of the society in which he functioned. Barzun's account of Berlioz as an embodiment of the nineteenth-century spirit[28] accomplishes this so well that one cannot separate the philosophies, behavior patterns, character, and music of Berlioz from the mainstream of life in his time. This is re-evaluation of another sort, adding dimension to biographical studies.

When an author writes from personal acquaintance rather than from documentation, as Liszt did in his treatment of Chopin,[29] he does not necessarily strive for objectivity. He may give a biased opinion and be quite aware that he is doing so. Although the student may not accept the writer's assessment at face value, he does get a contemporary's reaction to his subject and achieve an insight into his character, his techniques, and ultimately his music. Likewise, an anecdotal, intimate work like *Duet with Nicky*[30] may prove rewarding for the same reasons.

[26]An example is Mikhail O. Zetlin, *The Five: The Evolution of the Russian School of Music*, trans. George Panin (New York: International Universities Press, 1959).

[27]Harold E. Johnson, *Jean Sibelius* (New York: Alfred A. Knopf, Inc., 1959).

[28]Jacques Barzun, *Berlioz and the Romantic Century* (Boston: Little, Brown and Company, 1950).

[29]Franz Liszt, *Frederic Chopin*, trans. Edward N. Waters (New York: The Free Press of Glencoe, 1963).

[30]Alice Berezowsky, *Duet with Nicky* (Philadelphia: J. B. Lippincott Company, 1943).

Autobiographies and memoirs are valuable revelations of a person's character, artistic credo, and relations with his contemporaries. Circumstances of composition and the musician's self-assessment are two important types of information which may be impossible to glean from a biography. Rimsky-Korsakov,[31] for example, is sometimes critical of his own works, evaluating certain pieces with amazing candor. Stravinsky[32] tells in some detail the reasons and occasions for which he wrote some of his works and comments upon the reception by performers and audiences.

The purpose and viewpoint of a biographer may be revealed in his preface. If his tone is belligerent or he clamors for attention, the reader may expect some bias. On the other hand, if he gives indication of a serious aim, citing the sources of his documentation, the reader may expect at the least an honest attempt at a scholarly biography. Although a writer, being human, cannot avoid some subjectivity, he should be willing to use such primary sources as correspondence and records to achieve a measure of objective accuracy.

Fictionalized biographies must be read with caution. A novelist feels free to manipulate his materials to achieve a dramatic story even at the expense of truth. Less reliable still are works deliberately aimed at debunking or degrading the subject. Such works are usually exaggerated, even sensational; facts used out of context may become distorted and be used as barbs to puncture one's reputation, and criticism may turn into attack. Scurrilous writing is not a characteristic of the reliable biographer.

The achievement of historical perspective is important to research. Musical taste changes constantly. New data continue to be made available. Each writer tends to view his subject from his point of view and to express opinions in the light of his own times. To study only a single biography (unless it is the only one available) is to limit oneself unwisely. An investigator should read as many works as possible to learn all available facts, simultaneously being discriminating and receptive.

# Analytical Guides

To assist in harmonic, contrapuntal, structural, formal, and stylistic analysis (including technical devices, instrumentation, and other elements) as an adjunct to interpretation and understanding of music, there are works which in many libraries are classified as *analytical guides*. Such guides and

[31]Nikolai A. Rimsky-Korsakov, *My Musical Life*, trans. Judah A. Joffe (New York: Alfred A. Knopf, Inc., 1942).
[32]Igor Stravinsky, *Igor Stravinsky: An Autobiography* (New York: W. W. Norton & Company, Inc., 1962).

handbooks became popular during the nineteenth century when music under royal patronage waned, and concert activity as we know it today became increasingly important. They may cover large repertoires including a variety of forms and styles, the works of a selected group of composers, the music of individual writers, or a single major work.

Some analytical guides are simply written and are addressed to the cultured layman, while others, aimed at the musical scholar, are highly technical. Some are derived from program annotations, and some constitute chapters or sections of biographies and history texts. For guides published separately, the student may consult the library catalog; in libraries using subject headings of the Library of Congress there should be subject entries under ANALYTICAL GUIDES. For items included as parts of books, one must investigate the indexes and tables of contents of the pertinent volumes.

Some typical examples of guides follow:

Hermann Kretzschmar, *Führer durch den Concertsaal.* Leipzig: Liebeskind, 1887–1890. A general guide, surveying the province of concert music; includes symphony and suite, sacred music (Passion settings, Masses, hymns, Psalms, motets), choral works (cantatas, oratorios, and miscellaneous choruses); one of the early standard guides.

Phillip Hale, *Great Concert Music.* New York: Garden City Books, 1939. Based upon the author's program notes for the Boston Symphony Orchestra; a guide to selected concert pieces.

Rudolf Kloiber, *Handbuch der klassischen und romantischen Symphonie.* Wiesbaden: Breitkopf und Härtel, 1964. A guide to selected symphonic works.

Ezra William Doty, *The Analysis of Form in Music.* New York: Appleton-Century-Crofts, Inc., 1947. Example of a formal guide.

Allen Forte, *Contemporary Tone Structures.* New York: Columbia University Press, 1955. Example of guide to compositional devices, with analysis of selected works.

Leopold Auer, *Violin Master Works and Their Interpretation.* New York: Carl Fischer, Inc., 1925. Example of a guide for the performer.

Alfred Cortot, *Studies in Musical Interpretation.* London: George G. Harrap and Co., Ltd., 1937. Handbook of piano music and its interpretation; principally for the performer.

Eric Blom, *Beethoven's Pianoforte Sonatas Discussed.* London: J. M. Dent & Sons, Ltd., 1938. Handbook for one form of music for one medium.

Johann Nepomuk David, *Die Jupiter-Symphonie: Eine Studie über die thematisch-melodischen Zusammenhänge.* Göttingen: Deuerlichsche Verlagsbuchhandlung, 1953. An analytical study of a single composition from a thematic point of view.

In addition to providing assistance in analysis and interpretation, analytical guides often include bibliographies and discographies for further investigation. Many handbooks contain musical examples, graphs, charts, or other visual devices.

## Commemorative Volumes

Interesting, informative essays and bibliographies are found in commemorative volumes or *Festschriften*, compiled and published to honor a person (on the occasion of an anniversary, a birthday, or retirement from active service) or to celebrate a significant event (a centennial of a publishing house, for example). Papers are contributed by colleagues, friends, or pupils of the one being honored, or by people associated with the event being celebrated. Some *Festschriften*, those for which each author is asked to write about a topic of his own choice (usually in the field in which he is an authority), become collections of essays on a variety of subjects. Others, for which writers prepare an appreciation, tribute, memoir, or summary of the honored person's accomplishments, become a unified symposium on life and works of the subject.

Commemorative writings became popular during the nineteenth century, and increased in both number and variety during the twentieth. Because they bear titles not necessarily descriptive of their contents, and because the individual essays may not appear in ordinary bibliographical tools, there has arisen a demand for a comprehensive listing and index to *Festschriften*. Ernst Krohn's article in *Notes*[33] is a discussion and survey, with a catalog, of commemorative publications. It has been followed by Walter Gerboth's extensive index,[34] a comprehensive classified bibliographical treatment for locating individual essays in specific volumes. The excellence and easy availability of both the Krohn article and the Gerboth index make further discussion of *Festschriften* unnecessary, except for the reminder that essays in such volumes should not be overlooked in research.

[33]Ernst C. Krohn, "Musical Festschriften and Related Publications," *Notes*, XVIII (1964), 94–108.

[34]Walter Gerboth, "Index of Festschriften and Some Similar Publications," *Aspects of Medieval and Renaissance Music: A Birthday Offering to Gustave Reese* (New York: W. W. Norton & Company, Inc., 1966), pp. 183–307.

## Publications of Information
## Centers and Composers' Groups

In several culturally active countries, national information or documentation centers for music or societies of composers and publishers exist to promote performance opportunities for creative artists, the publication of music for consumption both at home and abroad, and the dissemination of information about musical activities. Support for such an agency may be public (or state) or private. In some countries several societies may operate as centers.

Documentation centers characteristically publish catalogs, bio-bibliographical lists for outstanding musicians, and bulletins or journals. Whatever form the materials take, they are valuable to the scholar, sometimes providing otherwise unobtainable biographical and bibliographical data. Some agencies also issue music, which may be procured for study or for performance.

The American Music Center, Inc., designated by the National Music Council as the documentation center for music in the United States, publishes *Music Today* (1958–    ), a bimonthly bulletin giving information on grants, contests, and commissions; first performances of works by American composers; and news of the International Society for Contemporary Music (ISCM).

The American Composers Alliance, with a membership of some 120 American composers, publishes a *Bulletin* (1953–    ). Nearly every issue contains a biographical sketch and an annotated catalog of one or two composers who are members of the Alliance, and in some cases the *Bulletin* is the source of the most comprehensive data about them. Moreover, articles and current news are featured, with accounts of premières and lists of recent works.

Broadcast Music, Inc. (BMI), a licensing organization, publishes an annual brochure (*Concert Music, U.S.A.*), a bulletin entitled *News About BMI Music and BMI Writers*, with brief notices about composers, new music, performances, and prizes and commissions, and a large series of bio-bibliographical leaflets on individual composers whose performing rights have been entrusted to the society. Containing a short biography, a photograph, and an annotated list of major works, the leaflets are valuable for the study of contemporary American music.

The American Society of Composers, Authors, and Publishers (ASCAP), a copyright-protection organization with a large membership including more than a thousand composers, has a biographical dictionary with a list of composition up to the middle 1960's.[35]

A regional organization, the Southeastern Composers League publishes an occasional bulletin, and in 1962 it issued a catalog. Some 80 composers from Alabama, Arkansas, Florida, Kentucky, Louisiana, Mississippi, North Carolina, South Carolina, Tennessee, Virginia, and West Virginia are represented in a list of works arranged by form and medium and giving the number of movements, instrumentation, grade of difficulty, and the publisher or agency where pieces may be obtained.

Other representative bio-bibliographical catalogs may be mentioned:

> *Latin-American Orchestral Music Available in the United States.* Washington: Pan American Union, 1956.
>
> *Composers of the Americas.* Washington: Pan American Union, 1955–
>
> *Catalogue des oeuvres de compositeurs belges.* Brussels: Fonds Danièle Cohen-Deswarts, 1953–  . Individual pamphlets compiled for the Centre Belge de Documentation Musicale (CeBeDeM).
>
> *Catalogue van Werken van Nederlandse Componisten.* Amsterdam: Donemus, 1954–  . Individual pamphlets for contemporary Dutch composers.
>
> Eduard Reeser and Wouter Paap, comps., *Contemporary Music from Holland.* Amsterdam: Donemus, 1953. Material on twelve Dutch composers.
>
> *40 Swiss Composers.* Amriswil: Bodensee-Verlag, 1956. Accounts of composers whose works have been chosen over a quarter-century (1930–1954) by three national juries for the annual festivals of the Swiss Composers' League or for the festivals of the International Society for Contemporary Music.
>
> Tauno Karila, comp., *Composers of Finland.* Helsinki: Suomen Säveltäjät, 1961. Issued under auspices of the Association of Finnish Composers; introductory pages contain brief history of Finnish music.
>
> *Catalogue of Finnish Orchestral Works and Vocal Works.* Helsinki: Teosto, 1961. Published by the Composers' Copyright Bureau; includes data about twentieth-century Finnish composers, most of whom were active in 1960.
>
> *Catalogue.* Copenhagen: Samfundet til Udgivelse af Dansk

---

[35]Daniel I. McNamara, ed., *ASCAP Biographical Dictionary of Composers, Authors, and Publishers* (2nd ed.), (New York: Thomas Y. Crowell Co., 1952), (3rd ed., comp. and ed. by The Lynn Farnol Group, Inc.), (New York: The American Society of Composers, Authors, and Publishers, 1966).

> Musik, 1956; supplement, 1964. Prepared by Dan Fog, a leading Danish music bibliographer for the Society for Publishing Danish Music; includes works published by the society.

The above represents a sampling of items. Some libraries classify and catalog such works, in which case one may consult the catalog cards. In libraries in which lists are treated as pamphlet literature, one should look in the pamphlet file or ask the librarian for assistance in locating them.

The periodicals issued by documentation centers and composers' societies are a source of information on contemporary activity in their respective countries. Some typical examples are:

> *Composer: The Journal of the Composers' Guild of Great Britain* (1958–    ). Includes articles, lists of new works, composer-profiles, announcements of competitions, and reviews.

> *Sonorum speculum: Mirror of Dutch Musical Life* (1958–    ). A quarterly journal issued in Amsterdam by Donemus; gives data on new works by Dutch composers and their performances over the world, historical aspects of Dutch music, and composer profiles.

> *Musical Denmark* (1950–    ). The bulletin of Det Danske Selskab, Institute for Information about Denmark and Cultural Cooperation with Other Countries; includes summary of Danish musical activity, lists of new music, recent books, and music.

# BIBLIOGRAPHY

Bruun, Carl L., and John Gray, "A Bibliography of Discographies," *Recorded Sound* (Summer, 1962), 206–213.

Coover, James, *Music Lexicography, Including a Study of Lacunae in Music Lexicography and a Bibliography of Music Dictionaries.* Denver: Denver Public Library, 1958.

Duckles, Vincent, *Music Reference and Research Materials.* New York: The Free Press of Glencoe, 1964.

Eggebrecht, Hans Heinrich, "Lexika der Musik," *Die Musik in Geschichte und Gegenwart: Allgemeine Enzyklopädie der Musik* (1960), VIII, cols. 685–699.

Gerboth, Walter, "Index of Festschriften and Some Similar Publications," *Aspects of Medieval and Renaissance Music: A Birthday Offering to Gustave Reese.* New York: W. W. Norton & Company, Inc., 1966, pp. 183–307.

Haydon, Glen, *Introduction to Musicology.* Englewood Cliffs, N. J.: Prentice-Hall, Inc., 1941.

King, Alexander Hyatt, "Dictionaries and Encyclopedias," *Grove's Dictionary of Music and Musicians* (1954), II, 691–700.

Krohn, Ernst C., "Musical Festschriften and Related Publications," *Notes*, XVIII (1964), 94–108.

Schaal, Richard, "The Fore-runners of the Grove-Blom: A Bibliography of Musical Dictionaries in Chronological Order," *Hinrichsen's Musical Year Book*, VII (1952), 594–601.

Spiess, Lincoln B., *Historical Musicology*. Brooklyn, N. Y.: The Institute of Mediaeval Music, 1962.

Winchell, Constance, *Guide to Reference Books*, and supplements. Chicago: American Library Association, 1951–    .

# 17

## Survey of Contemporary
## Music Periodicals

### Introduction

Music periodicals have existed since the eighteenth century.[1] Johann Mattheson's *Critica musica* began publication in 1772,[2] Johann Adolf Schiebe's *Der critische Musicus* in 1737, and the *Journal de musique française et italienne* in 1764. There were others. During the nineteenth century their number was augmented, and their importance increased as critics and scholars expounded their ideas in print. Periodicals were issued for the amusement and enlightenment of the cultured musical amateur in America as well as abroad. Among the products of this century were the *American Musical Times* (New York, 1847) and *Dwight's Journal of Music* (Boston, 1852).

The growth of periodical literature in the twentieth century has been rapid, in spite of grave setbacks during both World Wars. The number of journals begun in the past two decades is remarkable, though admittedly not as large in the arts as in the sciences. One finds an urgency in the way articles are being written. New techniques and interests, a growing public, increased efficiency of communication, and perhaps the compulsion felt by scholars to publish have conspired to add so many new journals that now literally hundreds of them deal with music.

Because a study of the complete range of music periodicals is impossible in this book, the following is but a sampling of basic types of contempo-

[1] For a history of music journals, see Alexander Hyatt King, "Periodicals," *Grove's Dictionary of Music and Musicians* (1954), VI, 637–672; supplement 344–347.
[2] Johann Mattheson, *Critica musica* (Hamburg, 1722–1725) is now available in reprint (Hilversum, The Netherlands, Frits A. M. Knuf, 1964).

rary serials, with brief notes about those journals most likely to be found in American libraries.[3] Because the value of any periodical is realized only after study by the researcher, the comments indicate merely general character and policy.

## The Musical Current-Events Periodical[4]

Every musically active nation has periodicals designed to keep readers informed on activities of the concert world. Publications aimed at national circulation have extensive coverage, while those localized in distribution have correspondingly limited coverage. In general, musical news journals of national scope have the following traits:

1. Feature articles are of interest to the concert-goer and treat many subjects. A sampling of current issues reveals a heterogeneous list of topics ranging from folk song to electronic music, from Bach to Bartók, and from international festivals to small recitals.

2. Signed reviews of concerts and festivals are of sufficient depth to indicate the nature of the music as well as the excellence of the performance. An accumulation of such reviews over a period of years reflects changes in musical styles and tastes.

3. Reviews of new books, music, and records are regularly included.

4. Although notices from other countries may appear in the news and foreign publications may be included in the reviews, the emphasis is usually upon the national, or domestic, scene.

5. Concert calendars, previews of future programs, announcements of commissions and awards, and vital statistics are included.

*Musical Courier* (1880–1962) and *Musical America* (1898–    ) are examples of American current-events journals, combining articles of general musical importance with a chronicle of activities: concert critiques,

[3]Those often consulted in the 110 libraries represented at Music Library Workshops (Eastman School of Music Summer Sessions, 1957–1959, 1961, 1963, 1965) and those frequently requested at the Sibley Music Library. Only journals in print as of July, 1966, are cited, with the exception of a few others used for illustrative purposes.

[4]Journals on musical events issued by national information centers, societies of publishers and composers, and special organizations were discussed in Chapter 16. Popular and jazz periodicals are not included.

notices of premières, and reviews of books and records. Illustrated with photographs of people and scenes from stage productions, both publications provide a pictorial as well as a verbal record of concert life. Unfortunately, *Musical Courier* ceased publication in 1962.

In August, 1965, *Musical America* was incorporated into *High Fidelity*, issued monthly from Great Barrington, Massachusetts. Divided into two sections, the new periodical serves a dual purpose. The *High Fidelity* section deals with sound reproduction (see below, p. 204). The *Musical America* section continues the policy of the original journal and includes articles on music and musicians, "Mephisto's Musings," concert reviews, a necrology, and some international music news.

*Music Journal* (1943–    ), originally *Music Publishers Journal*, appears ten times yearly from New York. It offers articles on a wide variety of subjects, some newsworthy, some technical, and some controversial. *Music Journal* differs from the usual current-events periodical in that articles of topical interest are given more importance than the reporting of concerts; the *Journal* is a forum for discussion of contemporary musical questions (not necessarily dealing with new music), with prominent leaders contributing their opinions. Some issues are devoted to special topics (e.g., brass-instrument literature, instruction, and history in the issue for January, 1966). By reading the many articles, one may keep abreast of current thinking on musical subjects. Other features of the *Journal* include reviews of new books, music, and records (both discs and tapes); announcements of competitions, grants, and commissions; accounts of premières; news of music schools; an opera and concert calendar for New York; news of the music industry; and notes on jazz.

An example of localized news coverage is the monthly *Musical Leader* (1896–    ). Though widely circulated, its emphasis is upon music of the Middle West, with attention focused on events in and around Chicago. Concerts in the Far West and the East receive brief notice. Personal news, "Periscopes," and activities of national fraternal organizations and conservatories are featured.

*Musical Times* (1844–    ), originally *Musical Times and Singing Class Circular*, is a British journal found in many American libraries. A monthly publication, it contains articles on music and musicians of the past and present; concert criticism, foreign as well as British; reviews of new records (including jazz), books, and music; a department for organ and choral music, with reviews of occasional music (principally works for Easter, Christmas, and other holidays); vital statistics; letters; an "Amateurs' Exchange"; and a "London Diary" of events in the English capital. Sometimes a source study (e.g., Hudson's Stanford bibliography[5]) is

---

[5]Frederick Hudson, "C. V. Stanford, Nova Bibliographica," *Musical Times*, CIV (October, 1963), 728–831.

included. Because of its long, continuous publication, *Musical Times* can be used to trace trends and changing tastes in Britain. A musical supplement accompanies each issue.

*Music and Musicians* (1952–    ) is issued monthly by Hansom Books Ltd., London, as one of a family of seven journals on the arts.[6] With a British emphasis but wide coverage, it contains signed articles on musical styles, composers, and performers; "Commentary"—editorial comments; "Counterpoint"—news items; and "Musicguide"—a day-to-day calendar of concerts and opera performances published at least a month in advance. Reviews are extensive, with events in London receiving the greatest attention. Critiques on records comprise a large section, while reviews of books and music are somewhat shorter. Because of its attractive format, with many illustrations and photographs, *Music and Musicians* is a favorite with American readers wishing to know about English musical events.

*Musical Opinion* (1877–    ), formerly *Musical Opinion and Music Trade Review*, is published monthly in London and comprises articles on concerts, opera, and ballet in London and music news from the Continent; a chronicle of brass and military band music; brief reviews of scores arranged by classification; radio in retrospect; extensive criticisms of records; and book reviews. "Organ World" contains notices of organ recitals and recently published organ music. "Music Trade Forum" deals with the music industry and instrument making.

The venerable *Neue Zeitschrift für Musik* (1834–    ), published monthly in Mainz, is a journal of musical criticism emphasizing West German activities. A periodical with a complicated history, founded by Robert Schumann and continuing his serious critical policy, it includes articles on many subjects; "Musikleben"—concert and festival reviews from international music centers; information about premières, works in progress, celebrations, and activities in conservatories; and reviews of selected books, scores, and records. The *Neue Zeitschrift* is important as a continuous chronicle of German music and criticism. In its earliest years it was the repository of Schumann's prophetic comments. A "Notenbeilage" or musical supplement accompanies each issue. Most libraries which implement music research subscribe to the journal.

The East German *Musik und Gesellschaft*, issued monthly in Berlin, contains articles and reviews serving a purpose similar to that of *Musical Times* for Britain.

The Netherlands journal, *Mens en Melodie* (1946–    ), published monthly in Utrecht, contains brief articles, conservatory news, reviews of scores and records, criticisms of both Dutch and foreign concerts, and

---

[6]Others: *Art and Artists, Dance and Dancers, Films and Filming, Plays and Players, Records and Recording, and Books and Bookmen*, the whole assembled into *The Seven Arts.*

personal notes. Another periodical, *Euphonia* (1919–    ), combined with *Symphonia* (1917–    ), gives a monthly summary of current events. Although *Mens en Melodie* and *Euphonia/Symphonia* appear slim, considering the brisk musical activity in The Netherlands, they offer adequate coverage. The effective Dutch information agency, Donemus, publicizes contemporary music and musicians in its periodical, *Sonorum speculum* (see Chapter 16), and together these various publications offer a good survey of musical life.

The Swedish *Musik Revy: Nordisk Tidskrift för Musik och Grammofon* (1946–    ), is published eight times a year in Stockholm. It includes articles, current news, reviews of concerts and records, and notices of new scores. Some issues are devoted to special subjects. During 1965, Number 2 was on Hungarian composers, Number 3 on festivals, and Number 7 on recording and sound equipment.

*La Revue musicale de Suisse Romande* (1948–    ), issued quarterly in Lausanne, consists of an editorial; articles on contemporary and past musicians and their works, as well as on timely general topics affecting concert-goers; notices of concerts and festivals, both Swiss and international; reviews of programs in the French-speaking parts of Switzerland; reviews of books and records; and a news miscellany entitled "Echos et nouvelles du monde musical."

Although several Latin-American republics have their own music journals, the Latin-American periodical most readily available to the North American reader is the bimonthly *Boletín interamericano de música* (1957–    ), issued in Spanish by the Pan American Union in Washington as the successor to the *Boletín de música y artes visuales* (1950–1957). With international coverage, it contains accounts of the most important presentations of music and ballet in the Americas, with reviews arranged in alphabetical order by countries. A summary of European music activity, lists of new scores, books, and recordings, and catalogs of outstanding composers' works are included. The *Boletín* is accompanied by the *Inter-American Music Bulletin*, an English supplement with contents differing from those of the Spanish journal. In the *Bulletin* such topics as Pan-American music festivals, Latin-American periodicals, or significant composers' groups are treated. Number 17 (May, 1960) is a periodical index, "Latin-American Performing Arts, An Analytical Index: 1957–1958," compiled by S. Yancey Belknap.

In addition, some South American periodicals should be mentioned, for they are available in many libraries.[7] *La Revista musical Chilena* (1945–    ), published bimonthly by the Music Faculty of the University of

---

[7]For a list and description of other Latin-American journals, see Irene Zimmerman, *A Guide to Current Latin-American Periodicals: Humanities and Social Sciences* (Gainesville, Fla.: Kallman Publishing Co., 1961).

Chile at Santiago, consists of articles on music pedagogy, contemporary styles, and music history. Chilean musical activity is reviewed in critiques, notes from conservatories, and announcements. International events are summarized, with attention given to festivals in Western Europe and the United States. Nearly every issue contains brief notes on books and scores, and some also include concise record reviews. "Revista de revistas" gives a résumé of the principal contents of selected journals from other countries.

*Buenos Aires musical* (1946–     ), issued either monthly or bimonthly depending upon circumstances, contains an editorial, news of events in Buenos Aires, "Síntesis crítica de conciertos"—notes on concerts, and reviews of new compositions and recordings. Some special issues are devoted to musical activity in other countries.

The *Boletín de programas* (1944–     ), appearing every few months from the Instituto Nacional de Radio y Televisión in Bogotá, Columbia, is a profusely illustrated journal with many articles on all aspects of music. In spite of its title, which suggests merely a program booklet, the *Boletín* is in fact a combination schedule of broadcast concerts, festival calendar, musicological journal, and news magazine. Topics for discussion are chosen with catholic taste, and music is treated not only alone but in relation to the other arts and to cultural history as well.

From 1956 to 1962 the *Canadian Music Journal*, published quarterly in Toronto by the Canadian Music Council, gave an excellent account of music in Canada. The coverage was extensive and the articles well documented. Unfortunately the journal is defunct and has not been replaced by a comparable periodical.

*Canon: Australian Music Journal* (1947–     ), published monthly in Sydney, contains news articles, accounts of festivals in Australia, and brief notices of events elsewhere, with concert criticisms, book and music reviews, and a necrology. From time to time the greater portion of an issue may be devoted to a single topic, with special articles and features pertaining to it.

A quick overview of the world's musical activity may be obtained through *The World of Music* (1959–     ), bimonthly bulletin of the International Music Council. A leading article and notes on events of the season, publications, radio, and recordings are included, together with some illustrations. A list of first performances and competitions is included. All articles are given in English, French, and German.

Though not strictly a news journal, the *Bulletin* of the National Music Council (1940–     ), published irregularly, keeps one up on such important items as the latest proposed legislation affecting music, activities of the 54 member organizations of the Council, news of UNESCO, and the like. The Council, a nonprofit group, is made up of representatives from the most important American national societies of music and presents a cross-section of thought and action in the field. Though American in representation, its interests may have international significance.

## The Current-Events-Scholarly Journal

Some periodicals treat both scholarly topics (historical, theoretical, analytical) and current musical events. Possessing qualities of both learned journal and news magazine, they are neither strictly one nor the other. An example is the *Oesterreichische Musikzeitschrift* (1946–    ), issued monthly except when double numbers appear. Leading scholars contribute articles on a variety of subjects, some being documented with musical examples, illustrations, and bibliographies. On special occasions the entire issue may be devoted to a single event; the number for June-July, 1962, for example, deals with the reopening of the Theater an der Wien. Some issues are celebration numbers honoring one person (e.g., the issue for September, 1963, commemorates Otto Erich Deutsch's eightieth birthday). Still others contain subject bibliographies. Side by side with such features are extensive reviews of concerts in Austria, with some notice given to programs in other countries, general news items, activities of music academies, and reviews of recently published books and scores. The *Zeitscrift* has an annual index.

*Musica: Zweimonatsschrift für alle Gebiete des Musiklebens* (1947–    ), combined with *Hausmusik* (1932–    ), is published bimonthly by Bärenreiter-Verlag in Kassel. Articles dealing with many aspects of music are featured in each issue. Information is given on congresses, festivals, and meetings. Personal data (birthdays, celebrations, and obituaries, with appropriate biographical material) are a regular feature. The many reviews comprise criticisms of current books and scores, records, and outstanding musical tapes. Equipment—record players, amplifiers, speakers, and transistor sets—also receives comment. Although the coverage is predominantly West German, significant events in other parts of the world are noted.

The *Schweizerische Musikzeitung/ Revue musicale suisse* (1961–    ), published bimonthly in Zurich, is the journal of the Association of Swiss Musicians, the Swiss Society of Music Pedagogy, and SUISA, the national organization of authors and editors. Its contents include analytical essays on contemporary composers and their techniques, articles on performance practices, pedagogy of music, reviews of new Swiss music, lists of works by Swiss writers performed in recital and concert programs, a bibliography of new books on music, and lists of articles from selected periodicals. Musical examples and illustrations are used. Although other languages may sometimes be used, German and French predominate. The journal has an annual index.

*Dansk Musiktidsskrift* (1925–      ) merged in 1959 with *Nordisk Musikkultur* (1952–      ). The new journal, published eight times per year in Copenhagen, reflects the interests of the Danish Young Musicians Society (the Danish section of the International Society for Contemporary Music). It contains articles of scholarly value, some being analyses of compositions; lists of major concerts and festivals; a music calendar; and a summary of selected articles appearing in various foreign music periodicals. Reviews of books, music, and records are quite extensive, as are some of the discussions of music teaching and comments on pedagogical literature.

## The Scholarly or Learned Journal

Learned journals in music are usually concerned with musicology, ethnomusicology, theory, and "new music." Musicology in this case means the systematic study of music in its various aspects—historical, analytical, and acoustical. The journals have the following characteristics:

1. They may be the official organ of a national or international learned society.
2. The principal papers, based upon scholarly research, usually contain musical examples and illustrations. They often include bibliographies, discographies, catalogs, and lists of works.
3. Because of the nature and magnitude of feature articles and the absence of urgently felt necessity for keeping abreast of current events, the learned journals are usually bimonthly or quarterly publications.
4. Reviews of records, books, and scores are directed to the scholar, specialist, or learned amateur.
5. The journals are indexed in such bibliographical lists as *Music Index* and the *Bibliographie des Musikschrifttums*. Some have annual indexes of their own, and a few have cumulative indexes.

### Musicological Journals

*Acta musicologica*, quarterly review of the International Musicological Society (1928–      ), was founded as the society's *Mitteilungen* and continued in 1931 under its present title. Started in Leipzig, its place of issue has changed several times and is now in Kassel. Fully documented feature articles in French, German, English, or Italian, according to the preference of the author, are of musicological and historical interest. Brief essays also appear, as do notices of the society's activities. An annual index of names is printed at the end of the year's cumulation of issues.

The *Journal* of the American Musicological Society (1948–    ), filling the need for a purely musicological periodical in the United States, is published three times a year. Each issue contains several articles, with examples, illustrations, bibliographies, and discographies; extensive reviews of books and of editions of music; communications; and a list, sometimes also abstracts, of papers read at chapter meetings in various parts of the country. From time to time the year's supplement to Helen Hewitt's "Doctoral Dissertations in Musicology" is printed.[8] The entire Volume 13 (1960) is a *Festschrift*: "A Musical Offering to Otto Kinkeldey Upon the Occasion of his 80th Anniversary." The *Journal* has an annual index.

*Current Musicology* (1965–    ), issued semiannually by Columbia University in New York, is devoted to the present state of musicological research. In addition to articles, the journal includes bibliographies (e.g., a list of foreign dissertations in I, No. 1 (1965), 118–120). Departments contain criticisms and announcements. Projected lists include masters' theses in musicology.

*Musical Quarterly* (1915–    ), published by G. Schirmer in New York, is the standard scholarly periodical in music of the United States and is found in nearly every music library. It contains feature articles by acknowledged scholars on contemporary music as well as on historical, theoretical, and aesthetic subjects. All papers are in English; those submitted in another language are translated. The "Current Chronicle" contains reviews of recitals, concerts, and festivals, with emphasis upon first performances and contemporary works. Reviews of books and recordings appear regularly, and there is a quarterly booklist. The cumulative index (1915–1959) and supplement by Goodkind is useful, as is the Kinscella Americana index.

A journal considered by some to be a British parallel to the *Musical Quarterly* is the *Music Review* (1940–    ), published four times yearly by W. Heffer & Sons, Ltd., Cambridge. Besides a half-dozen papers on musicological subjects, each issue contains several departments: "The New in Reviews"—recent works and young artists represented by succinct notices; a section on opera; correspondence; and extensive critiques of books, scores, and records. Some numbers also include a "Miscellany" in which festivals and outstanding concert series are reviewed. In 1950 the index for Volumes 1 to 5 (1940 to 1944) was issued, consisting of a list of contents and of illustrations.

*Music and Letters* (1920–    ), published quarterly by Oxford Uni-

---

[8]These supplements serve until the list is accumulated and a new edition appears in book form.

versity Press, is widely circulated in the United States. Its articles, international in coverage, treat musical styles, contributions of outstanding musicians, and subjects of historical significance. In spite of its title and constant references to texts and libretti, the periodical's emphasis is musical. The extensive critical essays on recent books are not confined to titles of British origin. Reviews of music are arranged by such classifications as collected editions, chamber music, and choral music. Volume 5 contains the index to the first five years' issues; Volume 10 contains the index to the second five years' issues. The cumulative index to Volumes 1 to 40 is published separately.

Among leading German periodicals is the *Archiv für Musikwissenschaft* (1918–    ), published quarterly in Wiesbaden by Franz Steiner Verlag. Its first eight volumes (each covering two years) were published in Bückeburg and Leipzig. In 1927 the journal was discontinued. After a quarter-century it was resumed and the volume numbers continued; thus, Volume 9 is dated 1952. Each issue, approximately 100 pages, contains lengthy articles of a musicological nature. All papers are in German; when the original is submitted in another language, it is translated. Musical examples and charts are plentifully used to illustrate the essays. From time to time an annotated list of new books and editions of music appears. The volumes now run annually rather than biennially, each volume containing an index for the year.

*Die Musikforschung* (1948–    ), published quarterly by Bärenreiter-Verlag in Kassel, is the journal of the Gesellschaft für Musikforschung and the Institut für Musikforschung of Berlin, Kiel, and Regensburg. The periodical is in German, with articles submitted in other languages being translated. The papers are extensive and well illustrated. Shorter notices of musicological interest are included. Reviews of books and music are ample and their selection is musicological. *Die Musikforschung* and the *Archiv für Musikwissenschaft* are found in many American university and public libraries as well as in the larger music collections.

The major learned journal of East Germany, subscribed to by some music libraries in America, is the quarterly *Beiträge zur Musikwissenschaft* (1959–    ), published in Berlin by the Association of German Composers and Musicologists. Its articles deal with contemporary music, theoretical, analytical, historical, and bibliographical matters. Notices are given of curricula of the universities in the German Democratic Republic, congresses (both national and international), and other matters of scholarly interest. The journal is strong in catalogs of composers' works[9] and in special topics with ideological implications.[10]

---

[9]For example, H. Ullrich, "Maria Theresia Paradis: Werkverzeichnis," *Beiträge zur Musikwissenschaft*, V (1963), 117–154.

[10]In II (1961) *Heft* 2 was on Chinese opera, *Heft* 3/4 on workers' songs.

The journal of the French Musicological Society is published semi-annually in Paris. Originally called the *Bulletin* (1917–    ), its title was changed in 1922 to *Revue de musicologie*. It was suspended in 1939 but resumed in 1945 with Number 73/74, 27ᵉ année.[11] The *Revue* contains musicological features, including long articles; notices of courses and congresses; reviews of new books and music; and a section compiled by the Department of Music of the Bibliothèque Nationale entitled "Périodiques," listing other journals and their principal musicological contents. News of society meetings and a necrology are also included. Sometimes a *numéro spécial* is devoted to an outstanding musician, with articles, bibliographies, and other features on the subject; for example, Number 47 (July-December, 1962) was on Debussy.

*La Revue musicale* (1920–    ; suspended 1941–1945) is issued in Paris in "numbers," ten numbers constituting an annual series, of which five are *numéros spéciaux* and five are *carnets critiques*. The numbering is by individual issues rather than by annual volumes. Special issues are usually devoted to a single composer, movement in music, or type of music, with a large selection of papers on the topic. Sometimes, if the special number and the *carnet* are on the same subject, the former contains the major articles and the latter the documentation or comments. Topics considered may be theoretical, historical, or contemporary. Reviews are included.

*Revue belge de musicologie/Belgisch Tijdschrift voor Muziekwetenschap* (1946–    ), issued quarterly in Brussels, is the journal of the Belgian Musicological Society. Articles contributed by scholars from all over the world are in various languages, with French, Flemish, and English predominating. The "Miscellanea" includes short essays on a variety of topics. Book reviews, like the papers, are in the language of the author. The business of the society is summarized periodically in the "Acta." Depending upon the publication schedule and the nature of the materials to be issued, several numbers may be combined into a large double, triple, or even quadruple issue. Each annual volume has its own index.

The *Tijdschrift van de Vereniging voor Nederlandse Muziekgeschiedenis* is published quarterly in Amsterdam as a society journal. The Vereniging, founded in 1868, began its original magazine in 1882, continuing until 1946. Each volume encompassed issues for four years rather than one. In 1948 the format was changed, and the present title was adopted. A multilingual periodical, its articles appear in the language of the author and deal with historical subjects as well as with the lives and works of important musicians. A bibliography of works published by the society from

---

[11]The *Rapports et communications*, published 1940–1944 to keep the members in touch during World War II, are not discussed here.

1869 to 1960, including an index of articles appearing in the *Tijdschrift* from 1882 to 1959, was issued in 1961 as part of Volume 19.

Three Italian periodicals may be cited in the context of musicology. *La Rassegna musicale* (1928–1962) was the successor to *Il Pianoforte* (1920–1928). After being suspended in 1944–46, it was resumed in 1947 but stopped publication in 1962. In most issues the articles (in Italian) treated subjects of historical, musicological, and contemporary significance, with a heavy leaning toward Italian opera. Departments included accounts of congresses, news, observations, and commentaries in a section called "Note e commenti." "Ricensioni" sections contained reviews of books, scores, and recordings. Sometimes several issues were combined to make a double or triple number, as in the case of Volume 32, in which three issues constituted a special opera number. The journal had an annual index, and Allorto compiled a cumulative index for 1928–1952.[12] After its suspension in 1962, there was a short period of inactivity. In 1964 the *Quaderni della Rassegna musicale* was started as a journal of contemporary music (see below, p. 192).

*L'Approdo musicale: Quaderni di musica*, is a leading musicological journal. Founded in Turin in 1958 as *L'Approdo musicale: Rivista trimestrale di musica*, it moved its headquarters to Rome, where it is published by Edizioni RAI (Radiotelevisione italiana). Most issues are devoted to a single topic or to a leading musician. A noteworthy example is the July-September issue, 1958, on Paul Hindemith, with an essay on his style, analysis of some major works, and a discography. A more recent example is Number 19/20 (1965), including articles, documents, and illustrations on the French "Six." Essays of general musical interest range from popular and primitive music to radio and electronics. The journal features chronological tables, bibliographies, and discographies. Reviews of current musical events, opera, books, and recordings lean heavily toward works of Italian origin.

*Jucunda laudatio: Rassegna di musica antica* (1963–    ), published every three months in Milan, is a journal of historical musicology with emphasis upon older music. Articles are illustrated with musical examples.

The outstanding Hungarian journal available in the United States is *Studia musicologica* (1960–    ), published in Budapest. The number of issues appearing annually varies. Articles based upon musicological research are in French, German, English, or Russian, depending upon the language of the contributor. In addition to papers on musicology, the journal also includes essays on ethnomusicological subjects. Because it is a periodical of Hungarian studies, the *Studia* naturally shows a native bias. It regularly contains book reviews and discographies.

[12]Riccardo Allorto, *Indice generale delle annate 1928–1952* (Torino, n.d.).

The Polish *Muzyka* (1950–    ) and the Jugoslav *Zvuk* (1955–    ) are other Eastern European journals found in some libraries.[13] With the impetus that is being given to historical and ethnomusicological research in these countries, such periodicals should increase in importance.

### Journals of Ethnomusicology and Folk Music

The study of folk music, primitive music, and non-Western music has assumed important proportions within the past two decades in the United States as well as in other countries. Several journals are devoted to this type of research, among them *Ethnomusicology*, the organ of the Society for Ethnomusicology, published three times a year in Middletown, Connecticut. From 1953 to 1957 it was issued as the *Newsletter*, and assumed its present format and title thereafter. It contains, in addition to feature articles, many bibliographies and discographies. At present it is perhaps the most widely circulated journal of ethnomusicology in the United States.

A periodical restricted in circulation because of its specialized subject-matter but valuable for certain types of study is the *Folklore and Folk Music Archivist* (1958–    ), published jointly by the Folklore Archive and the Archives of Folk and Primitive Music, both divisions of the Research Center in Anthropology, Folklore, and Linguistics at Indiana University. Appearing three times a year, it is devoted to the collection, documentation, indexing, and cataloging of folklore and folk music in institutions where such materials are available for research. It contains articles and lists of publications.

*English Folk Dance and Song* (1936–    ), journal of the English Folk Dance and Song Society, is usually issued quarterly. As the news periodical for the society, it reports folklore activities and programs given in various parts of Britain. The annual of the same society is its research publication.

### Journals of New Music

Considering the many recent innovations in musical techniques and their attendant "modern" aesthetics, it is not surprising that learned journals for new music should exist. They have some traits in common:

1. Articles of considerable length, written by authoritative critics or chief exponents, deal with contemporary techniques, philosophies of composition, and the resulting music. Not only are composers made the subjects of biographical accounts and their works analyzed, but often

[13]For a long list of East European journals, see Coover's bibliography in *Fontes artis musicae*, 1956–1962.

they are authors of essays in which they emerge as articulate defenders of their artistic beliefs.

2. Focus is on first performances, with attention paid to critical comment and/or appreciation; in some cases reviews are extensive and analytical.

3. Reviews of scores, books, and records deal with contemporary issues, although they are not always confined to new or avant-garde music.

Most of the current-events periodicals discussed above include news of contemporary music, and musicological journals contain discussions of new techniques and contributions of present-day composers. The publications noted below are, however, those emphasizing new music primarily and showing a predominating interest in it.

*Perspectives of New Music* (1962–      ), published semiannually by Princeton University Press for the Fromm Music Foundation, contains articles by composers, critics, musical scholars, and teachers on the many aspects of modern music. Some of the papers are highly specialized, requiring in the reader a knowledge of contemporary styles and the terminology employed to describe them. Other articles are quite understandable by the average music student. Works of contemporary composers are analyzed, performances are reviewed, artistic tenets are explained, and methods of both composition and notation are discussed. Illustrations are abundantly used. Reviews and communications are included.

*Tempo: A Quarterly Review of Modern Music* (1939–      ), published by Boosey and Hawkes in London, contains articles of contemporary interest. Some are detailed analyses of new works, amply illustrated with musical examples. First performances are noted in signed critical reviews, with emphasis upon works presented in England, though not necessarily those composed by British writers. In some issues a single subject receives primary attention: American music in Number 64 (Spring, 1963) and Bartók and the piano in Number 65 (Summer, 1963). Departments include reviews of books (not all on modern music; Chailley's *40,000 Years of Music* as well as Howes' *The Music of William Walton* are reviewed in Number 74, for Fall, 1965), a record guide, and a "Select List of Articles on Contemporary Music in Foreign Periodicals."

The German monthly periodical, *Melos: Zeitschrift für neue Musik* (1920–1934; 1946–      ), is published in Mainz. It assumed its present form as a journal for new music in 1946 after being suspended for more than a decade. Liberally illustrated with pictures and musical examples, the articles—usually of considerable length—deal with contemporary writing techniques and composers, modern choreography, and "new" staging. "Blick in ausländische Muzikzeitschriften" contains excerpts from periodicals of other countries, quoting reviews of first performances, festivals, and concerts. Critiques of new publications, as well as of modern music on records, are a regular feature. Selected premières are given extensive coverage, sometimes with detailed musical or choreographic analysis. Some issues are devoted to special subjects. A periodical of large scope, *Melos* deals with all aspects of new music and all media of musical expression. In some quarters it is regarded as the prototype of the modern-music journal.

*Le Courrier musical de France* (1963–    ), issued quarterly, contains illustrated articles on historical aspects of music as well as extensive accounts of new works, with annotations on duration and first performance, description of the score, and critique. Catalogs of works by contemporary composers are featured. News items cover celebrations and congresses; obituaries are included; new books and recordings are reviewed. As the title of the journal may indicate, the emphasis is upon French music and musicians.

The Italian *Quaderni della Rassegna musicale* (1964–    ) is issued three or four times a year. Its articles emphasize new music, and its reviews are on contemporary works.

*Nutida Musik*, published in Stockholm by the Swedish Radio, contains information about aspects of contemporary music, with an international coverage. John Cage and Charles Ives are given as much attention as Lutoslawski, Boulez, and Nono.

Publications of documentation centers, societies for the dissemination of national music, and composers' organizations also deal with modern music (see above, Chapter 16).

### Journal of Music Theory

The close association of theory with history causes many problems of a theoretical nature to be discussed in musicological periodicals. Contemporary theories, such as those underlying serial composition, are treated in journals of new music, and bibliographical aspects of theory are treated in music library publications.

In a class by itself is the *Journal of Music Theory* (1957–    ), devoted almost exclusively to theory and published semiannually at Yale University. Each issue contains a half-dozen research papers on theoretical problems, both contemporary and historical. Some are expositions of a large area of theory; others deal with a single theorist or with the evaluation of a specific school of thought. Book reviews are long and analytical; written by scholars and teachers, they are aimed at the learned reader. Bibliography is an important feature.

*Journal of Music Therapy*

The National Association for Music Therapy publishes a quarterly formerly called the *Bulletin* (1952–    ), with papers on therapy and related fields, training, practices, and ideals of the profession, and announcements. There is an annual volume index. The title was changed to *Journal* in 1965.

## Library Journals

Some periodicals issued for the music librarian are important to the research scholar for bibliographical purposes. *Fontes artis musicae* (1954–    ), the multilingual review of the International Association of Music Libraries, is published by Bärenreiter-Verlag in Kassel. Until 1964 it was issued semiannually; since then it has appeared three times a year. English, French, and German predominate, with some articles presented in all three. Its papers by research librarians, musicologists, theorists, and directors of information centers deal mostly with bibliographical matters. Reviews are in the form of critical essays, with high standards of judgment. The "Liste internationale selective" includes such classifications as theater and film works, instrumental music, vocal music, folklore, works about music, and didactic writings, with entries arranged by country of origin. Editions and re-editions of early music before 1800 occupy a separate section; another section is devoted to modern editions of music from the nineteenth and twentieth centuries. Special bibliographies are often featured. There is an annual table of contents.

*Notes* (first series, 1934–1942; second series, 1943–    ), organ of the Music Library Association, is a valuable quarterly journal for the scholar regardless of his research area. Reference has been made in several previous chapters to specific features useful to the investigator. Although designed to assist the librarian in the selection of music materials, the periodical includes articles, lists, and critical essays helpful to all professional musicians. The bibliographies prepared by subject authorities are scholarly tools. "Record Ratings" provides evaluation of discs. Book and music reviews, on a wide variety of publications, are detailed and extensive, sometimes containing valuable critical analysis. The influence of *Notes* is international, and copies are found in most American and foreign music libraries.

*Brio*, journal of the United Kingdom Branch of the International Association of Music Libraries (1964–    ) serves a practical purpose for both librarian and scholar. Some of its articles are bibliographical; others deal with such subjects as the arrangement of collections and acquisition of materials.

## Journals of Music
## Education and Pedagogy

"Music education" is a broad term, embracing many aspects of musical art, psychology, philosophy, and pedagogy. As a result, journals devoted to music education are varied in aim and in coverage. Some deal primarily with teaching materials (graded lists of pieces, recommended texts, educational recordings, instrumental handbooks), while others are devoted to educational methods and philosophies, and still others exist for the researcher in educational history and psychology. The coverage may be international, national, statewide, or local.

The *International Music Educator* (1960–    ), organ of the International Society for Music Education, is published semiannually under the auspices of UNESCO. Predominating languages are English, French, and German, with some articles appearing in all three. "Music education" is interpreted liberally to include theater, dance, ethnomusicology, new techniques and concepts of style, and instruments, as well as pedagogy. The journal gives an overview of the educational aspects of all subjects related to music.

A broad view is taken also in the *Journal of Research in Music Education* (1953–    ), published by the Music Educators' National Conference. Formerly a semiannual, it became a quarterly with Volume 12. It contains long, fully documented articles of a serious nature, some being condensed versions of doctoral dissertations; reviews of many kinds of books—histories, educational studies, handbooks, and works of a general musical interest; and news of the music education field. Bibliographies of research are often featured, some occupying an entire issue. The *Journal* is the learned periodical for music education in the United States.

A "practical" journal is the *Music Educators' Journal*, published six times yearly by the Music Educators' National Conference. Continued from the *Music Supervisors' Journal* in 1934, it contains papers on pedagogy, concert reviews, accounts of activities in schools of music, announcements of contests and awards, and personal notes. A calendar of events of the Conference is included. Lists of teaching materials appear regularly.

The Canadian counterpart of the *Music Educators' Journal* is *The Canadian Music Educator*, official organ of the Canadian Music Educators' Association. Begun in 1959/60, with editorial offices in Toronto, it is issued eight times during the school year and contains articles, announcements, curriculum studies, reviews of materials, and accounts of meetings.

A similar journal is the English *Music in Education*, issued six times yearly and containing short articles of general interest, news of activities of the School Music Association, and lists of teaching works.

*Musart* (1948/49–     ) is the journal of the National Catholic Music Educators' Association, with articles on music teaching at all levels, reviews of books and records, and news of musical events in the Catholic colleges and parochial schools of America.

The United States is rich in periodicals issued by state groups. Music teachers in nearly every state are members of a professional association or a chapter of the Music Educators' National Conference. Many such organizations have their own journals for publicizing teaching materials and equipment, new methods, meetings, contests, and awards. Because much attention is paid to activities of members and of the schools they represent, the periodicals have more local appeal than do the national journals.

The *American Music Teacher* (1951–     ), organ of the Music Teachers' National Association, is issued six times each year. Since a considerable number of the society's members are private music teachers, the periodical is not aimed at the public school music educator alone but contains articles on the training of individual pupils in the studio as well. In addition to articles, there are reports and announcements of meetings, conventions, contests, and association activities. A regular feature is a section of book and music reviews.

In continental Europe, where music training is offered in many kinds of institutions, each with its particular emphasis (e.g., denominational or parochial schools, private academies, conservatories), articles on pedagogy are likely to be included in the publications of the individual organizations. Some important journals on the theory and practice of music education do exist, however. The German monthly periodical, *Musik in der Schule* (1949–     ) published in Berlin, and the Austrian *Musikerziehung* (1947–     ), issued in Vienna five times per year, are examples.

## Church Music Periodicals[14]

Periodicals of church music are usually denominational and cover a variety of subjects: liturgy, theological concepts as they touch upon music, and sacred composition in different styles. The working relations of the organist and the choir is sometimes emphasized, although this is not a universal characteristic among the journals.

The *Catholic Choirmaster* (1915–     ), quarterly bulletin of the

---

[14]Journals devoted to the church organ are mentioned below, with periodicals on instruments.

Society of St. Gregory of America, is devoted to liturgy and sacred music. It contains articles, lists of music, a chronicle, reviews, and necrology. A music supplement is included with each issue. For the practical purpose of finding new music for performance, this journal is most useful.

*Caecilia: A Review of Catholic Church Music* (1874–    ), is published quarterly in Omaha. It includes articles, reviews of books (not necessarily on church music and not necessarily Catholic), reviews of Catholic compositions (generally Masses and motets suitable for performance), and a list of music received, with the names and addresses of the publishers. The articles, written by outstanding scholars in the United States, are brief and to the point.

*Music Ministry* (1960–    ) is a Methodist journal published monthly in Nashville, Tennessee. With major emphasis on music in the church and the church school, its articles are on choral, liturgical, and organ compositions. An account is given of music in the junior grades and in the small church. Annotated lists of choral collections and short reviews of individual compositions and books are regularly featured.

The *Journal of Church Music* (1959–    ) is published in Philadelphia monthly except in July and August, when the issues for the two months are combined into one. Its articles have historical, practical, and general interest; departments include organ music reviews and annotations on anthems. A musical supplement provides anthems in octavo format.

*The Hymn* (1949–    ), quarterly of The Hymn Society of America, is published in New York, and includes articles on hymn writers, past and present; advice on the selection and the teaching of hymns; studies on historical aspects of hymnology (interdenominational); and discussions on hymns in general. Hymn texts as well as tunes are treated. Items reviewed are books on hymnology, dissertations on sacred music, hymnals, and church compositions.

*Response, In Worship, Music and the Arts* (1959–    ) is a semiannual publication of the Lutheran Society for Worship, Music, and the Arts in St. Paul, Minnesota. It contains valuable reviews of music and of books. Its articles deal with the association of music and the arts with worship. An index exists for Volumes 1 and 2 and for Volumes 3 and 4.

*Gregoriusblad: Tijdschrift tot bevordering der Kerkmuziek* (1876–    ), the scholarly journal of Catholic church music in Holland, is published in Amsterdam by the Nederlandse Sint-Gregoriusvereniging. Its avowed aim is the advancement of church music; its editor is the musicologist, J. Smits van Waesberghe. Articles deal with historical developments in church music; theoretical and technical aspects, including analysis of Masses and other major sacred works; and liturgy in its various ramifications. Departments treat choral music, organ music, liturgy, current events, and selected reviews of new materials.

The Belgian *Musica sacra* (1900–1965) was published quarterly in Bruges. In Flemish and French, its papers include research in sacred music, lists of specifications of new church organs, theories of plainchant, and other topics pertaining to Catholic church music. There is a chronicle and reviews of concerts. A summary of contents of other journals (*De Praestant, Gregoriusblad, Revue grégorienne*) gives some insight into related literature. Critical comments on new music are a feature. The non-musical supplements include such items as a catalog of certain important musicians' works, especially emphasizing their contributions to church music. With the cessation of this journal, scholarship in sacred music has suffered a loss.

The Italian *Musica sacra* (1877–    ) is a bimonthly journal published in Milan. It contains articles, reviews of music and books, notices, a "rivista delle riviste"—quoting articles from other periodicals, and a musical supplement. Its emphasis is Catholic.

The bimonthly German *Musik und Kirche* (1931–    ) is published by Bärenreiter-Verlag in Kassel. It has combined with an earlier periodical, *Zeitschrift für evangelische Kirchenmusik* (1876–    ). On a high scholarly level, it contains fairly long articles on composers, historical matters, and performance practice in church music. Works of such men as Hugo Distler and Buxtehude (to name two from widely separated periods) are analyzed. Departments include an organists' corner, a miscellany and current-events chronicle, "Bücher und Note" (reviews), personal notes, and accounts of new church organs. The journal comes bound with *Der Kirchenchor* (1941–    ), dealing with choral matters.

The French *Revue grégorienne* (1911–1964) was published six times yearly at the Abbey of Saint Pierre de Solesmes as the official journal of the School of Solesmes and of the Gregorian Institute of Paris. Although it was discontinued at the end of 1964, it is recent enough to be included here. Devoted to studies of the chant and liturgy, it contains articles of a technical and historical nature, often illustrated with excerpts of chant and holding to the interpretation of plainsong typical of the Solesmes School. The journal was intended for the scholar rather than the layman.

## Periodicals on Opera

Opera news and reviews are included in periodicals of current musical events and in nearly all of the learned journals. The titles discussed here are those devoted primarily to the composition, performance, and staging of opera.

Opera journals are usually illustrated and may present a large variety of subjects, for opera involves not only music and the performance of the score but also librettos, stage settings, costumes, acting, and ballet. Opera is typically a rich art, thought of as perhaps the most glamorous (and perhaps most sybaritic) area of music. Periodicals devoted to it are apt to be luxuriously printed, with large format and many pictures, often on fine paper.

In the United States, where the Metropolitan Opera is the foundation of the nation's operatic activity, the longest season is in New York. The standard periodical is *Opera News* (1936–     ), issued by the Metropolitan Opera Guild. Its publication coincides with the season: monthly issues appear in September, October, November, and May; weekly issues appear from December through mid-April. The monthly numbers are concerned with the national and international operatic scene and opera history. The weekly numbers are primarily focused on the featured (and broadcast) opera of the week, with a historical note, summary of plot, cast, and photographs of settings and principal singers. News of international operatic activities is included, with shorter essays on subjects of interest to theatergoers such as stars of the past and present, librettists, and other personalities of the operatic stage—designers, costumers, conductors, and managers.

*Opera* (1950–     ), published in London, supersedes in part the journal entitled *Ballet and Opera*. It contains reviews of performances in musical centers, not only in Britain but on the Continent as well, and articles on operatic composition and production. At appropriate times a special issue may appear. The issue for August, 1962, for example, was devoted to summer festivals, with attention directed to Salzburg, and included a list of works played at the Salzburg Festivals from 1920 to 1960.

*Opernwelt: Monatszeitschrift für Oper, Operette, Ballett* (1960–     ), published in Stuttgart, is a de luxe periodical. With an opera company in nearly every city, Germany can support such a journal. It contains illustrated articles on personalities (composers, librettists, singers, dancers, conductors, choreographers, stage designers), on historical aspects of opera and famous theaters. In spite of its glamor, the journal maintains high standards in its leading articles. Reviews of recordings appear regularly, along with criticisms of performances. A new opera, regardless of its place of origin, is likely to receive a long, analytical review, illustrated with photographs and musical examples. During the festival season a calendar of offerings may be given, with emphasis on such popular summer opera centers as Bayreuth, Munich, and Salzburg. Although the greatest attention is paid to Continental Europe in general and West Germany in particular, both British and American activities are reported in some reviews and summaries.

Although it was discontinued in Spring, 1963, *La Scala: Rivista dell'op-*

*era* (1949–1963), published in Milan, is recent enough for consideration. Beautifully illustrated, with articles on many operatic subjects and including reviews of performances, recordings, and books, it was a rival of *Opernwelt*. At the end of each issue was a summary in English, German, and French, of the leading articles, no attempt being made otherwise at translation from the Italian.

## Periodicals on Instruments

The number of journals devoted to musical instruments, instrument making, and instrumental music is increasing. On the one hand, instruments continue to be improved and music is being written to exploit new techniques. On the other hand, historical research reveals data hitherto unknown about earlier instruments and their music. Technical proficiency, widespread development of bands and orchestras, and improved teaching in the schools have acted together to support the periodicals.

The French bimonthly *Musique et instruments* (1964–    ), published in Paris, serves editors and instrument makers. It contains news, discusses organizations using instruments, reviews new works, and accounts for records and methods of instrument manufacture.

*Das Musikinstrument und Phono* (1952–    ), a monthly journal published in Frankfurt-am-Main, serves the instrument industry. Reports of developments in manufacturing are featured, as are scientifically documented papers on tone production and technical improvements. Book reviews, current events, a necrology, descriptions of instruments in museums, lists of international patents on instrumental devices, and production news constitute the departments of the journal, and an annual classified index is included. The journal is issued in three editions: A is in German, B is in German and English, and C is in German and French. In the bilingual editions some of the articles appear in both languages, while others appear in one or the other.

A practical American periodical for the teacher of instrumental music is *The Instrumentalist* (1946–    ), issued eleven times a year in Glen Ellyn, Illinois, by the Association for the Advancement of Instrumental Music. Articles and "clinics" treat performance, conducting, and teaching. Departments include reviews of books, records, and music (classified and graded); an audio-visual guide; personal notes; and some observations about the instruments and supply industry. Bibliographical material and lists of music (e.g., Gary Echols's list of bassoon music[15]) are regularly

[15]Gary Echols, "Solo and Ensemble Literature for Bassoon," *The Instrumentalist*, XVIII (September, 1963), 91–95.

featured, with some practical pedagogical suggestions and graded studies.

*Woodwind World* (1957–    ) published five times a year in Bedford Hills, New York, specializes almost exclusively in articles on woodwind performance and teaching. Departments report news of college activity, accounts of festivals and coming musical events, notices of new products and supplies, and lists of new music for woodwind instruction and ensemble playing. *Woodwind World* superseded *The Clarinet.*

*Brass Quarterly* (1957–    ), published in Durham, New Hampshire, contains articles on brass music, instruments, history and performance; reviews of music, books, and recordings of brass works; and valuable subject bibliographies. In addition to the special bibliographical compilations, each Fall issue includes a "Brass Bibliography," listing articles in journals, books, and theses on brass instruments and their music issued during the previous year.

The *American Recorder* (1959–    ), quarterly organ of the American Recorder Society, consists of articles on the history of the instrument, the literature for and about it, and reviews of books related to the recorder and recorder playing. Concert notes and letters are included.

The *NACWPI Bulletin* (1952–    ), journal of the National Association of College Wind and Percussion Instructors, is issued quarterly. Articles are devoted to the literature and performance of wind and percussion instruments, news of the Association, and personal notes. Lists of new music and materials appear. Because the periodical is a compact one, its papers are brief and to the point; some longer essays may be continued serially through several issues.

*Journal of Band Research* (1965–    ), published twice each year by the American Bandmasters Association, is devoted to scholarly papers on band history, analyses of outstanding compositions for band, and studies of band performance practices. Some association news and announcements are included, but the chief aim of the journal is the publication of research.

*Das Orchester* (1953–    ), a German monthly journal for orchestral, stage, and radio-television music, contains articles of timely and historical interest, some illustrated with musical examples; "Spiegel des Musiklebens" —reviews of performances with pictures of principal soloists and stage settings; "Pressestimmen"—concise quotations from criticisms in European newspapers; reviews of selected records, books, and scores; and briefly noted news items. A good cross-section of European orchestral activity is disclosed, with major emphasis upon West German centers. With offices in Mainz, the periodical is supervised by a distinguished editorial board.

*American String Teacher* (1950–    ), quarterly of the American String Teachers' Association, is a practical journal for string pedagogy.

Articles dwell on the techniques, teaching, ensemble problems, and current developments affecting the instruments. Book reviews and lists of new music with brief annotations are found.

The British *Strad: A Monthly Journal for Professionals and Amateurs of All Stringed Instruments Played with the Bow* (1890–    ), issued in London, is the standard periodical for strings. Its title is almost entirely self-explanatory: articles are on instruments, orchestras, techniques of performance, compositions for strings, and the history of instruments and their literature. Departments include reviews of music and books, news of associations, announcements of festivals, and editorial notes.

*The Guitar Review* (1946–    ), publication of the Society of the Classic Guitar, appears irregularly. Its articles are on the history of the guitar and guitar-related instruments (e.g., the lute), on notable books of tablature and methods, and on composers and their works. Reviews of music are included. The musical supplements consist of pieces representing various styles of composition.

*Harp News* (1960–    ), issued twice yearly by the Northern California Harpists' Association, is a news bulletin on activities involving the harp. Articles treat problems and repertoire. Concert schedules and short lists of new works and recordings are a regular feature, together with announcements of recitals and workshops.

The number of journals devoted to the piano is surprisingly small. One reason may be the extensive coverage of piano and piano literature in the *American Music Teacher*; another may be the emphasis placed upon piano pedagogy and teaching pieces by directors of the many workshops throughout the country and by publishers in their graded lists, advertising leaflets, and "thematics."

*Piano Quarterly: A Critique of Piano Literature* (1952–    ), is published by the Piano Teachers Information Service, New York. It contains lists of recommended music (pedagogical volumes and recital pieces) arranged by grade, with "thematics" of several works; articles on outstanding pianists; historical studies of the instrument and techniques of playing; books reviews and music reviews; and a record list.

*The Piano Teacher* (1959–    ), bimonthly journal issued by the Summy-Birchard Company in Evanston, Illinois, deals with piano teaching. Among its features are accounts of workshops and lists of new music.

*Clavier: A Magazine for Pianists and Organists* (1962–    ), published bimonthly by The Instrumentalist Company, is the learned journal for keyboard teachers and performers. Instruction, performance, and appreciation of all styles of music are the principal subjects treated in the articles. Some papers on individual compositions are analytical, with attention given to style, form, and harmonic or contrapuntal idiom. Others are critical, while still others offer suggestions on interpretation. Biographical sketches of famous artists and composers, as well as historical studies involving them, are often featured. In addition to notes on new books, there are reviews of new pieces for piano and for organ; outstanding recordings are criticised. Miscellaneous current events and news of the keyboard instrument industry may be included.

The American Guild of Organists publishes two periodicals. *Diapason: A Monthly Publication Devoted to the Organ and the Interests of Organists* (1909–    ), is the news journal of the Guild and the Royal Canadian College of Organists. It deals with activities of the two organizations and their members. Its articles pertain to organ playing. Reviews of recitals form an important chronicle of performance and composition in the United States and Canada.

*The American Guild of Organists Quarterly* (1956–    ) is the learned journal of the society, with emphasis upon historical and cultural aspects of the organ and the performance practices of outstanding artists. Books related to the history, development, and playing of the organ are reviewed, as are new recordings and compositions. Contest and festival announcements appear occasionally.

The *Organ Institute Quarterly* (1951–    ), published in Andover, Massachusetts, journal of the Institute, contains papers on organ technique, evolution of the instrument, and performance, with a short section entitled "Editorial Briefs." It reflects the views of the Organ Institute.

*The American Organist* (1918–    ), issued in Staten Island, New York, is a news periodical rather than a society journal. It features articles, recital reviews, current musical events, and personal notes on organists, teachers, and composers.

The *Choral and Organ Guide* (1948–    ), monthly journal of the American Academy of Organists and the Choral Conductors' Guild, is exactly what its title implies: a guide to music for choir and organ, with recommendations and criticisms of music for church holidays in particular. It contains articles, reviews, and lists of publishers of sacred music.

*The Organ: Quarterly Review for its Makers, its Players and its Lovers* (1921–    ), is published by Musical Opinion in London. The standard British periodical for the organist, it contains rather lengthy articles on aspects of the organist's art, on the mechanics of the instrument, and on specifications of famous church organs. Sometimes an outstanding historical study appears. Letters to the editor often contain worthwhile bits of information and opinion.

*L'Orgue: Revue trimestrielle*, is published in Paris. Started in 1947 as a continuation of the *Journal de l'Association des amis de l'orgue*, it deals with the history of the instrument, various performance problems, and the aesthetic value of the organ as an expressive musical medium. Its articles deal with outstanding organists, specifications of instruments, and the history of organ playing and literature. Departments include brief reviews, announcements, and a necrology. Although its major emphasis is naturally European, reflecting the ideas of the so-called French school, the journal may prove interesting to American organists as well.

The bimonthly *Musik und Gottesdienst* (1947–     ) is the journal of the Evangelical Organists Society of German Switzerland and is published in Zurich by Zwingli Verlag. It contains articles of interest to an organist in an evangelical church, lists of music recommended for service playing and for holidays, news and notes, and a miscellany.

The *American Choral Review* (1958–     ), the quarterly organ of the Association of Choral Conductors, contain some highly technical and analytical articles on important compositions, with copious musical examples illustrating musical styles. Book reviews, critiques of school music, choral news, and lists of new publications are other features of this learned journal.

## Audio Journals

The twentieth century has brought a phenomenal development of recording techniques and acoustical sciences from which music has derived considerable benefit. Attendant upon this growth has been the appearance of periodicals devoted to recordings, tapes, and all manner of sound production and reproduction. Some journals are technical, with data on equipment, recording procedures and standards, acoustical research, and mechanical improvements. Others are cultural, being concerned primarily with record reviews, while still others are discographical, specializing in lists of records. An example of each basic type follows.

*Audio* (1917–     ), published monthly in Mineola, New York, is one of the oldest journals for audio science and equipment. Dealing with radio, phonorecords (both high fidelity and stereophonic), acoustics, and acoustical engineering, it contains a variety of articles. Regularly featured are descriptions of new products and a section of record reviews.

The *American Record Guide: An Independent Journal of Opinion* (1935–     ) superseded the *Music Lover's Guide*. From 1935 to 1944 it was called *American Music Lover*; for one issue (September, 1944) it was entitled *The Listener's Record Guide*; its present title was adopted in October, 1944. Each issue contains some fairly lengthy, serious reviews of records, as well as some concise comments on stereo tapes. Recordings of jazz are covered in the reviews, along with classical records, and the reviews are noted in "Record Ratings" of *Notes*. In addition, there are book reviews. The journal is useful to one searching for recorded works and critical comment; it is an aid to the record collector and record librarian.

The *High Fidelity* section of *High Fidelity/Musical America* is valuable for the information it gives about music and musicians heard on recordings and about sound production and reproduction, and for its reviews of recordings on discs and on tape.

*HiFi/Stereo Review* (1949–    ), published monthly by Ziff-Davis Publishing Company in New York, is divided into four principal sections: "The Music," with articles on compositions and performers; "The Equipment," on new products, technical data, and equipment; "The Reviews," with critical comment on classical recordings, "entertainment" recordings, and tapes; and "The Regulars," with editorial comments and letters. Profusely illustrated, it is a useful periodical for anyone interested in sound reproduction.

The British *Records and Recording* is part of *The Seven Arts* (see above, p. 181) and contains news of the record industry, as well as articles on discs and criticisms of records of all sorts.

The British *Hi-Fi News* represents a merger of *Tapes and Tape Records*, *Audio News*, and *Stereo News*. Published in London, it deals primarily with acoustics, engineering problems, new equipment, and recordings. It includes some valuable information on music but is a technical journal rather than a musical one.

*Recorded Sound* (1961–    ), the journal of the British Institute of Recorded Sound, is a successor to the *Bulletin of the Friends of the Institute* (1956–1961) and is now a quarterly publication. Devoted to a thorough study of recording in its many aspects, almost every issue contains at least one detailed, critical discography in conjunction with biographical material on an artist or a composer. Moreover, the journal includes interesting feature articles, information on record archives, historical accounts of recording, abstracts of articles on record libraries, and a section of book reviews. A cumulative index for Volume I (1961–1962) appears in the issue for Autumn, 1962.

The Italian *Discoteca: Rivista mensile di dischi e musica* (1960–    ), published monthly in Rome, contains articles about artists, composers, and their works, and reviews of both recent disks and books. Items selected for criticism include speech and jazz records as well as disks of operatic and classical music.

The *Gravesano Review* (1955–1966), published every several months in Mainz, is concerned with studies of acoustics, tuning, sound properties of concert halls, and synthetic sounds, including those produced electronically. The articles, in German and English, are technical and scientific.

On the other hand, the French *Musique et radio: Revue technique et professionnelle de musique* (1911–    ) leans in the direction of music. Published monthly by Horizons de France, it contains studies of composers and their works on records, movements in music history, opera in various countries, and a variety of subjects interesting to a musician. The feature articles may be supplemented by a classified catalog and a discography, as in the June, 1963, issue, which focuses on Carlos Surinach. Reviews of music, books, and records are given. Because of its extensive discographies, the journal has been discussed here rather than with current-events periodicals.

## Current Nonmusical Journals
## Including Articles on Music

When music is studied as part of a humanities project, it may be treated in learned journals whose emphasis is not purely musical. Some society publications devoted to a national culture, to a period of history, or to a subject related to the arts often contain articles on music. A few selected examples follow.

*Speculum: A Journal of Mediaeval Studies* (1926–    ), quarterly organ of the Mediaeval Academy of America, Cambridge, Massachusetts, contains some important contributions to the theory and history of music during the Middle Ages. Arthur S. Wolff has prepared a checklist of articles and book reviews pertaining to music (1926–1964) (see above, p. 100). The journal includes an annual index in its October issue.

*Renaissance News* (1948–    ), quarterly journal of the Renaissance Society of America, is rich in articles on music. That music is part of the interests served by the society is attested to by the presence of outstanding musical scholars on the Renaissance Society Council, and articles on music and the socio-cultural-economic backgrounds of music often appear, though not necessarily in every issue. Reviews of records and books include items on music, and some attention is paid to music prizes and performances.

*Studies in Romanticism* (1961–    ), published by the Graduate School of Boston University to stimulate research on the nineteenth century, includes articles on music from time to time.

Another type of journal is represented by the *New Hungarian Quarterly* (1960–    ), published in English. Music is among the many cultural interests it serves. Considerable material about Béla Bartók, for example, may be found in the issue for September, 1963.

The *American Scandinavian Review* (1913–    ), published quarterly in New York, regularly includes a section on music in addition to an occasional feature article on some aspect of Scandinavian music. The *Review* encompasses activities of Denmark, Iceland, and Finland as well as of Norway and Sweden.

*Américas* (1949–    ), monthly publication of the Pan American Union in Washington, appears in three language editions: English, Portuguese, and Spanish. A section on music is regularly included, and from time to time a leading feature article deals with a musical subject.

*Revista nacional de cultura* (1939–    ), published in Caracas, Venezuela, is a bimonthly journal of cultural affairs. Each issue contains a music section, giving accounts of concerts, meetings, and congresses. Occasionally a special article on music is featured.

*Dance Perspectives* (1959–    ), a quarterly published in New York, is representative of journals devoted to a music-related art. Many of its articles deal directly with music, while some treat dancing with reference to its musical setting.

*The Journal of Aesthetics and Art Criticism* (1941–    ), organ of the American Society for Aesthetics, contains many articles on musical subjects, as well as reviews of books on music. Peter Louis Ciurczak has prepared an index to articles and reviews on music (1941–1964) (see above, pp. 100).

Critical magazines like the *Saturday Review* and news magazines like *Time* have regular sections devoted to music.

The foregoing examples demonstrate to what extent nonmusical journals may be useful to a musician. Further testimony is given in a recent list of 1074 items of musical interest found in Italian periodicals: Ernst-Ludwig Berg's "Bibliographie der Aufsätze zur Musik in aussermusikalischen italienischen Zeitschriften," *Analecta musicologica*, II (Köln: Böhlau Verlag, 1965), 144–228.

# Yearbooks

As the term clearly indicates, yearbooks are annual publications. Because of the long interval between issues, some bibliographers consider them in a separate category, distinguishing them from periodicals which appear more frequently. Others, however, treat them as they would treat magazines, and indeed some yearbooks bear the title *Journal*. Some are society organs featuring research papers by members or reporting the organizations' activities in a scholarly manner. Some are yearly symposia. Still others are publishers' annuals. Because of their publishing schedule and their scope, yearbooks often reach monographic proportions and contain longer articles than do ordinary periodicals.

In addition to yearbooks or annuals which appear at regularly scheduled times, there are irregular issues, appearing more or less on a yearly basis. The volumes of *Die Reihe* and of *Chord and Discord* are examples.

### Musicological Yearbooks

Like journals of musicology, the yearbooks are devoted primarily to an exposition of scholarly research. Examples below will give a cross-section view.

*Musica disciplina* (1946–    ), organ of the American Institute of Musicology in Rome, began as the *Journal of Renaissance and Baroque Music*, published in Cambridge, Massachusetts. From 1948 to 1952 it was issued irregularly. Since 1953 it has appeared annually, with its coverage expanded to include the entire province of music history; witness its subtitle: *A Yearbook of the History of Music*. The papers, by scholars from over the world, are lengthy, profusely illustrated with musical examples, and documented with bibliographies and other scholarly aids. An international bibliography of books and articles for the preceding year is included.

The Royal Music Association's *Research Chronicle* (1961–    ) is a society publication containing material of bibliographic and reference value to musicologists. Being British in origin, its emphasis is upon British music history.

The *Deutsches Jahrbuch der Musikwissenschaft*, published in Leipzig by Edition Peters, was begun in 1956 as the successor to the *Jahrbuch der Musikbibliothek Peters*, which had been instituted in 1894 and had run continuously except for interruptions by war. In addition to articles it contains a section of necrology and vital statistics and a valuable list of German dissertations for the previous year.

*Anuario musical* (1946–    ), published in Barcelona by the Consejo Superior de Investigaciones Científicas, Instituto Español de Musicología, is devoted to historical studies (not necessarily on Spanish subjects) with emphasis upon periods from the Middle Ages through the Baroque; to folklore; and to catalogs and bibliographies. Some issues are entirely or almost entirely given over to a single subject; the 1962 volume is on Juán Cabanilles and organists of the seventeenth and eighteenth centuries, while the 1963 volume was a *Festschrift* honoring José Subirá on his eightieth birthday. A multilingual annual, its articles usually appear in Spanish, French, or German.

*Svensk Tidskrift för Musikforskning* (Swedish Journal of Musicology)

(1910–      ) is issued by the Swedish Society for Musicology in Uppsala. Each issue contains articles on historical or theoretical subjects, an ample section of long reviews or critical essays on musical editions and recordings, a list of Swedish works composed during the previous year, a list of earlier works performed during the previous year, and a bibliography of music history appearing in Swedish journals. The *Tidskrift* is multilingual, with the majority of its articles in Swedish, English, or German, depending upon the language of the author.

*Dansk Aarbog for Musikforskning*, published in Copenhagen by the Dansk Selskab for Musikforskning, is also a multilingual annual. Scholarly articles, in the language of the writer, represent historical, bibliographical, and analytical studies, and are illustrated with musical examples. Some book reviews also appear.

The *Yearbook* of the Inter-American Institute for Musical Research (1965–      ) is published at Tulane University in New Orleans. Articles on music in the first issue were mostly on Latin-American subjects. A summary of the Inter-American Institute conference is given, together with book reviews, lists of publications received, and communications. The yearbook is multilingual, using the languages of the American republics.

*Studies in the Renaissance* (1954–      ) is a publication of the Renaissance Society of America. Among the interests served by the Society is music, either alone or in relation to other subjects. Each issue contains a paper on a musical subject.

## Yearbooks on New Music

*Die Reihe: Information über serielle Musik* (1955–1964), published by Universal-Edition in Vienna, has an English translation: *Die Reihe: A Periodical Devoted to Developments in Contemporary Music* (1958–      ), issued by Theodore Presser in Bryn Mawr, Pennsylvania. Although it is designated as a periodical, it has not appeared on a regular publication schedule but has been issued irregularly, on the average of once a year. In content it resembles an annual, each issue being devoted to a special subject: electronic music, Anton Webern, musical craftsmanship, young composers, speech and music, etc. The English translation appears considerably later than the publication of the German original.

The *Darmstädter Beiträge zur neuen Musik* (1958–      ), published in Mainz by B. Schott's Söhne, is the official organ of the International Course for New Music in Darmstadt. It contains useful information about contemporary style, compositional devices, and new composers. Special attention is paid to world premières and German first presentations of contemporary works. Subjects covered in the well-illustrated articles are international; discussion is not limited to German subjects but cover the field of new music. There is a "Kranichsteiner Chronik" for each year, giving the programs of music presented at the International Course.

### Some Subject Yearbooks

*Jahrbuch für Liturgik und Hymnologie* (1956–    ), published in Kassel by the Johannes Stauda-Verlag, is devoted to liturgy and hymnology but includes also the entire province of sacred music. It treats music in relation to theology, worship, and church history. In addition to articles, there are long lists and bibliographies regularly featured as a scholarly tool.

*Jahrbuch für musikalische Volks- und Völkerkunde* (1963–    ), issued by Walter de Gruyter in Berlin, is an annual of ethnic studies. International coverage, including ethnic music from over the world, characterizes the articles, which are printed in the language of the author.

*Folk Music Journal*, formerly the *Journal of the English Folk Dance and Song Society* (1932–    ), is the annual publication of the Society. It contains articles, correspondence, and reviews of books and recordings pertaining to English folk dance and folk song.

The annual *Journal* of the International Folk Music Council (1949–    ), published in England, contains proceedings and/or papers read at the Council's conferences, an obituary section, and a comprehensive section of reviews of books, pamphlets, and recordings of folk music. Its critiques of periodicals (including such publications as the Hungarian *Ethnographia*, the Bulgarian *Izvestiya na Instituta za Musika*, the Finnish *Studia fennica*, and the Austrian *Jahrbuch des Oesterreichischen Volksliedwerkes*) are outstanding. The *Journal*, though published mainly in English with only occasional articles in another language, has an international coverage which reflects both the Council's affiliation with UNESCO and the annual or biennial conferences of folk music held in Europe, the Near East, and both North and South American. Folk music (folk song, folk dance, and instrumental music) is viewed from many angles, including history, performance practice, present interpretation, and collection of archives.

*Consort: Annual Journal of the Dolmetsch Foundation*, contains an editorial; articles on music, composers, and instruments; and reviews of books, music, and recordings. It reflects the interests of the Foundation, an international society for early music and instruments. Leading articles are illustrated with both pictures and musical examples.

The *Galpin Society Journal* is the yearbook for the Society, which was founded in 1946 for research in musical instruments and the publication of such studies. The papers are international in coverage. Departments include notes and queries; reviews of music and books; and correspondence. Critical essays are long and detailed.

The English *Opera Annual* (1954–    ), published by John Calder in London, is an illustrated yearbook devoted to contemporary opera. Its articles concern new works, opera houses, financial conditions in the operatic field, and the general state of opera from various points of view. Some essays are analytical, others critical. Appendixes include a list of premières for the year, a necrology, and an occasional list of opera houses, celebrations, and the like.

The *College Music Symposium* is an example of still another sort of annual. It was begun in 1961 as the successor to the *Proceedings* of the College Music Society (formerly Society for Music in the Liberal Arts College), whose aim is the consideration of music as an integral part of the humanities and liberal arts curricula in universities and colleges in the United States. The articles deal with subjects of interest to the college music professor. Reviews of books are lengthy and detailed. Being a society yearbook, the *Symposium* also includes news and proceedings of the organization.

## Yearbooks Devoted to Composers

Annual publications devoted to studies of one composer are often the most fruitful source of information about the subject, once an authoritative biography and the music have been studied. Some important examples are:

> *Bach-Jahrbuch* (1904–    ). Leipzig, New York: Breitkopf und Härtel.
>
> *Beethoven-Jahrbuch* (1953/54–    ). Bonn: Beethovenhaus.
>
> *Handel-Jahrbuch* (1955–    ). Leipzig: Deutsche Verlag für Musik.
>
> *Das Haydn Jahrbuch* (1962–    ). Vienna: Universal-Edition.
>
> *Mozart-Jahrbuch* (1951    ). Salzburg: Mozarteum.

As a general rule, the yearbooks strive to promote a better understanding of the composer and his music by giving newly discovered data concerning specific works, correcting any errors which might have crept into the collected editions of the music, and offering critical opinions. The articles are often long and scholarly, although some shorter essays and commentaries may also be included. Reviews are usually of books, editions of music, and recordings pertaining to the composer. Bibliographies may be included.

Although *Chord and Discord* (1932–    ) is not strictly an annual, its issues appear about once a year. Subtitled *A Journal of Modern Musical Progress*, it is devoted to the cause of Bruckner and Mahler, with articles on various aspects of their music and including criticisms, analyses, and lists of programs on which their works have been presented. Books on the two composers and occasionally on some figure associated with them are reviewed.

### Other Types of Yearbooks

*Hinrichsen's Year Book* (1944–1961), issued by Hinrichsen Edition in London, is an annual publication in which each issue contains material relating to some main topic or several principal subjects. To discover the contents, one may easily consult the individual volumes; the interesting array of articles, lists, and miscellany is sure to be rewarding even if the student's topic may not be directly served. The bibliographical data are useful.

Annuals issued by current periodicals are another type of publication. Sometimes taking the form of a de luxe special issue, with photographs and special articles, they are usually called annual directories. In addition to summing up the previous year's activities, they feature contemporary concert artists, concert managers, recording companies, and other groups of people associated with the current music life.

The term "yearbook" or "annual" may be applied to concert calendars and musical almanacs, although such publications are being absorbed into the current events periodicals to keep abreast of the vigorous activity in our music centers.

There are many other yearbooks; for further notations, one may consult Ulrich's *International Periodicals Directory* and the *International Directory of Irregular Serials, Annuals and Yearbooks*, published by R. R. Bowker Company in 1966.

# BIBLIOGRAPHY

*Bibliographie des Musikschrifttums.* Leipzig, Frankfurt-am-Main: F. Hofmeister, 1936–1941; 1954–

Coover, James B., "A Bibliography of East European Music Periodicals," *Fontes artis musicae* III (1956), 219–226; IV (1957), 97–102; V (1958), 44–45, 93–99; VI (1959), 27–28; VII (1960), 16–21, 69–70; VIII (1961), 75–90; IX (1962), 78–80.

King, Alexander Hyatt, "Periodicals," *Grove's Dictionary of Music and Musicians* (1954), VI, 637–672; supplement, 344–347.

*Music Index: The Key to Current Music Periodical Literature.* Detroit: Information Service, Inc., 1949–    .

Wunderlich, Charles E., *A History and Bibliography of Early American Musical Periodicals, 1782–1852.* Ann Arbor: University Microfilms, Inc., 1962.

Zimmerman, Irene, *A Guide to Current Latin-American Periodicals: Humanities and Social Sciences.* Gainesville, Fla.: Kallman Publishing Co., 1961.

# Index of Proper Names

# Index of Works and Periodicals

# Index of Subjects